GW00938954

Beating the Nazi Invader

For Michelle Bullivant

Beating the Nazi Invader

Hitler's Spies, Saboteurs and Secrets in Britain 1940

Neil R Storey

Pen & Sword
MILITARY

First published in Great Britain in 2020 and reprinted in 2021 by
Pen & Sword Military
An imprint of
Pen & Sword Books Ltd
Yorkshire – Philadelphia

ISBN 978 1 52677 294 7

Typeset by Mac Style
Printed and bound in the UK by TJ Books Ltd,
Padstow, Cornwall.

Pen & Sword Books Limited incorporates the imprints of Atlas,
Archaeology, Aviation, Discovery, Family History, Fiction, History,
Maritime, Military, Military Classics, Politics, Select, Transport,
True Crime, Air World, Frontline Publishing, Leo Cooper, Remember
When, Seaforth Publishing, The Praetorian Press, Wharncliffe
Local History, Wharncliffe Transport, Wharncliffe True Crime
and White Owl.

For a complete list of Pen & Sword titles please contact

PEN & SWORD BOOKS LIMITED
47 Church Street, Barnsley, South Yorkshire, S70 2AS, England
E-mail: enquiries@pen-and-sword.co.uk
Website: www.pen-and-sword.co.uk

Or

PEN AND SWORD BOOKS
1950 Lawrence Rd, Havertown, PA 19083, USA
E-mail: Uspen-and-sword@casematepublishers.com
Website: www.penandswordbooks.com

Contents

Acknowledgements

The author would like to express his personal thanks to the following: The National Archives, Imperial War Museum, Aberdeen City and Aberdeenshire Archives, Manx National Heritage Library and Archives, Newcastle Local Studies Library, Gerry Jackson, BBC Look North, BBC Radio Norfolk, MVC Studios, Norfolk Record Office, Lizzy Baker, Archives Lead, Tyne & Wear Archives, German Occupation Museum, Guernsey, Milton Keynes Museum, Lieutenant Colonel Martin Valles, Kim Valles, David Hepworth, Derek Tree, John Warwicker, Richard Underwood, David Schrader, Tim Bennett, Steve and Eve Bacon, David and Christine Parmenter, Ian Johnson, Marc Hope, Richard Cobb, Ellengard Gertz, Oliver Rogge, Mark Cudworth, Susanne Köhler, Austin Ruddy, Michelle Bullivant, Henry Wilson, Matt Jones, Irene Moore, my old friends Stewart P. Evans, Bob Collis and James Hayward, my loving family and partner Fiona for all her love and support.

The author also would like to place on record his thanks to the many Second World War veterans of Britain, America, France, Belgium, Holland and Germany and their families who have shared their wartime stories, letters, memoirs and photographs with him over the years.

'The August Moon' Punch, *21 August 1940*.

Introduction

Though much is taken, much abides; and though
We are not now that strength which in old days
Moved earth and heaven, that which we are, we are,
One equal temper of heroic hearts,
Made weak by time and fate, but strong in will
To strive, to seek, to find, and not to yield.

Ulysses, Alfred Lord Tennyson (1809–1892)

In the years after the end of the First World War when many strove hard for peace and government spending was reduced year on year under the 'Geddes Axe' of the Committee on National Expenditure (chaired by Sir Eric Geddes), the Security Service, because its operations were seen by many as an expedient of war not peace and because of its secret nature, was not fully understood by the public or many MPs. It only clung on to its existence by a thread, its saving graces being the distinguished war record of the service co-founder and director, Major General Sir Vernon Kell, the high regard he was still held in[1] and a particularly successful operation in 1929 that revealed Special Branch had been infiltrated by Soviet intelligence.[2]

This stood the service in good stead, especially as subversive Communist groups were on the increase in Britain, so when the intelligence was reorganised in 1931 the Security Service, increasingly referred to as simply MI5, was given full responsibility for counter subversion. MI5 proved its worth again and again throughout the 1930s, with notable achievements combatting subversive Communist elements, infiltrating Oswald Mosley's British Union of Fascists (BUF) and the penetration of the Nazi German Embassy. The problem that constantly confronted MI5 during the 1930s was that it only had limited staff to deal with new threats as they emerged, especially the Nazi Party *Auslandsorganisation* in Britain. Coercive methods were employed by the Nazi government over Germans resident, working or studying in Britain. German agents were also sent over to spy on German émigrés; especially those who had fled for political reasons. There were also agents gathering intelligence, not just of military value, but also about British

The Gatehouse of Wormwood Scrubs Prison, where A, B and C Blocks provided an unusual home for MI5 in 1940.

cities, towns, transport and communications systems, industries, utilities, religious, social, academic and political organisations and individuals.

In early 1939 MI5 had a total staff of just 36 officers backed up by 103 administrative and registry staff working in offices on the top floor of the South Block of Thames House on Horseferry Road, Westminster. As the storm clouds of war gathered and staff numbers and workload expanded MI5 needed more office space, as did numerous other government departments, so they found a novel solution by moving half their staff to Blenheim Palace in Oxfordshire and the other to A, B and C Blocks of Wormwood Scrubs Prison. At least they could be sure the latter location, that was soon known simply as 'The Centre', was secure; indeed there were amusing instances when some of the staff ended up being locked in their offices that had received little or no conversion from their former use as cells. Some had no handles on the inside, so occupants had to carefully watch the latch locks on some of the doors.

Every officer had his own office cell and the secretaries were usually two to a cell. There was plenty of work to be done and they all worked hard at it, but The Centre was recalled by those there in the early days as having something of a family atmosphere about the place. Director Vernon Kell was very much the father of the establishment in his tweed suits and round horn-rimmed spectacles; the secretaries would enjoy sitting in the prison garden during their lunch breaks on sunny days. Among the staff who stood out was the debonair MI5 officer, Major Thomas Argyll Robertson (Tommy or TAR to his friends and colleagues) who was recalled striding manfully along the lofty corridors of the old prison wings wearing the slim cut tartan trews of his old regiment, the Seaforth Highlanders. The secretaries nicknamed him 'passion pants'.

There too, before he became Commandant of Camp 020, was Colonel Robin Stevens, known as 'Tin-Eye' after the monocle he habitually notched into his right eye socket, who *used to walk about with a large hiatus between his sweater and the top of his trousers, putting up minutes about "loathly Germans" and "scrofulous Bosches"*.[3]

There was also the unassuming figure of Guy Liddell, a decorated Royal Field Artillery officer during the First World War, who joined the Special Branch of the Metropolitan Police after the conflict and transferred to MI5 in 1931. His obituary in *The Times* described some of his qualities: *'He possessed to an unusual degree a clear mind, sound judgement and mastery of detail.'*[4] Counter espionage was his life and Liddell did much to build bridges between MI5 and the intelligence branches in all three services and internationally with the likes of the Royal Canadian Mounted Police and the FBI in the United States.[5] He even went on a research mission to Berlin in 1933 during which he met with Ribbentrop and officials of the Nazi security service.[6]

In 1939 Liddell was deputy to MI5 Deputy Director 'Jasper' Harker and was made director of B Branch, the counter-espionage and counter-intelligence branch of MI5 in June 1940; they could not have had a better man for the job. The challenges of wartime, especially concerns over the 'Fifth Column' of Nazi agents, collaborators and saboteurs feared to be in Britain at the time of the invasion scares of 1940, saw B Branch expand its numbers of personnel to cope with the burgeoning workload. Liddell took especial interest in the recruitment of every officer and *'is credited with holding together the disparate collection of gifted amateurs drafted in from the universities'*. Although he undoubtedly fitted the mould of the senior intelligence officers at the time, holding deep patriotic beliefs, conservatism and Christian faith dear to his heart, he remained a very human figure in a world of espionage. His style of management was described as 'bureaucratic, democratic' and his love of more aesthetic pleasures of fine art, music and being a fine cellist certainly appealed to the dons and earned him the nickname of 'Darling Guy' among subordinates.'[7]

W. Somerset Maugham met Liddell for lunch in August 1940 when he was researching four articles for the American press, one of them about the Fifth Column. The result was a pen picture of Liddell and his colleagues:

> *I examined a number of secret reports dealing with the Fifth Column and I was fortunate enough to meet some of the men whose job it is to watch their activities in Britain and to take the necessary steps to counter them. I cannot tell their names; I can only say that in appearance they do not resemble the secret agents of fiction. If you met them, you would never dream they have anything to do with the occupation they follow. Another was a plump man with grey hair and a moon face, in rather shabby clothes. He had an ingratiating way with him, a pleasant laugh and a soft voice. I do not know what you would have taken him for but if you had found him standing in a doorway where you had sought refuge from a sudden shower – a motor salesman perhaps, or a retired tea planter.*[8]

The agreeable personality would be one recognised by all who knew Guy, but while Maugham was rather cutting about his appearance, others would recall him as a dapper gentleman who wore well-tailored suits and hand-made shoes. Perhaps Maugham wanted to evoke more of his hands-on nature of getting things done under difficult circumstances rather than paint him as a preening fop of a civil servant. The daily diary Liddell dictated provides a rare and revealing insight into the work of MI5 throughout the war years and into the Cold War. Some of those who served with Liddell were moved to pay tribute to him in *The Times* describing him as '*a person of sterling worth and flawless integrity who deserves well of his country, which in times of exceptional difficulty, he served with loyalty, efficiency, devotion and distinction.*'[9]

Vernon Kell had been thirty years at the helm of MI5, indeed he was Britain's longest serving head of any government department, but he was past retirement. Churchill felt it was time for Kell to go and he was 'retired' (without any say in the matter) on 10 June 1940. Deputy Director 'Jasper' Harker was appointed Acting Director General; naturally there would be comparisons but sadly although younger, Harker was never the man that Kell was and the permanent appointment was given to Sir David Petrie in 1941.

By September 1940 decentralisation of MI5 had been discussed for a while. Regional Security Liaison Officers (RSLO), in effect field officers of MI5, had been attached to the staff of every regional commissioner to provide a direct link and filter on matters of national security. However, it was at MI5 headquarters where the administration problems lay, especially with the limited number of telephone lines at Blenheim which frustrated communication. Complaints had also been received from other government departments regarding the lack of response or the time it took to receive a reply to enquiries sent to MI5. Liddell's diary entry for 24 September reveals much about the situation:

I myself had recently been told by somebody in the FO that it was no longer any use writing to MI5 because no one ever got an answer. Most people in B Branch were very keen about their work and it was very disappointing for them to see the whole organisation blackened in the eyes of outside departments ... but it had to be remembered that everybody here had given their services voluntarily and for small remuneration, that not only the temporary but the permanent staff were on a month's notice and had been for years and that therefore the organisation could not be expected to run quite like a military unit. It was necessary to take into consideration the various peculiarities of certain officers with a view to getting the best out of them. This meant that one could not always build one's organisation quite logically.

Ironically it was during the night of 24–25 September 1940 that the situation was further exacerbated when Wormwood Scrubs had incendiary bombs drop on it during an air raid and it was the great misfortune for MI5 that the wing that the bombs fell on contained the registry, destroying the card index of file numbers and titles that enabled the quick look up of all files, names of persons of interest and cross references. Fortunately the index had been photographed and could be reprinted, but approximately 1,000 files that were also destroyed in the conflagration had not been copied.[10] After the bombing most of MI5 joined their colleagues at Blenheim, the registry was installed in the palace building and the staff housed in the courtyard that had originally been erected for Repton School when it was evacuated there. Residential accommodation for MI5 staff was found at Keble College, Oxford and at 'billets' in the homes of local families.

After the bombing of the Scrubs, Guy Liddell was keen for B Branch to retain a base in London. In practice some were despatched to Blenheim, but the director general, Liddell and some of his counter espionage operations officers remained in London along with a small secretarial staff in a former

Blenheim Palace, near Oxford where the majority of the offices and registry of MI5 moved after Wormwoods Scrubs was bombed in September 1940.

MGM Building on St James's Street for the rest of the war. After the move the communications problem was further exacerbated. Blenheim was now the co-ordination centre of Britain's internal counter espionage operations but as Guy Liddell records in his diary entry for 7 October 1940:

> *Communication with Blenheim Palace is frightful. At the moment there are only two lines and one of them is not working. Whenever you ring you are told that your name will be put on the waiting list. We have been promised five lines but quite clearly we need twenty. What seems to have been overlooked is that everybody down at Blenheim has to keep in touch with his outside contacts and that if connection is not made those in the country will become completely isolated.*

Against this backdrop of bombed records, changes in senior management, relocation and new staff recruitment, B Branch was faced with what became a huge remit of investigating Nazi agents, collaborators and all manner of enemies of the state within Britain under the pressure of what was believed to be an imminent threat of invasion.

It is worth considering how the MI5 offices operated in the 1940s. Decades before a computer would be on every office desk, letters and reports would be drafted longhand then walked to the secretaries who would type them up on a manual typewriter and walk them back so they could be signed ready for despatch. Cross references and drawing files from the registry would only be carried out by registry staff upon submission of a written request on the correct pro-forma form. A priority search could only be carried out upon a specific request being made. Every case investigated and every person of interest would have a hard copy file containing correspondence and reports relevant to the subject with hand-written minute sheets just inside the file cover that annotated the contents and comments of those handling the case, all held in place with treasury tags. Some cases and individuals ran to several files and frequently spanned a number of years. Problems also emerged, especially among regional officers, who held on to files 'just in case' there were further developments when cases stalled or lines of enquiry appeared to dry up, rather than get them down to registry. The problem was compounded yet further as fears over Fifth Columnists, suspicious individuals and spies mounted up and backlogs of files pending investigation piled up on every officer's desk.

Permission to monitor telephone calls could be obtained via a Home Office Warrant (HOW) but the task was vast. There were not huge quantities of the technology available to record the conversations, it was not always reliable and for the most part conversations listened into for 'key elements' of conversation that may be value to the intelligence services, which would then be repeated by the listener as he recorded it onto a 12″ double acetate recording disc, which would then be transcribed. This was not an easy task when the conversations were conducted in foreign languages and the listener was not an adept linguist and translator.

One of the greatest weapons in the counter espionage armoury was postal censorship, the process by which mail to and from foreign destinations would be examined and, if found to contain suspicious or sensitive information that could be of use to the enemy, would have the detail obliterated. If the letter was considered to be of sufficient concern, it would be passed up the line to the intelligence services. The 3,000 staff of postal censorship were drawn from people of all walks of life, from those who opened the mail and searched parcels (mostly female staff) to the huge team of experts involved in the examination of letters for hidden codes and the detection of secret inks.

Magazine and newspaper articles presented the story of this impregnable wall of postal censorship,[11] but the truth was somewhat different. In February 1940 the Stephenson Committee published its report on the work of censorship which concluded 'admittedly more importance is attached to the work of MEW [Hugh Dalton's Ministry of Economic Warfare] than for the Security Service.' In fact, censorship had only been dealing with about 10–15 per cent of correspondence to certain specified countries which achieved 'indifferent results'. Liddell was of the opinion *Their work as regards letters has amounted to little more than a lucky dip.*[12]

The situation was addressed the following month by the original censorship centre established in the Littlewood's Football Pools building in Liverpool being complemented by a sister operation to share the load established in the massive Prudential Assurance building in Holborn.[13] There were still concerns over exactly who was sorting the mail and the GPO worked with MI5 to flush out BUF members on the staff who may well be subverting the censorship process, by bringing about their internment, having them moved to a harmless job in the Post Office or by simply dismissing them.[14] The idea was good but in practice the difficulty was identifying who were BUF members and harder still who were non BUF members but pro-Nazi or BUF collaborators.

A mobile census team, known within MI5 as 'The Travelling Circus' that would descend on regional General Post Office sorting offices around the country to bring their expert eye to the mail, was also established in July 1940 and within its first months of existence exposed a case of sabotage in the Hull area.[15]

MI5 operations were often generated in response to reports from Special Branch, chief constables and the Regional Security Liaison Officers (RSLO). Investigations drew on contacts, informants and double agents, but observation and especially the following of suspects, was seriously hindered by the blackout. The information MI5 was presented with was a problematical blend of 'jitters', supposed Fifth Column activities and suspects which when investigated had innocent explanations. Add into that mix people listening to and taking as fact the reports from a number of radio stations broadcasting from Germany, sabotage of machinery by disgruntled employees, malicious reports and hoaxes, some deliberately originated by former members of the British Union of Fascists. However, amongst the tangle of intrigues were genuine operatives of the Third Reich and pro-Nazi terrorist groups that posed a credible threat.

This book examines the stories of Nazis, agents and Fifth Columnist saboteurs in Britain from the 1930s up to 1940. Set in the context of the war of nerves so quaintly known at the time as the 'jitter war', it investigates the plans the Nazis and British authorities made in the event of the invasion and occupation. You may never see the story of 1940 in quite the same way again.

Neil R. Storey
2020

WANTED!

FOR MURDER . . . FOR KIDNAPPING . . . FOR THEFT AND FOR ARSON

ADOLF HITLER
ALIAS
Adolf Schicklegruber, Adolf Hittler or Hidler

Last heard of in Berlin, September 3, 1939. Aged fifty, height 5ft. 8½in., dark hair, frequently brushes one lock over left forehead. Blue eyes. Sallow complexion, stout build, weighs about 11st. 3lb. Suffering from acute monomania, with periodic fits of melancholia. Frequently bursts into tears when crossed. Harsh, guttural voice, and has a habit of raising right hand to shoulder level. DANGEROUS!

Can be recognised full face by habitual scowl. Rarely smiles. Talks rapidly, and when angered screams like a child.

Profile from a recent photograph. Black moustache. Jowl inclines to fatness. Wide nostrils. Deep-set, menacing eyes.

FOR MURDER Wanted for the murder of over a thousand of his fellow countrymen on the night of the Blood Bath, June 30, 1934. Wanted for the murder of countless political opponents in concentration camps.

He is indicted for the murder of Jews, Germans, Austrians, Czechs, Spaniards and Poles. He is now urgently wanted for homicide against citizens of the British Empire.

Hitler is a gunman who shoots to kill. He acts first and talks afterwards. No appeals to sentiment can move him. This gangster, surrounded by armed hoodlums, is a natural killer. The reward for his apprehension, dead or alive, is the peace of mankind.

FOR KIDNAPPING Wanted for the kidnapping of Dr. Kur' Schuschnigg, late Chancellor of Austria. Wanted for the kidnapping of Pastor Niemoller, a heroic martyr who was not afraid to put God before Hitler. Wanted for the attempted kidnapping of Dr. Benes, late President of Czechoslovakia. The kidnapping tendencies of this established criminal are marked and violent. The symptoms before an attempt are threats, blackmail and ultimatums. He offers his victims the alternatives of complete surrender or timeless incarceration in the horrors of concentration camps.

FOR THEFT Wanted for the larceny of eighty millions of Czech gold in March, 1939. Wanted for the armed robbery of material resources of the Czech State. Wanted for the stealing of Memelland. Wanted for robbing mankind of peace, of humanity, and for the attempted assault on civilisation itself. This dangerous lunatic masks his raids by spurious appeals to honour, to patriotism and to duty. At the moment when his protestations of peace and friendship are at their most vehement, he is most likely to commit his smash and grab.

His tactics are known and easily recognised. But Europe has already been wrecked and plundered by the depredations of this armed thug who smashes in without scruple.

FOR ARSON Wanted as the incendiary who started the Reichstag fire on the night of February 27, 1933. This crime was the key point, and the starting signal for a series of outrages and brutalities that are unsurpassed in the records of criminal degenerates. As a direct and immediate result of this calculated act of arson, an innocent dupe, Van der Lubbe, was murdered in cold blood. But as an indirect outcome of this carefully-planned offence, Europe itself is ablaze. The fires that this man has kindled cannot be extinguished until he himself is apprehended—dead or alive!

THIS RECKLESS CRIMINAL IS WANTED—DEAD OR ALIVE!

All the above information has been obtained from official sources and has been collated by CASSANDRA

The Hitler War Criminal wanted poster published in **The Daily Mirror** *newspaper the day after war broke out.*

Chapter 1

Nazis in Britain 1930–1939

Oh, what a tangled web we weave. When first we practise to deceive!
Marmion, Sir Walter Scott

The dramatic rise of Oswald Mosley's British Union of Fascists, his Blackshirt bullyboys and rabid anti-Semitism combine to leave a foul legacy that dominates many accounts of right-wing activities in Britain during the 1930s. But in the shadow of these events was a covert and sinister infiltration. The establishment of an overseas branch or *Ostgruppe* of the Nazi Party and Nazi intelligence gathering in the United Kingdom during the 1930s is far less known and its true extent has only been revealed by the release

Reichsleiter *Alfred Rosenberg giving an address in Berlin, 1934.*

of secret files over the past twenty years. The Nazi Party gained its majority in the Reichstag in September 1930 and that same month, in an attempt to improve their international profile they sent Hans Wilhelm Thost to London to become their first full-time correspondent of the official Party newspaper, *Völkischer Beobachter*, in Britain, an action that also meant he became the first officially sponsored member of the Nazi Party in the country.

Thost would be given specific tasks or channels of inquiry to research by his superiors and he would send his reports back by post. Every three or four months he would return to Germany to meet with his superiors, notably his editor-in-chief, Alfred Rosenberg, the Nazi Party's chief racial theorist. He was the proponent of the Nordic theory and notions of the 'master race' as well as being the architect of the anti-Jewish theories that the Nazis used to justify their racial and ethnic policies. At these meetings Thost would present a more detailed debrief, would answer questions and the next subjects to be researched would be discussed. Thost proved himself invaluable as one of the Nazi Party's most direct sources for news of British social and political matters and the mood of the British people. He would be the first of many.

Thost's activities remained undetected by the British intelligence services for several months. The reasons for this are simple; in retrospect we have the advantage of being able to see that the machinations of the National-Sozialistische Deutsche Arbeiterpartei (NSDAP, commonly referred to as the Nazi Party in English) in Germany in 1930 was the first toe hold of the ascent to power of the Nazis. However, in the early 1930s the NSDAP was simply another political party in Germany that was far from securing enough votes to seize power. At the same time the manpower and resources of MI5 were limited.

As the Nazis built on their successes in Germany, so they also sought to court the support of, and disseminate propaganda to, German nationals living and working abroad. They did so by establishing officially recognised Nazi Party groups or *Ostgruppe* in countries outside the Fatherland. Early in September 1931 Nazi party activist, 21-year-old Rolf Wunderer, was sent to London to muster members. His infectious fervour and enthusiasm talking to German nationals, particularly in the restaurants and tea houses of Soho, and his engagement with extant British Fascist groups enabled him to find numerous German nationals sympathetic to the Nazi cause.

The London *Ostgruppe* held its first meeting at a Viennese restaurant in Soho in October 1931 with around twenty-eight members present. It was an evening where the hallmark Nazi ploy of blurring traditional German nationalism with Nazism was very much in evidence. As those present drank German beer and sang traditional German songs, the *Ostgruppe* was established and Thost was elected as leader or *Ortsgruppenleiter* and Wunderer as secretary.

Rosenberg was delighted to hear of Thost's appointment and, to endorse the fledgling group and encourage its growth, he came to London for a week-long visit in November 1931. It was hardly headline news, indeed it was six days before any of the national newspapers picked up on his visit. Rosenberg gave interviews to a number of reporters claiming to the *Manchester Guardian* that his visit had '*no political significance at all*',[1] but in the *Daily Herald* he was reported as saying: '*I came here to inform myself about the state of mind of Britain* [but I have] *not seen any British public men and women of note*.'[2] Rosenberg had undoubtedly come to Britain to disseminate Hitler's ideas to the new party faithful, but both newspapers and the Foreign Office were of the opinion he was also on a personal fact-finding mission to try and ascertain what the political and financial reaction in Britain would be if the Nazis came to power.

Horace Rumbold, the British Ambassador in Berlin, shared this opinion and in response to a Foreign Office enquiry into Rosenberg's motives he also warned of darker undertones, describing the visit as being:

> *... to prepare the way for his Chief* [Hitler] *who may very likely wish to visit England and, if possible, to make the acquaintance of leading British statesmen before the time, which may be soon, comes for his party to take an active part in controlling the destiny of Germany*.[3]

Perhaps these were the first glimmers the British people had of Nazi German intentions involving Britain in their future plans for domination in Europe. The *Führer* himself held a strong personal belief that Britain would be won over to join with Nazi Germany by persuading those in power to embrace the Nazi way of thinking or, if the government remained obstinate in pursuing a war with Germany, he hoped the British people would rise up, dislodge the government and enter into a pact with Germany. Hitler's feelings are summed up well in an incident recalled by General Franz Halder, chief of the *Oberkommando des Heeres* staff and the senior German army planner of Operation Sealion.

He entered the *Führer*'s office to find him reading a copy of the *Illustrated London News*; as he looked up Hitler mused '*That we have to make war against such personages, isn't it a pity?*'[4] As late as May 1940 Field Marshal Gerd von Rundstedt would recall a meeting with Hitler at Charleville where he expressed his admiration of the British Empire and his hopes for an earlier peace. General Günther Blumentritt, Operations Officer of Army Group A, wrote with regard to himself and his planning staff of how the *Führer*:

'astonished us by speaking of his admiration for the British Empire, of the necessity for its existence and of the civilization that Britain had brought to the world.'[5]

The first headquarters of the London *Ostgruppe* was established in two rooms at 46, Cleveland Square, W2 in December 1931. Over the ensuing months the Nazi Party in London steadily increased its membership and began to hold political meetings behind closed doors in public buildings such as Porchester Hall, Bayswater. There had been rumblings of concern in the corridors of both the Home Office and the Foreign Office, but at the time the feeling was very much that as long as they didn't break the law or attempt to subvert His Majesty's Government they could be left alone by the authorities. In correspondence between the Foreign Office and the Home Office regarding *Orstgruppenleiter* Thost in 1932 it was pointed out:

> *He would, of course, be breaking the law of England if he were to publish defamatory libels against the German Government which might affect friendly relations between that Government and His Majesty's Government but there is no evidence he is doing this, and, as you know, prosecutions for this type of seditious libel are very rare and the authorities are always unwilling to launch them, as they may well do more harm than good.*[6]

The Nazi Party gained majority power in Germany early in 1933 and the London *Ostgruppe* continued to grow. Meetings and social events were held regularly and membership rose to around 120 by April 1933. A new party headquarters was established at the Park Gate Hotel, Stanhope Terrace, near Lancaster Gate, Bayswater W2.

April 1933 also saw concerns expressed in the House of Commons over the actions of the Nazi Party in Germany, especially its anti-Semitism and talk of expansion and 'colonization schemes' beyond Germany's extant frontiers. The Nazi press was far from pleased by any suggestion of criticism of Nazi policy, but did not give up hope of Britain coming around to their way of thinking, as articulated in the *Deutsche Allgemeine Zeitung*:

> *The Brown House in Munich regards it a happy sign that precisely at this moment a small but energetic group has been formed in England which also preaches anti-Semitic Fascism and in the near future will certainly win a large following. Just as England has abandoned 'free trade' so she will abandon free racial theories for the principle of keeping the race pure.*

In late April the press picked up on the establishment of the new *Ostgruppe* headquarters, *The Times* reported a 'Nazi Club in London' but having made enquiries 'in German circles' they were assured there was no intention of establishing a 'Brown House' (like the Munich Party headquarters known as *Braunes Haus*) in London. The new club chairman *Ortsgruppenleiter* Otto Bene was at pains to stress '*the members had no desire to interfere with British politics*' and pointed out '*there were no British members*'.[7]

With the heavy-footed diplomacy that rapidly became synonymous with the Nazis, Hitler despatched Rosenberg to London in May 1933 in an attempt to assure the British people the Nazis were no threat, to try to build bridges between the new regime and Great Britain and assess how the ascent of Nazism was being received in Britain itself. Rosenberg, who had unsurprisingly won no affection among the British on his last visit, had recently been appointed leader of the Nazi Party's foreign political office. On 10 May 25,000 'un-German' books by Jewish, Marxist, pacifist and other authors who did not meet with Nazi Party approval were burned in the square at the State Opera in Berlin. The books had been 'collected' from libraries and private collections by Nazi-led students of Berlin University and were publicly burned amid much flag waving, Nazi saluting, cheering and singing in the presence of Dr Goebbels, the Minister for Propaganda.[8]

It was also on 10 May that Rosenberg, as part of his visit to London but with no prior consultation with British authorities, formally laid a wreath on behalf of Hitler on The Cenotaph and gave a Nazi salute. As 11 May

Reichsleiter *Rosenberg laying the wreath on behalf of Hitler at The Cenotaph, 10 May 1933.*

dawned newspapers in Britain and around the world told the story of the Nazis burning books in Berlin and at 11am a car was spotted driving slowly along Whitehall. It slowed near the Cenotaph and a man was spotted grabbing the Nazi wreath, it was taken into the car which sped off. Returning to the Cenotaph a short while later First World War veteran, Captain James Sears (57), chairman of the Aylsham Branch of the British Legion in Norfolk and prospective Parliamentary candidate for South-West St Pancras, gave himself up to the police. The wreath was later recovered in a dishevelled state from the Thames.

Brought before Bow Street Magistrates on 11 May, Sears was clear about his reasons for his actions:

> *... as a deliberate protest against the desecration of our national war memorial by the placing on it of a wreath by Hitler's emissary, especially in view of the fact that the Hitler Government are contriving to do those things and foster those feelings which occurred in Germany before the war, for which so many of our fellows suffered and lost their lives.* [9]

Sears appears to have received support among the general public for what he had done, but in the wake of a number of public protests, including demonstrators carrying banners emblazoned with 'Down with Hitler' outside Claridge's where Rosenberg was staying, the court was mindful of maintaining order and could not dismiss the incident. The magistrate, with a stiff upper lip, pointed out, '*Whatever the defendant's private opinions were, it was an improper and unmanly thing to do,*' and handed down of a fine of forty shillings for wilful damage.

German authorities were furious, the Berlin *Tageblatt* stated somewhat ominously '*A similar act would be punished more severely in Germany*' and warned there would be diplomatic ramifications.[10]

Hitler was enraged and British Ambassador Sir Horace Rumbold was called to account for the way the wreath incident had been dealt with. Sir Horace informed him: '*There had been an unmistakable swing in English*

Sir Horace Rumbold, The British Ambassador in Berlin, 1928–1933.

public opinion, based upon British concepts of freedom of the individual and consideration for other races.'[11]

It was the most diplomatic way of telling Hitler that the behaviour and persecution policies of the Nazi Party were jarring with the British public. Rumbold had warned the British Government of the sinister actions of the Nazis as they rose to power but their response remained one of appeasement. Rumbold's warnings went unheeded and having presented Hitler with such a reality check he was removed as British Ambassador in Berlin soon after. His replacement, Sir Eric Phipps, was also disquieted by what he saw and he was replaced in 1937 by Nevile Henderson, a man far more content to toe the appeasement line.

Meanwhile, during the Rosenberg visit to London in 1933, the wax figure of Adolf Hitler at Madame Tussaud's was doused in blood red paint and a placard hung around his neck proclaiming: 'Hitler, the Mass Murderer'. A number of London bookshops, which attempted to capitalise on the publicity by displaying volumes featuring Hitler in their windows, had to send assistants out regularly with wet cloths and sponges to wipe spit from the plate glass.

A leader in *The Spectator* eloquently summed up the mood of Britain in the wake of the Rosenberg visit:

> *Herr Hitler's unofficial foreign secretary has been in London this week sounding British opinion regarding Germany. He can have had little difficulty reaching a conclusion. Rarely has this nation been more nearly of one mind on anything than it has been in reprobation of the excesses that have marked the political upheaval which Adolf Hitler has inspired.*

This led to further concern over the activities of the Nazi *Ostgruppe* in Britain and questions were asked of Sir John Gilmour, the Home Secretary, in the House of Commons of whether a 'Brown House' was being established by Nazis in London. After an initial rebuttal to buy some time, when the Home Secretary was questioned again on the matter the following week his reply was that he declined to interfere with what were in effect private meetings. However, behind the scenes discussions had been held with MI6 with the conclusion being rather than banning the *Ostgruppe* and driving it underground, it was far better to keep it in the open so they could keep an eye on its activities. A member of Special Branch was charged with the duty of infiltrating the *Ostgruppe*, attending its meetings and reporting back.

The British national newspapers, notably the *Daily Herald*, continued to run scare stories about the activities of the *Ostgruppe*, bringing the group a lot of unwelcome attention which resulted in them being evicted from the Park Gate Hotel. They moved to 27, Westbourne Terrace W2 in January 1934

Cleveland Terrace, Bayswater W2, where the Nazi Party had its London Headquarters between 1934 and 1939.

intending to keep a low profile, but the following month national newspapers were reporting 'Nazi Stormtroopers in London' accompanied by the story of how two Nazi Stormtroopers, the first to land in England in full uniform complete with Nazi arm bands, had arrived in Croydon airport. It turned out they had come under their own initiative after having been invited by a Mr Thomas, an English Fascist they had met in Germany, to come and stay in Stanhope Gardens S.W. Their arrival understandably drew quite some attention and via a translator they stated that they were on an eight-day visit during which they were hoping to make contact with British Fascists and others in sympathy with Hitler's policies.

The report in *The Times* concluded: '*After their arrival they were taken care of by responsible German people in London. They will be sent back to Germany immediately.*'[12]

More unwanted attention was brought on the Nazi HQ in London and they were ousted yet again. Finally, they managed to obtain rooms at 5, Cleveland Terrace (just around the corner from their original headquarters on Cleveland Square) where they remained until 1939.

Chapter 2

Victims of Nazi Vengeance

I told you so. You damned fools.

H.G. Wells

The Great War had changed the face of modern warfare. The development of modern weapons of war meant that although there would be those who would cling on to older ideas of infantry warfare, those who had the vision could see that in any future war the winner would be the country with the most up-to-date weaponry, armoured fighting vehicles, tanks and aircraft, particularly bombers. Britain had been subjected to bombing from the air for the first time in January 1915. The Zeppelins that droned over

The Graf Zeppelin over the East Coast of England, July 1931.

Britain at night during the war were far more a weapon of terror than an effective weapon of war, but the daylight raids on London by German Gotha bombers were far more deadly, and an ominous portent of the shape of aerial warfare to come.

After the Armistice in 1918 and the Treaty of Versailles in 1919 beyond the cheering crowds of victory celebrations there were already rumblings of disquiet amongst returned veterans of defeated countries. There was significant discontent at the way they felt that they had been treated, many could see that The Great War was sadly not going to be 'the war to end all wars'.

In 1921 a joint War Office and Air Ministry committee was set up to consider the defence of South East England, south of a line drawn from Portland Bill to The Wash. The Home Defence Sub-committee report on a potential 'continental air menace' in 1923 declared '*a highly organised system is essential for the rapid collection and distribution of information and intelligence regarding the movements of hostile and friendly aircraft throughout the whole area of possible air operations.*'[1]

It was from these early findings that the first air observation posts were set up around London. In those early days, as civil flight began to find its feet again, these posts and the volunteers manning them felt more like hobbyist aeroplane spotters armed with flask, lunch box and a pair of binoculars. It was not long, however, before they stepped up to become a more formal organisation when the Observer Corps was formed in 1925. In part a move to use an extant national organisation to organise the new corps, it was also with our nation's security in mind that members of the Observer Corps would be recruited as Special Constables from 1926.

Instead of the Zeppelin being banned forever after Versailles, Germany revived the lighter-than-air craft as a means of passenger transport for transatlantic flights in the 1920s. However, when film of the new Zeppelins was seen in the UK, many felt a shudder as they recalled the horror of the air raids they had seen and heard about during the Great War. When the 236.6m long *Graf Zeppelin*, with that same ominous drone that many remembered only too well, came over to Britain on a 'good will' flight and toured the East Coast in 1931 many were filled with apprehension.

In the early 1930s military aircraft were also developing apace. In 1933, the year the Nazis gained power in Germany, the only development in the defence of Britain from air attack air was the Air Defence Intelligence System. Observer Corps posts were extended to include the counties of Dorset, Norfolk and Suffolk in October 1933, but threats from the air were ignored at our peril. H.G. Wells, the author of *War of the Worlds* (1897), published *The Shape of Things to Come* (1933) in which he, albeit fictionally, explored the potential changes wrought in the nature of warfare and included harrowing descriptions of cities destroyed by bombing. This was something that he had predicted as early as 1907 in his book *The War in the Air*, republished in 1921 and 1941. In the latter edition, produced in the aftermath of the blitz on London, he would add to his preface: *I told you so. You damned fools.*[2]

*   *   *

In the last weeks of March 1935 Britain was buzzing with plans to celebrate the Silver Jubilee of King George V. Hitler had announced on 16 March that Germany would re-arm, even though it was in contravention of the Treaty of Versailles. Rather than nipping this in the bud, Britain's national government chose appeasement and, as one of the leading lights of the League of Nations, sent Foreign Affairs Minister Anthony Eden on a two-week mission during which he visited Hitler in Berlin, Stalin in Moscow and a number of countries across central Europe to discuss their anxieties and sound out how they would greet pacts and accords with their European neighbours with a view to maintaining peace. With the usual panorama of national and local news stories that vied for coverage, when the story of the deaths of two women named in the press as Dr Dora Fabian and Miss Mathilde Wurm broke over 4–5 April 1935, the story was picked up by most nationals, but it was not front page headline news for most of the papers.

Then, as now, the plight of refugees was not a high priority for many in Britain of the mid-1930s. Most people, although not keen on Herr Hitler and the activities of the Nazis in Germany, really did not see it as a problem that affected them and, as chilling as it may be in hindsight, there were thousands in Britain who were sympathetic to the Fascist cause and apathetic to both the situation and the people fleeing from it. The way the news of the deaths of Fabian and Wurm was reported did not help matters either; there was a suggestion of the involvement of Nazi agents in some of the reportage but typical of the headlines was 'Two Women Dead in Bed'.[3]

In a time when homosexuality was a criminal offence and lesbian relationships were seen as taboo in Britain, the story already had a grubby patina that encouraged an instant distaste among readers. The sub heading of 'Refugees from Germany' just added grist to the mill for those who chose the conceit that refugees brought trouble with them. Over the next two days papers were running with column headers for the story (still buried among the lower columns) such as *Two dead women, what did Scotland Yard think: German refugees who feared their permits to stay here might not be renewed.*[4] and *German Women's Death: Police Theory of Suicide.*[5]

Few papers published a photograph with the story, those that did seemed unable to find an image of Dr Fabian. They did however seem able to locate a photograph of Miss Wurms and Dr Fabian's friend, the anti-war activist and Secretary of the Independent Labour Party, Fenner Brockway. Although having a kindly face, the picture and name of middle-aged Miss Wurm hardly stirred the suggestion of a crime of passion or *femme fatale* that might capture the imagination of the sensationalist press, and the socialist inclinations of both women did not endear them to the wider readership. It was also reported Sylvia Pankhurst, a friend of Dr Fabian, had commented that in her opinion, '*She must have come to the end of her resources but was too proud to speak about it.*' Once it was revealed the flat was locked and the key found inside, it appeared a tragic *fait accompli* and the story was consigned to the sidelines by most of the broadsheets before the inquest was held, let alone before a verdict had been passed.

The story of two middle aged German refugee women committing suicide by poison while in bed together in their down-market flat may have been accepted and consigned to history by many papers, but the truth is far less straight forward. This may well be the first case of Nazi agents committing an act of murder on British soil. Few papers picked up on the story that Fabian had incriminating evidence against the regime, their plans for rearmament and the operations of their spies in the UK and around the world. Only the more sensational newspapers dared to ask *Were they victims of Nazi vengeance?*[6] and although this notion did generate some creative stories around the case, there was indeed a darker truth to be uncovered by piecing together the story from the released MI5 files and Metropolitan Police file on the investigation.

The two women concerned were no ordinary refugees; in fairness to the press there had been some mention of both women's academic and political lives in Germany, but little detail. Frau Mathilde Sara Wurm (60), who styled herself Miss Matilda Wurm after fleeing to the UK, was Jewish and the widow of political journalist and politician Emanuel Wurm. A journalist in her own right, Wurm was also an active member of the Social Democratic Party of Germany (SPD). She successfully stood for election and took her place in the Reichstag where she was a prominent opponent of the Nazis and voted against the Enabling Act of March 1933 which, in effect, imbued the Chancellor with the power to enact laws without consultation with the Reichstag.

Dr Dora Fabian (33) was Jewish and a divorcee. She had been born in Berlin and was also an active member of the SPD and a pacifist and received her doctorate in economics from the University of Giessen in 1928. She had worked as secretary to Dr Rosenfeldt, a former Socialist member of the Reichstag and Minister of Justice for Prussia, and had published several works on political economy in her own right.

Fabian and Wurms were great friends, not lovers. They had fled independently to Britain; money was tight, but living was not impossible if they shared a flat. Dr Fabian had always been a fierce critic of the Nazis and had been imprisoned shortly after the party gained control in 1933 for being an editor of the pacifist paper *Das Andere Deutschland* (The Other Germany). In his introduction to his *Letters from Prison* Fabian's friend the dramatist Ernst Toller claimed Fabian was actually incarcerated for removing two cases of his papers from his flat after it was raided by stormtroopers of the *Sturmabteilung* (SA). When police authorities heard of what she had done she was imprisoned but convinced them that she had actually destroyed the papers. Thanks to her friends exploiting the confusion that existed as a result of the duplication of prison control by the Nazis and the regular police, Dr Fabian was released ten days later and it was then she took the opportunity to flee; indeed, as she boarded her train to Switzerland Nazi security forces had gone to her house to re-arrest her. By some miracle she got away and managed to take the papers with her.

After a time in Switzerland Dr Fabian arrived in the UK in September 1933. Miss Wurm was the widow of Herr Emanuel Wurm, Under Secretary of State immediately after the Nazis came to power, had arrived in the UK in February 1934 and in April she applied to the Home Office to extend her stay, stating that having formerly been a member of the Reichstag and as a socialist of partly Jewish origin, she did not wish to return to Germany. She claimed she had the sum of £200 in the Russell Square branch of Barclay's Bank and with investments in America and the articles she wrote for German and foreign periodicals on political and economic questions, she would have an income of £6 a month. She also worked as a dressmaker to earn some extra income. The pair started sharing rooms on Guildford Street in 1934.

Even though some would decry the newspapers that raised the question of the deaths being the actions of Nazi agents working in Britain as deliberately sensational, the concerns were not raised without grounds. A number of killings and suspicious deaths had already taken place in Europe, such as that of the philosopher, refugee campaigner and ardent anti-Nazi critic Theodor Lessing, who had fled to the village of Marienbad, Czechoslovakia. He had continued to write articles for German language newspapers outside Germany but was assassinated by Sudeten German Nazi sympathisers in August 1933.

After working for SA head Ernst Röhm, engineer Dr Georg Bell had his eyes opened to the Nazis and made a high-profile break from the party in October 1932, but the knowledge he had of the SA leadership made him a dangerous man outside the control of the party. He narrowly evaded capture and arrest when members of the SA raided the offices of the newspaper he worked for in March 1933. He fled over the border from Germany into Austria where he was traced by members of an *Einsatzkommando* to Glashof Blattwirt near Durchholzen where, according to the account given to the coroner by members of the *Einsatzkommando*, he was persuaded to return with them to Germany. But as he was packing to leave another member of the police team entered the room, shot him five times in the back and then escaped over the border to Germany.

As the refugees fleeing from Nazi Germany travelled further across Europe, some of them took damning secrets and military information with them. It seemed highly likely that the long arm of the Nazis would find it much harder to cross far less sympathetic borders and consequently they would have to become more subtle.

Whether Hans Wesemann was ever a committed socialist writer, pacifist and anti-Nazi, or originally held those beliefs but 'turned' or was put under pressure to 'turn' and become a Gestapo operative, is unclear. What is known is that he could be highly plausible. He would claim, and had paperwork that appeared to confirm, that he had been expelled from Germany in 1933 and fled to Britain to avoid persecution by the Nazis. In reality, according to Foreign Office documents,[7] he came to the UK in 1933 when he stated his reason for visiting was to improve his English. Whilst in England he was requested by newspapers in Berlin to write articles for publication and was finally appointed official correspondent to *Dammerts Presse Dienste*, Berlin.

His remit was to observe the German refugee community and report back to his masters in Germany. Maintaining his cover as a socialist and anti-war campaigner, he attended the Peace Conference at Oxford in July 1933 and the Trade Union Congress at Weymouth in October 1934. In the MI5 file on Wesemann, John Court Curry described his *modus operandi* as:

> *... to incite political refugees from Germany to write articles attacking the Nazi regime, to assist them in getting the articles published and then to report on their activities to the Nazi authorities. He would tell them he had good connections with pacifist or humanitarian associations and suggest journalistic and literary openings, and then, having won their confidence, he appears to have schemed to get them into the power of the Nazi authorities.[8]*

One of those who fell prey to Wesemann's professed beliefs and connections was Dr Dora Fabian who had submitted articles to him for publication and was known to have associated with Wesemann while he was in the UK.[9] She was not alone. During his time in England Wesemann used a variety of cover addresses, attempted to establish connections with a number of refugees and used various aliases, chiefly Rudolf Schroeder, under which name he became known to Henry Wickham Steed, the former editor of *The Times* who was one of the first to ring the alarm bells regarding the Nazis and rearmament in the British press.

Wesemann was also known to veteran pacifist campaigner Otto Lehmann-Russbüldt. German by birth, Lehmann was residing in London where he had numerous contacts who supplied him with material for his articles revealing Nazi plans for rearmament, new weapons and the development of bacterial warfare, which he also shared with Wickham-Steed. Lehmann's findings were condensed into the book *Germany's Air Force* published in 1935.

Naturally, Wesemann wished to try to identify Lehmann's sources. MI5 listed individuals he was believed to have approached, among them Otto Katz and Willi Münzenberg who regularly brought anti-Nazi material for activists and the British press. Lehmann was also fortunate to have German Jewish reporter Berthold Jakob as one of his key sources. Jakob had written a number of well-informed articles exposing Nazi plans for rearmament and secret weaponry and had fled to Switzerland shortly after the Nazis gained power in Germany, establishing an independent press agency in Strasbourg.

In February 1934 Seymour Cocks MP brought documents before the House of Commons that revealed the secret building programme for the German air force. The claims had been made previously in some of the British national papers but had been dismissed as exaggerations or out-and-out falsehoods. Presented with reliable documents from a reliable source they could no longer be ignored. In his book *Germany's Air Force*, Lehmann points out the documents quoted by Cocks in the House had been 'obtained through Dr Dora Fabian', but what he did not reveal is that she had obtained them from Berthold Jakob.

That same month the flat shared by Fabian and Wurm was broken into. Despite there being items of value visible, all that was taken were some of the papers relating to the

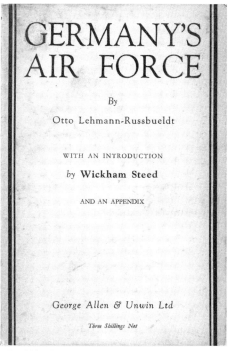

The 1935 book that revealed the extent of the expansion of Germany's air force and contained a tribute to the bravery of Dr Dora Fabian for her contributions.

15

rearmament of Germany. Concerned that German agents were responsible and could return again, Dr Fabian and Miss Wurm moved to another flat on Coram Street, where a second robbery occurred and yet again secret and sensitive papers were the target rather than valuables. After this robbery they moved yet again. When they took on their new four-room flat on the 4th floor of 12, Great Ormond Street the landlady would recall how they were concerned about security; they requested the light over their door to be boarded up and they had all their locks examined to see that they were secure.

Meanwhile, Wesemann had made regular trips to Germany throughout 1934. On 17 January 1935 his landlady Mrs Doris Crisp recalled she received a telegram in German which she handed to Wesemann who left hurriedly for Hamburg for a meeting with Dr Walter Richter and Hans Joachim Manz. It was on their instructions he went to Copenhagen where he caught up with German trade unionist Karl Balleng whom he had met at the Trade Union Congress in October 1935. Wesemann used his skills of persuasion to befriend Balleng and lured him near to near the border where he was snatched back into Germany and placed in a concentration camp. Balleng's wife was then decoyed to Flensberg by a telegram which purported to have come from her husband claiming he had been let out of prison but prohibited from leaving. While she was gone Wesemann visited the Ballengs' apartment where he opened all the trunks and drawers with keys in his possession and took away their correspondence.

The next mission saw Wesemann sent to Strasbourg where he presented himself as a German refugee from London and befriended Berthold Jakob whom he enticed to Basle with a promise he could procure him a false German or Czechoslovakian passport. On 9 March Wesemann took Jakob to meet two other men he claimed were political refugees with important information of interest to Jakob. The group talked for hours and, drunk or drugged, Jakob was persuaded to accept an invitation to go with the two men to visit someone in the city. Once he was in the car Jakob was gagged and driven over the border into Germany where he was charged with entering with no papers and, when his identity was allegedly discovered, he was charged with high treason and imprisoned. It is also intriguing to note that Frau Wesemann, the divorced wife of Hans Otto Wesemann, was admitted to the Necker Hospital, Paris having attempted to commit suicide by taking poison. Hans Otto Wesemann was arrested by Swiss authorities and was held at Basle.

Dr Fabian had been warning fellow refugees of her suspicions about Wesemann for some time. Both she and Miss Wurm had been interviewed by Dr Anton Roy Ganz of the Basle Department of Justice when he came to England on 25–30 March 1935 to investigate Wesemann, his connections and life in London. Perhaps blaming herself for careless talk about her sources to Wesemann and the resulting fate of Jakob, Dr Fabian worked tirelessly running a campaign to apply pressure for his release.

Divisional Detective Inspector Clarence Campion of 'E' Division arrived at 12 Ormond Street at 2.30pm with Detective Inspector Hawkyard and went up to the front bedroom of the flat on the top floor. In his statement of 9 April he recorded:

They were lying side by side on the bed with the clothes pulled up around them. Wurm was fully dressed with the exception of her shoes and lying on her left side. The Coroner's Officer was informed and the bodies removed to the mortuary.[10]

On their finances Inspector Campion commented:

I have made inquiries in this case and find that the flat was taken over by Mrs Wurm on 16 July last, at a rental of 19 shillings per week and that the rent was paid up to the 15th April next. With the exception of a few shillings, no money was found in the flat ... I have learned that Mrs Wurm had no financial resources and her account at the bank is overdrawn. Dora Fabian appears to have been a very brilliant woman, who endeavoured to earn her livelihood with the assistance of a refugee society in London.[11]

Campion's enquiries also led him to believe that Fabian was trying to borrow money in late March to pay off debts and to live for the next two months while she wrote her new book. Elizabeth Allworth who was employed by Dr Fabian as a cleaner on Tuesdays and Thursdays gave a statement to the police:

On Friday 29 March 1935 when I went to the flat to work as usual, whilst cleaning the floor of the bathroom, I heard a man's voice coming from the bedroom. A little later Miss Fabian came out of the bedroom dressed only in her vest and knickers, entered the bathroom and asked me to excuse her whilst she washed her hands; whilst she was washing her hands, I saw a man, whose name I do not know, but who was fair, very tall and had a small moustache ... That day whilst I was there, I saw the man go in and out of the room several times. This man was staying at the flat the Friday before the women were discovered dead, but I do not know the actual day he left. I don't know who the man was, or his name, as they always spoke in German.[12]

It was known by a number within the refugee community in London that Karl Korsch, the exiled German Marxist theoretician, a man with a wife back in Germany, was having an affair with Dora Fabian who on occasion had acted as his secretary. When questioned about this Korsch downplayed any relationship he had with Fabian claiming: '*We were friendly and she used to do some typewriting for me. She formed an infatuation for me.*'[13] Nonetheless he continued to have her assist him in his work.

Police enquiries revealed Dora Fabian had told Ika Olden on 25 March 1935 that she was meeting a friend arriving from Denmark on 28 March. Mrs Olden knew Fabian was having a relationship with Korsch and the friend she was talking about was Karl Korsch. Mrs Olden had spoken to Miss Wurms at 11.30am on Sunday 31 March and they had arranged to meet on 1 April.[14] In a letter from Karl Korsch to Dora Fabian dated 31 March 1935, in which Korsch told Fabian that he did not wish to live with her, he stated '*I thank you for the key and the books, the last I will bring back to you after having read them.*'

Korsch claimed he went to see Fabian at her room on 30 March when she made a scene by trying to prevent him leaving the house. On Monday 1 April Korsch received what appears to be a suicide note from Fabian in shorthand, it was unsigned and undated.

Miss Wurm visited her nephew Arthur Campbell in Harlesden on 30 March. She appeared to be in normal health and spirits, he would recall, but before leaving she had said: '*Don't come on Monday, I shall be engaged, phone me on Thursday morning.*'[15] On 2 April Mrs Allworth went to clean as usual and, even though there was not the usual note left to let her know they were going away, Mrs Allworth assumed that was the case. It was also unusual that when she tried to enter the bedroom she found it locked '*a most unusual thing as they have never locked the bedroom before*',[16] but nonetheless she just cleaned the rest of the flat. There was no disorder and nothing out of the ordinary apart from the bedroom door being locked.

Mrs Mary Omerod, the Honorary Secretary of The Society of Friends, German Emergency Committee, was a friend of Dr Fabian and Miss Wurm and knew that both women had been associated with Berthold Jakob. She knew they had been in touch with Hans Wesemann and that they had been visited by Dr Anton Roy Ganz, the Assistant Public Prosecutor of the Basle Department of Justice who had come to England to investigate Wesemann, his antecedents and his involvement in the abduction of Jakob. Mrs Omerod added: '*I understand that several Germans resident in this country had received letters threatening them with reprisals if they gave evidence about the case of Jakob.*'[17]

It was also Mrs Omerod who, having telephoned Miss Wurm and not received a reply, told her friend Mrs Ika Olden who dropped into her office, that she had rung Dr Fabian a few times on the same number and not received an answer. The pair decided to visit the flat on Ormond Street but did not receive a reply. On the morning of Thursday 4 April she had still not heard anything so went to Grays Inn Road police station and returned with two constables who after repeated knocking, forced the door.

PC 157 George Hall of E Division entered but finding the bedroom door was locked, forced the door:

> … and on the bed I saw Dr Fabian dressed in pyjamas and Mrs Wurm fully dressed, except her shoes, lying apparently dead. I immediately called Dr White, who attended and pronounced life extinct. There was no disorder in the bedroom and the key of the door was on a shelf on the wall facing the door. The dead persons were lying in bed, covered in bedclothes to their necks. On a small box table on the side of the bed I found a cup containing a brown liquid … On a small box table near the window I found an empty tablet bottle, five empty glasses which had been used and a coffee pot.[18]

Lord Dudley Marley of the German Relief Committee also arrived at the flat and made no bones about his suspicion of foul play in comments he later made to the press. Mrs Omerod told PC West that Lord Marley was concerned '*that his association with Dr Dora Fabian was such that he was worried as to what correspondence was in her possession*'. PC Hall advised her that nothing could be touched.

Mrs Olden had spoken to Korsch after the murder and he told her he had received a letter in which Dr Fabian had said she was going to commit suicide. He also claimed he had called at the flat on Monday around 11am but had received no reply. According to Campion, Korsch told him that he and Fabian had quarrelled before and Fabian '*spoke as if she intended to commit suicide but he paid no attention to it and on the present occasion when he received the note he looked upon it as another idle threat.*'[19] He was given an envelope from Karl Korsch on 6 April containing the note which was written in shorthand, which Korsch claimed was the usual way they wrote to each other.

Campion found a large quantity of correspondence regarding various international associations for German refugees and communicated with Chief Inspector Foster of Special Branch '*as it seemed a matter that would interest that Branch*'. Foster sent Inspector Jempson and Sergeant East to investigate.

Inspector Jempson of Special Branch saw Mrs Omerod and Mrs Olden who, together, explained their theory and were explicit in their accusation:

> … that Dr Korsch was a Nazi agent, that he stayed with Dr Fabian from 28th March until 30th March and was concealed in the flat while Dr Ganz from Basle was interviewing Dr Fabian concerning the Jakob case. They therefore suggested that Dr Fabian realised that Dr Korsch was a Nazi Agent, and the knowledge that she had been living with such a man perturbed her and Mrs Wurm [so much] that this was really the cause of their suicide.[20]

Mary Omerod told the police in her statement: '*I know that the two dead women were not in any serious financial difficulties*' and clarified that she knew Wurm had received assistance from Jewish friends, that she had some capital and had received £25 from an insurance claim just a month previously, and that Dora Fabian had only recently received a grant of £25 from the Jewish Refugees Committee.

Some friends were quoted as being concerned about Fabian's financial status, but they were at a loss to provide an explanation for them entering into a suicide pact. Another friend, Ellen Wilkinson, was quoted as saying: '*I can only feel that there is some deep mystery behind the tragedy. There was no apparent reason why either of them should decide to end their lives.*'[21]

What is intriguing is the statement from a man who walked into Scotland Yard to offer information on the case on 5 April. His name was Heinz-Alex Nathan who claimed to be a German political refugee studying at the London School of Economics, but a few enquiries soon revealed he was suspected among the German refugee community of '*being a Nazi agent, because they knew nothing of his antecedents and is a frequent visitor to the German Embassy*'.[22]

Nathan had gone to give information in which he claimed Dr Fabian had asked him to loan her £50; he claimed he did not have the money but promised to procure it for her. If a cover story was being set up to provide a motive for the 'suicide' of Fabian and Wurm, Nathan would be doing exactly what his masters had instructed him to do.

The bodies of Dr Fabian and Miss Wurm were removed to Paddington mortuary for examination by Dr Taylor the pathologist. In the meantime, fears over safety from further attacks were raised among the refugee community. *The Daily Herald* ran a story headlined *Nazi Decoys at Work in London*, undoubtedly based on the research of Dr Fabian. The paper revealed:

> *The existence in this country of a widespread Nazi organisation for decoying political refugees back to Germany was responsible yesterday for further inquiries by officers of the Special Branch of Scotland Yard. Among the ruses so far discovered to entice refugees back to punishment are letters saying relatives are seriously ill in Germany. Other letters declare that refugees have become entitled to legacies which they may claim if they return to the Fatherland. The Daily Herald was told last night that the evidence already collected includes the names and addresses of a number of persons (mainly in London) who have been taking part in the organisation – many of them unwittingly.*[23]

Home Secretary, Sir John Gilmour was questioned and confirmed investigations by Scotland Yard officers had been taking place at the request of Dr Ganz and the Swiss authorities. During the course of their inquiries the trails led them to Paddington, Bloomsbury, North London suburbs and several provincial towns. Newspapers reported more stories of German refugees in Britain being shadowed, their addresses discovered, their friends identified, their habits recorded and fed back to German intelligence. Armed with this information, those of interest and considered 'subversive' were approached with a view to getting them back to Germany. This was done by using a corps of correspondents, many of them acting in good faith and quite unaware of any sinister motives, their letters being sent under cover from one address to another.

The Home Office, however, was quick to play down any suggestion of the involvement of Nazi agents in the deaths of Fabian and Wurm in their comments published in newspapers, but as the inquest approached questions were raised in the House of Commons:

Captain Charles Waterhouse MC (Conservative, Leicester South) asked if the Minister had any statement to make. Captain Harry Crookshank (Under-

Sonntag den 5. Mai 1935.

„Volksw

Julius Epstein:

Dora Fabian und Mathilde Wurm
sind ermordet worden!

In der Weltpresse ist es ruhig geworden um den Tod dieser beiden Frauen. Diese Ruhe liegt vor allem im Interesse des Dritten Reiches, außerdem aber in dem der englischen Regierung. Die derzeitige Regierung Seiner Majestät des Königs von England sagt sich mit Recht, wenn es sich vor der Welt herausstellte — woran, wie wir noch sehen werden kaum ein Zweifel gestattet ist —, daß Dora Fabian und Mathilde Wurm einem von der Gestapo raffiniert inszenierten Verbrechen zum Opfer gefallen sind, so verpflichtete sie dies in weit größerem Maße als die Entführung Jacobs die Schweiz zu energischem Protest in Berlin. Und nicht nur zu Protest, dessen äußerste Folge der Abbruch der diplomatischen Beziehungen wäre, sondern zu exemplarischen Sanktionen, die Berlin so bald nicht vergessen könnte. Dieser Protest und diese Sanktionen müßten aber zwangsläufig das englisch-deutsche Verhältnis in entscheidendem Maße trüben; nichts haßt aber die Regierung Macdonalds und Sir John Simons so, wie irgendeine Spannung der Beziehungen Englands zum Dritten Reich Der maklosen Angst davor sind ja

Abgesehen davon war es zu 99 Prozent sicher, daß sie die Verlängerungen ihrer Aufenthaltsbewilligungen erhalten hätten. Nichts — aber auch gar nichts sprach dagegen. Im übrigen hätte gerade Dora Fabian, die in der offiziösen englischen Darstellung als die treibende Kraft bei Entschluß und Durchführung des „Selbstmordes" dargestellt wird, jederzeit Aufnahme bei Freunden in der Schweiz oder in Paris gefunden Sie hatte sogar, wie heute feststeht, einer Freundin in der Schweiz ihren Osterbesuch angekündigt. (Selbst das Gericht, das die Todesursache offiziell festzustellen hat, mußte zugeben, daß Angst der beiden, nach Deutschland zurückkehren zu müssen, als Selbstmordmotiv vollständig ausscheide.)

Die zweite der Wahrheit ins Gesicht schlagende Meldung war die von den Behörden lancierte, es müsse sich schon deshalb um Selbstmord handeln, weil das Motiv zu einem Mord durch die Nazis nicht erfindlich sei, da doch die beiden Frauen sich überhaupt nicht politisch gegen das Dritte Reich betätigt hätten. Dies wurde von Dora Fabian gesagt, die bis zuletzt mit nie ver-

Julius Epstein argues the deaths of Dora Fabian and Mathilde Wurm were a 'political murder' in the Volkswille *German language newspaper published in Prague on 5 May 1935.*

21

Secretary Home Office) replied '*No sir. Those deaths will be investigated by the coroner in the ordinary way.*'

Captain Waterhouse pressed: '*In view of the statement made by responsible organs of the press this morning connecting those deaths with the activities of foreign secret political societies in this country, may I ask him to give this House an assurance that every step will be taken to ascertain the facts in order that we may be quite sure, and to make it quite clear that political crime will not be tolerated in England?*'

Captain Crookshank replied: '*That is what the inquest is for, to find out the facts.*'

Mr Emmott (Conservative, Springburn): '*Is not the function of the Coroner merely to inquire into the cause of death and not enter into other matters?*'

Crookshank: '*That is quite true, but if the allegations to which Captain Waterhouse refers have anything in them, they would naturally come before the coroner.*'

Waterhouse: '*Will he now give us an assurance that he will investigate those allegations, in view of the fact that responsible newspapers are putting a sinister connection on this?*'

Mr Isaac Foot (Labour, Bodmin) (father of Michael Foot, the former Labour Party leader 1980–83) pressed further: '*Assuming that the coroner feels that his duty confines him to the cause of death, will the Home Office recognise any responsibility in respect of these statements and make the inquiry asked for?*'[24]

There was no reply and an unsigned note in the Metropolitan Police (MEPO) file of the case states unequivocally: '*Having regard to the political excitement over this suicide it is unnecessary and undesirable to complicate the inquest by calling in a Special Branch Officer.*'[25]

The inquest was opened at the Paddington Coroner's Court by Mr Ingleby Oddie, who sat with a jury, on 10 April 1935. Dr John Taylor the pathologist gave his opinion that in neither case was there any natural cause of death. Both women died from respiratory failure, following some

Dr Karl Korsch, 1935.

form of narcotic poisoning, which he considered was likely to be barbituric poisoning.

Korsch was questioned as to how the German press had obtained a transcription of the alleged suicide note so quickly that the contents of the note were published in the German press the day following the deaths. Korsch claimed he had informed Mrs Olden on Friday morning and was in no doubt it was she who conveyed the information. This caused Mrs Olden to angrily shout 'I did no such thing' and, requesting that she should be given the chance to give more evidence, she was permitted to return to the witness box. She was of the opinion Korsch had not told the truth and that in fact he was not the friend Dr Fabian believed him to be and that he had some ulterior motive for his journey to Sweden and Denmark so soon after the visit of Dr Ganz to Dr Fabian. To this the coroner said he could not have politics introduced into his court.[26]

The coroner addressed the jury offering the suggestion that as far as Dr Fabian was concerned, her death seemed to be a case of unrequited love and financial troubles, but he found it hard to suggest a motive for the death of Miss Wurm other than she allowed herself to be dominated by Fabian. The jury returned a verdict of suicide whilst of unsound mind in both cases. Dora Fabian and Mathilde Wurm were buried at East Ham Jewish Cemetery just two hours after the conclusion of the inquest.

In his final report on the case held in the Metropolitan Police file Divisional Detective Inspector Campion commented: '*The conduct of Dr Korsch in this case does not impress me as being straightforward and his particulars might be of interest to Special Branch.*'[27]

Among the final enclosures of the same file is a copy of a covering note from Sir Norman Kendal, Assistant Commissioner (Crime), Scotland Yard to senior civil servant (later appointed Cabinet Secretary 1947–62) Norman Brook at the Home Office: '*Here is a copy of a report showing the final report of the Inquest. You will already know all about it from the newspapers. I think it went very well.*'[28]

In the atmosphere of disquiet current in Europe at the time and when appeasement was the line taken from the very top in British politics, there was no way they were going to risk upsetting German diplomatic affairs with concerns surrounding the deaths of a couple of refugees. British authorities were happy to bury the matter. Charmian Brinson and Richard Dove, in their account of the case in their excellent book *A Matter of Intelligence* (Manchester 2014), found and translated the German report of the interview between an unnamed member of German Embassy staff, who had gone with the intent of clearing the German Embassy of any involvement in the affair, and Ralph Wigram at the Foreign Office:

Mr Wigram immediately declared that the Foreign Office did not attribute the slightest significance to the English press reports nor the questions in the House of Commons. For this reason the parliamentary question on 11 May had been deflected by the reply that it was necessary to await a report from the Legation in Berne. In fact, a report had not even been requested from the legation. Mr Wigram considered the matter as closed unless – as he put it – another foolish question should be asked in the Commons or some trashy newspaper or other should pick up the story again.[29]

The German refugee community in London remained unconvinced. Even as late as 1938 American reporter Clara Leiser was still attempting to get answers to some of the questions that lingered from the case. In a letter to Scotland Yard she raised nineteen points including such questions as:

Were fingerprints taken from the bottles in the flat that contained poison?

Was the shorthand note alleged to have been sent to Karl Korsch by Dora Fabian compared with other shorthand notes of Dr Fabian's?

Korsch said they had always corresponded in shorthand, although his own letter to her was in longhand?

Was the type on the envelope said to have contained the note compared with the type of Dr Fabian's typewriter?

Was there an investigation as to how the 'farewell' note, presumably made public in London for the first time on April 10 at the inquest and published in London newspapers for the first time on April 11, appeared in German newspapers on April 6?

The charlady, according to her testimony, washed up dishes for three people on the Tuesday following the supposed suicide. I do not believe this was mentioned at the inquest at all. Was there any effort made to find out who that third person was?

Could the shorthand note of Dora Fabian's now be examined by anyone and who could apply for such permission?

The reply she received from the Assistant Commissioner was brief:

I am directed by the Commissioner of Police of the Metropolis to say that he regrets that particulars such as you ask for are confidential and cannot be disclosed. I may add however, that, at an inquest held on 10 April 1935, a verdict of 'suicide whilst of unsound mind' was returned in both the cases you refer.[30]

None of her questions would be answered and they remain unanswered to this day. The MI5 files for Dora Fabian and Karl Korsch have been not been released, they have not been deposited at The National Archive (TNA) and consequently there is no date for them being opened. Indeed, it is not clear whether the files have been retained, are lost or have been destroyed.

Roy Ganz of the Basle Department of Justice was not satisfied either and returned to London on 18 April 1935 and conducted enquiries with Inspector Jempson. Jempson compiled a report based on his enquiries, those of Roy Ganz and the statement made by Wesemann to the Swiss authorities:

He has told the Swiss police that he was working for a secret department of the German police, which is exclusively concerned with watching German political refugees abroad, luring the most dangerous back to Germany or taking other steps to render them innocuous … He states that each agent works separately; reports direct to a police officer in Germany and does not know the other agents in the country in which he is active. He could not therefore give the names of other persons employed in England.[31]

The Swiss police were already aware of this German secret police department that had agents in all European countries. They had identified Dr Thiele as one of its chiefs and also had the names of two further members of the organisation, Richter and Manz who had acted with Wesemann to abduct Jakob.

It also appeared Wesemann had made visits to Germany on four separate occasions in August, September and November 1934. His passport was accompanied by a *Passe Partout* from the German Embassy in London which stated: '*Dr Hans Wesemann, German journalist, well known to us, is proceeding to Germany on an official mission. Please render him all facilities.*'

Before his departure on his first trip from London to Berlin in August 1934 he had passed a letter to Werner Hitzmeyer (Vernon Meyer) addressed to Herr von Marschall von Bieberstein, to be sent to the German Embassy in London if he did not return within fourteen days. On his first two visits to Berlin he met with Walter Richter. After his return from his second visit he was handed £22 or £23 from Richter via a German woman working in Britain named Elizabeth Anna Maria Gunther. (Shortly before his departure from London in January 1935 Wesemann also received a further £40 from Richter by post.)

Wesemann had handed two letters to the Swiss authorities from Fraulein Gunther who was passing messages and payments from Richter to Wesemann. Each letter was brief and would have seemed quite innocuous, the first stated: '*I must see you. Dr Richter sends friendly greetings through me and I would like to speak to you.*'

The second was for the handing over of the money that Richter had sent over: *'I have got something to hand over to you. Meet me at the Marble Arch at 3.00pm.'*[32]

Jempson and Ganz tracked Gunther to the house where she was working as a housekeeper in Horsham, Sussex from the return address on the letters. She was interviewed without the knowledge of her employer or other servants. After initial flat denials she reluctantly admitted she had known Dr Richter since 1933. He lived next door to Fraulein Gunther's family at Spandau, Berlin and was a great friend of her brother Walter. She knew Richter was what she referred to as a police *kommisar* when she first met him, but she did take pains to point out that she did not write to him, but corresponded with his wife. When Gunther went to Berlin in July–September 1934 she admitted she saw Richter almost every day but she claimed she had only written to Wesemann once, only met him to send the greetings of Dr Richter and swore she neither gave him any money nor carried a message to any other person in England.[33]

It would be interesting to be able to comment further on Fraulein Elizabeth Gunther but, like a number of the other files on those associated with this case, they are closed for 100 years and in this instance, even though an application was made under the Freedom of Information Act in 2017 her file will not be accessible until 2038.[34]

Others we are able to see and in the MEPO file Inspector Jempson was frank in his opinion of Karl Korsch:

This man played a sinister role in the suicides of Dr Dora Fabian and Frau Wurm … He was interviewed by Dr Ganz in my presence. He talked for a long time on the suicides without admitting anything … concerning his former relations with Dr Dora Fabian he would say nothing … The theory held by the German refugees in this country and abroad is that Korsch knew Dr Dora Fabian had given information to Dr Ganz concerning the Jakob case and reproached her for having done so. She discovered that Korsch was a Nazi agent and the shock of this, coupled with the fact that she had betrayed to him many things concerning German refugees in London caused her to commit suicide.[35]

There is even the possibility, especially with rumours of Jakob being tortured to extract information from him now he was in German hands, that Korsch had played on this when talking to the two women, perhaps suggesting it was only a matter of time before they too would be snatched. The combination of horror of what Fabian felt she had caused to happen to Jakob and the sheer terror at what may happen to both women, may have caused them to take their own lives. However, the answer could be far more prosaic.

Studies and statistics from the twentieth century show suicide pacts are rare[36] and it seems very strange to say the least that neither Wurm nor Fabian exhibited any signs of behaviour indicating they might be contemplating suicide before their deaths. Although some suicides can be impulsive in situations where two people are involved, one would think that a friend would try to talk the suicidal person out of their drastic actions rather than enter into a pact to end their life with them.[37] As T.E. Joiner points out in *Myths about Suicide* people become vulnerable because they consider suicide so regularly they eventually envisage it becoming a reality for them. They may not have told anyone about the way they were feeling, nor display any psychosis, but they don't just decide to end their lives out of the blue.[38]

Korsch was a man of average strength. Both women had not been eating well for some time, they were not large framed. Korsch could have simply put poison in the drinks of both, Fabian while she was in bed and Miss Wurm as she sat in the living room, and once they had lost consciousness or died he could have laid them in bed together. He would have been in no hurry, he could take time to remove shoes and set the rooms as he wished. The bedroom door key was known not to be regularly used and he could easily have borrowed it and had a copy made some time previously. He already had a key to the front door of the flat; he mentioned it in his last letter to Dora Fabian. Even if the cleaner had seen him at the flat in the days before the murder, it would not have proved too difficult for Korsch or one of his Nazi agent cronies to intimidate her enough to change her story slightly to divert suspicion from him to a man with the fair hair and moustache she described in her statement.

After his comments on Korsch, Jempson recounts the story of Nathan's information supplied to Scotland Yard, but he follows these with the comment: *'There is no evidence in the possession of the police to confirm the theory that the last two men are Nazi agents.'* [39] It does beg the tantalising question, did Jempson believe there was key evidence that had been removed or was known to be held elsewhere, or had key evidence been suppressed by a higher agency in the Home Office in the 'national interest' by appeasing Nazi Germany?

A note at the end of Jempson's report pointed out Gunther, Korsch and Nathan's visas all ran out later in 1935. Norman Kendal wrote a confidential memo to the Home Office on 29 April 1935 pointing out that the suspicion that Korsch, Nathan and Fraulein Gunther were Nazi agents 'is fairly strong' adding that they '*were all frequent visitors of Baron von Bieberstein at the German Embassy, First Secretary at the German Embassy who is supposed to be the man who controls the secret agents in this country … You may consider whether, when their permission to stay runs out, it is neccessary or advisable to allow them to stay any longer.*'[40]

Both Gunther and Korsch were not granted any further extensions to stay in the UK, only Nathan was permitted to stay, but MI5 continued to keep abreast of his movements and behaviour. He was interned as an enemy alien in 1940.

After a Freedom of Information (FOI) decision dated 2018, the MI5 file on Hans Joachim Wesemann aka Schroeder that is lodged with the National Archives remains closed for 100 years and will only be released in 2048. The translated copy of the deposition Wesemann gave to Swiss authorities, that they then supplied to the Metropolitan Police in 1936 is in the released case file and provides a valuable insight into how the German secret service was recruiting and operating in London:

In the summer of 1934 my passport ran out. I therefore went to the German Embassy in London in order to get a new one. I needed this passport urgently for a journey to Germany, where I wished to take leave of my fiancee and in addition, had urgent business to attend to. I also wished to take this opportunity of clearing up my personal position. I spoke at the Embassy, concerning the issue of a new passport, with Dr Rutter. Dr Rutter had no personal objection but declared that the Embassy could not issue passports to Germans living outside Germany, without first receiving authorisation from Berlin. He promised to arrange the matter through the Foreign Service in Berlin. We had, at this time, a very long and detailed conversation on general political affairs.

Later, through Dr Rutter, I was brought into touch with the Embassy Secretary, Freiherr von Marschall [Baron Marschall von Bieberstein the Secretary of the German Embassy in London] *who wrote to Berlin on my matter. One day he showed me a document from the Secret State Police, Berlin* [Geheime Staatspolizei, often abbreviated to Gestapo] *signed by Dr Walter Richter, in which this gentleman said he wished to have a personal interview with me in Berlin. At first I declined this as I had various doubts.*

After my conversation with von Marschall, he told me that the Embassy would stipulate a safe-conduct for me. This safe-conduct was expressly assured by the Gestapo and shown to me. This document was also signed by Dr Walter Richter. The correspondence came through the intermediary of the 'Foreign Service' of Berlin, which forwarded this correspondence to the Embassy. Mr von Marschall gave me a special document issued by the Embassy for my journey to Berlin. As I had a great fear of the Gestapo mainly because of information from refugees and news in the foreign press and looked forward to this meeting with Dr Richter with great reluctance, I tried to take steps for my own security. I therefore showed the special pass from the Embassy to a friend [Werner Hitzmeyer]. *At the same time I gave him a letter addressed to Freiherr von Marschall. In this letter, which was dated forward eight days, I begged Herr von Marschall to intervene on my behalf with the Foreign Service if, within eight days, reckoned from my leaving, I had not reported to him personally or in writing. I have, in addition, agreed personally with Mr von Marschall, that I would again report within a certain period, as proof that nothing had happened in Berlin. I travelled in August 1934, with the special pass from the German Embassy to Berlin and there met the, to me up to then unknown, Dr Walter Richter.*

My activity with the German Embassy in London lasted from August 1934 until the middle of January 1935 ... I continuously visited the Embassy and acted with the full knowledge and consent of the Ambassador von Hoesch and the Embassy Counsellor Prince von Bismark. All my discussions with the Embassy Secretary Freiherr von Marschall were carried on with the full approval of the previously named gentlemen. I did not speak personally with these two gentlemen because they, by reason of the extremely delicate nature of my work, did not wish to give it official sanction. However, the Embassy gave me every help unofficially.

I repeatedly carried out important political tasks in England for the Embassy. The Embassy brought me in touch, through the Foreign Service, with the Gestapo ... I visited the German Embassy in London regularly. I had a long conference with Freiherr von Marschall at least once a week. In addition to this gentleman, I repeatedly discussed matters with the General Consul Bielfeld, the successor of Dr Rutter. This gentleman was also fully informed of my collaboration with the Gestapo ... it was arranged between me and Dr Richter that especially confidential reports should be sent through the courier post of the German Embassy. Also, Dr Richter would pass especially confidential matters through the Embassy to me. This happened repeatedly.

Once, in London, I had a detailed conversation with Dr Sherpenberg, son-in-law of Dr Schact, President of the Reichsbank. [Dr Albert Hilger van Scherpenberg was second secretary to the Ambassador in 1935] *who is responsible for the observation of refugees and the police, and was, like myself a former social democrat ... In certain circles of the Gestapo it is suspected Dr Sherpenberg, even today, is in secret communication with prominent Marxists and gives them information ... Scherpenberg told me he felt himself embarrassed, as a former Marxist, that he could not negotiate with me in certain matters as he could not lay himself open to the reproach of having betrayed his former principles. Dr Scherpenberg was however, fully in agreement with my work and quite approved my motives. He emphasised also that the Embassy had the greatest interest in my collaboration and had included some of my information in their reports to the Foreign Service with the greatest success.*

The gentlemen at the Embassy, especially von Marschall, always told me they could not recognise officials of the Gestapo abroad and would not receive them in order not to be compromised. Therefore von Marschall also approved the principle of Dr Richter, that all discussions for certain work of the Gestapo in foreign countries, should be held in Germany. I remember Freiherr von Marschall, who regularly received certain reports of the Gestapo, once said 'It is not right that German officials of the Gestapo who are abroad should discuss any action to be taken. Such things must, once and for all, be decided upon in Germany' ... He also laid great stress on a distinct separation between tasks undertaken for the Embassy and the Gestapo. During the whole time, however, I was accredited by him and at the German Embassy as an Agent of the Gestapo. At the express wish of von Marschall I used the official cover-name of Dr Schroeder in my visits to the Embassy and was always announced as such.[41]

Wesemann only mentions interactions with Embassy Counsellor Prince Otto von Bismark, and First Secretaries Baron Marschall von Bieberstein and Harald Bielfeld, every one of them among the senior Nazi Party loyalist diplomats at the Embassy. Albert Hilger van Scherpenberg the former socialist who, according to Wesemann, had been 'turned' to toe the Nazi line but was still rumoured to be in communication with his socialist comrades, became head of the Scandinavian unit in the Department of Trade Policy of the Foreign Office. He was betrayed by Gestapo spy Paul Reckzeh as a member of the Resistance and was sentenced by the People's Court to two years in prison on 1 July 1944.

The German Embassy building viewed from The Mall c1945.

Leopold von Hoesch, the German Ambassador in London 1932–1936.

There is, perhaps, a dark postscript to this story. Wesemann was always kept at a distance from German Ambassador Leopold von Hoesch, who had never been happy dirtying his hands with Nazi business. Since his appointment in 1932 von Hoesch had mixed in well with London society; he carried himself with a distinguished bearing, he was always immaculately dressed and the hallmark of his hospitality at events he hosted at the embassy was refinement. His *Times* obituary described him as: '*an excellent speaker, with a quiet, convincing style. He spoke beautiful English in soft, modulated tones.*'[42]

His speeches always encouraged better Anglo-German relations, his easy manner saw many statesmen warm to his charm and in his diplomatic life he had built many bridges between Germany, France and Britain over the years after the First World War. Above all von Hoesch was not a Nazi nor had he been appointed by Nazis, but as Hitler began to assert his power and wanted more NSDAP men in the London Embassy Ambassador von Hoesch and his old fashioned ways seemed more and more out of step with the new regime. Not to mention von Hoesch was also becoming more and more critical of Hitler's actions, writing to his predecessor Ambassador Konstantin von Neurath, now Hitler's Foreign Minister, denouncng Hitler's occupation of the Rhineland on 7 March 1936 in violation of the Treaty of Versailles, as a calculated provocation of both the French and the British. This would have reached the *Führer*'s ears and yet again Hoesch would be proving to be a thorn in his side.

Having been active at official events as usual and showing no signs of illness von Hoesch died suddenly of a heart attack at the embassy less than a month later on 10 April 1936 at the age of 55. His death was so convenient it was suspicious and there were rumblings of a suggestion of poisoning, but these were rapidly brushed aside in the wake of a full-honours Nazi funeral which saw the incongruous sight of British Grenadier Guardsmen bearing a coffin draped in a swastika flag to a gun carriage. Hundreds crowded onto the balcony of the embassy to give the Nazi salute and a gun battery fired a salute of nineteen guns from Hyde Park. The Royal Horse Artillery then towed the gun carriage and flag-draped coffin, as the band of the Grenadier Guards

Leopold von Hoesch's the funeral courtège departing from the German Embassy, London on 15 April 1936.

played the funeral march, along The Mall, Buckingham Palace Road and through the streets of London to Victoria Station in a formal procession with cortège, uniformed members of the German forces and dignitary mourners.[43]

The images leave the legacy to the sight and imagination that Hoesch, rather than a fine diplomat and gentleman, was the hardline Nazi that he never was. His replacement as ambassador was already waiting in the wings, Hitler's favourite expert on Britain and the full-bore Nazi supporter Hitler had always wanted as ambassador, Joachim von Ribbentrop.

Joachim von Ribbentrop (the 'von' was his own affectation he was not entitled to it), Germany's new ambassador in London 1936.

32

Chapter 3

Sympathisers and 'Spyclists'

… something of an innocent abroad, proved much slower to bite on the bullet of disillusion.

Gordon Brook-Shepherd

In the years after the end of the First World War veterans' groups began pilgrimages to their old battlefields and cemeteries of their comrades. Widows and families of the fallen also began to visit where their loved ones had fought, died and were commemorated. They saw the devastated cities, towns and communities of France and Belgium for themselves and, of course, those who had not been were only too familiar with the images of these war-torn places through the popular illustrated magazines and papers of the war years.

As a result, movements, often raised on a local level in cities and major towns across Britain, began to build strong associations with particular cities and major towns synonymous with the the old battlefield salients such as Ypres in Belgium and Albert on the Somme. The aim was to help raise money for their reconstruction and they began to organise exchange visits. In this spirit many in Britain were also moved to build friendship links with Germany in the hope of continuing peace and understanding through similar groups and exchanges, especially with young people of the post war generation.

The problems began soon after the Nazi Party gained power. Its sinister objectives and persecution of Jewish people caused many British people, Jews and non-Jews, to break these ties and many Anglo-German groups made the decision to fold. The groups that remained or were founded after this time, no matter how they tried to dress-up their existence, were pro-Nazi. The problem was that there were those in Britain who, to give them the benefit of the doubt, stuck with maintaining friendly links with Nazis in the sincere hope that there could be understanding and to maintain peace. Others remained naïve and would not see the darker implications of these associations; some, both overt and tacit, were Nazi supporters willing to embrace the ideals of Nazism.

The right-wing groups such as the British Union of Fascists were only too obvious and were easily infiltrated and observed by Special Branch and MI5. There were also pro-Nazi groups that attempted to cloak their sympathies by claiming their aims were to foster non-political, commercial and sporting links with Germany. The most prominent of these was The Anglo-German Fellowship founded in 1935. Created by and aimed at recruiting influential people in British society, its membership included aristocrats, titled members of the landed gentry, retired senior personnel of the armed forces, businessmen and directors of a number of well-known British companies and several MPs.

Other organisations such as The Link (1937) and front organisations would follow. It is also clear that some newspapers, both nationals and local press, were under pressure from their owners or significant members of their readership and were apologetic for any negative reportage of the Nazis or pro-Nazi activities in Britain. It was no wonder appeasement was such a favoured and entrenched view held by some significant people in the British Government when dealing with Hitler in the late 1930s.

* * *

The high profile trial and conviction of Hermann Görtz at the Old Bailey for collecting information about the RAF Manston air station for German intelligence in March 1936[1] had been more an embarrassment than a great loss for the *Abwehr*, but it taught the Nazi intelligence services they would have to find new approaches if they were going to carry on their espionage activities. They were only too aware of the value of using young people who, inspired by the all-pervading imagery, sounds, pageantry and indoctrination of Nazism, could be filled with the ardour and sense of adventure to become spies for the Fatherland. A number were sent to Britain shortly after the Nazis came to power under the guise of being students or reporters for German newspapers. British intelligence soon became aware of this method of infiltration, some of the most dangerous were expelled, others were allowed to stay but their German masters knew they had to be canny if they were going to avoid further embarrassment or even risk a blanket ban.

Among the new vanguard of students-cum-reporters was Joachim Benemann. On first appearance his purpose for being in Britain was that of a student at the London University. He was in fact the representative of the *Reichsjugendführung* in Berlin who was here to co-ordinate German Hitler Youth activities in Britain, to forge links with youth groups for boys and to build links between the *Bund Deutscher Mädel* (BDM) (German League of Girls) with girls' groups in Britain.[2]

Benemann knew he would not be starting from scratch; as early as 1935 twenty German boys had attended a summer camp with a similar number of English lads in Surrey under the auspices of the German and British YMCA movements. In May 1936 Benemann had flown over to England specially to represent the Hitler Youth headquarters in Berlin. At Hove he collected a substantial cheque to inaugurate the Anglo-German Youth Camps from the newly formed Britannia Youth Movement (BYM) founded by Councillor (later Mayor of the Borough of Hove) H.C. Andrews. In August that same year fifty uniformed members of the Hitler Youth Movement encamped at Dymchurch with a similar number of British lads of the BYM.[3] What was hoped would be the first of many Anglo-German Youth Movement camps was proudly sponsored by local philanthropist Mr Capel Morris who even had an enamel badge bearing the Union Flag and the Nazi Flags specially struck by Thomas Fattorini Ltd of Birmingham to commemorate the event. The English boys were then reciprocally invited to Germany during which visit they attended the Olympic Games and other attractions in Berlin.

BUF leader Sir Oswald Mosley inspects his 'Blackshirts' on Royal Mint Street shortly before the clash on Cable Street, 4 October 1936.

Policemen arresting a demonstrator during the 'Battle of Cable Street' in London's East End, 4 October 1936.

Before they left, The Hitler Youth and Britannia Youth boys also visited London where they marched up Whitehall carrying their British and Nazi flags which they dipped when they laid their wreaths at the Cenotaph.[4] This would not be the last time Nazi flags would be seen at the Cenotaph, despite earlier misgivings over the wreath laid by Rosenberg on behalf of Hitler in 1933. German war veterans and British Union of Fascists and Britannia Youth Movement tried to ally themselves with the British Legion. In some areas they were warmly accepted and Nazi salutes and flags were included in Remembrance Services at the Cenotaph and in a number of British cities and and towns for the Armistice Sunday services before the outbreak of hostilities in 1939.

Despite the infamous 'Battle of Cable Street' taking place in the East End of London on 4 October 1936, where local communist, anarchist, socialist and Jewish groups clashed with the Metropolitan Police who had been sent to protect a marching parade of members of the British Union of Fascists, the membership of the BUF continued to grow. In fact membership increased steeply after Cable Street; in a Special Branch secret report to the Home Office (copied to MI5) it was revealed:

Confidential returns which have been prepared for the information of Sir Oswald Mosley show that the London Command has, since 5th October, increased its membership by a little over 2,000, the majority having been recruited by East London Branches.[5]

The year 1937 would see more pro-Nazi organisations emerge such as the anti-Semitic Nordic League which had its main driving force in Archibald Maule Ramsay MP. The pro-Nazi Christian movement and the Anglo-German Brotherhood merged with them as well as the Anglo German Link, usually known simply as 'The Link,' founded by Admiral Sir Barry Domvile, the former Director of Naval Intelligence. In April 1937 a 'goodwill' camp organised by the Anglo-German Circle was held at Dauntsey's School, West Lavington, Wiltshire where twenty young men from Germany and twenty from England aged 17 to 28, with a variety of backgrounds from factory hands to university students came together *'to work, play, hold discussions and make tours.'*[6]

Young men from Britain and Germany at the 'Good Will' camp organised by the Anglo-German Circle at Dauntsey's School, West Lavington, Wiltshire, April 1937.

Hitler Youth training required the boys to complete a series of skill-based activities to become fully fledged members. One of these was to successfully plan and execute treks over distance with challenging terrain and an extended *Fahrradtour* (bicycle tour) which some units carried out abroad in countries of Germany's old enemies; countries that, curiously (or not), became subject to German invasion after the outbreak of war. The boys and their leaders were encouraged to document their journey and they took a great interest in the historic and industrial areas they visited.

In 1937 *Unterbannführer* Joachim Benemann, now established in his own office and residence at 27, Mecklenburg Square, Bloomsbury WC1, worked with the Anglo-German Fellowship to arrange *Farradtouren* for Hitler Youth in Great Britain for the first time. MI5 had already obtained a Home Office Warrant (HOW) on Benemann and a number of his known associates and an intercepted letter from July 1937 revealed a list of tours for twelve different Hitler Youth cyclist groups as:

Trip 1:   Grimsby – Manchester
Trip 2:   Southampton to Londonderry
Trip 3:   Ostend – Dover – London – Liverpool
Trip 4:   London to Liverpool
Trip 5:   Grimsby – Leeds
Trip 6:   Hook of Holland – London – Sheffield – London – Ostende – Dover
Trip 7:   Canterbury – Birmingham – Newport
Trip 8:   Grimsby (TBA)
Trip 9:   Southampton – London
Trip 10: Grimsby –Manchester
Trip 11: Vlissingen – Harwich – London
Trip 12: Southampton – London[7]

Numerous British youth groups such as the League of Nations Youth Groups, Youth Hostels Association, YMCA, and Boy Scouts innocently and non-politically hosted the Hitler Youth groups, just as they would have hosted any other young groups visiting from aboard, organising days out and special events to share with the Hitler Youth visitors. Organisations such as the Rotary Club used their contacts in local councils, industries and emergency services to arrange tours of factories, utilities and the likes of new ambulance and fire stations.[8]

Although a few eyebrows were raised, in the main the welcome was very warm for the smart, clean cut young men from Germany. MI5 warned local constabularies of their anticipated arrival and their CID officers kept an eye on them. A typical report on a Hitler Youth cycle tour visit was sent to the Chief Constable of the City of Sheffield Police by Detective Sergeant Leonard Ward:

On 2 July 1937, 37 German schoolboys arrived in this city from Berlin, under the charge of two schoolmasters, Herr Friedrich and Herr Hahn. Boys were aged 15–18. Divided into two parties, 14 under Friedrich guested at King Edward VII school and 23 under Herr Hahn guested at Firth Park Secondary School. They visited local factories such as Bayley's Steel Works Ltd in Sheffield, Daniel Doncaster & Sons Ltd and the Electric Power Station at Blackburn Meadows. On Tuesday 20th they were

Photograph of a member of the Hitler Youth sent to a British friend he made during a cycle tour in 1937.

received by the Lord Mayor ... It is known that these masters and a number of the boys are in possession of cameras and it is known that Herr Hahn was found taking photographs of the surrounding country when he and the boys were on a visit to Edale recently and this was resented by residents.[9]

Another group of twenty-two members of the Hitler Youth spent a week's holiday as guests of Rydal School. The invitation had been extended by the headmaster the Rev A.J. Costain MA after some other German youths visited the school for a day the previous year. The *Colwyn Bay and North Wales Weekly News* described them:

The visitors were a well set up body of youths, all picked leaders of boys. They were divided among the various dormitories for sleeping and dined with the Rydal boys who quickly fraternised with the Germans. Only a few of the guests spoke English and conversations were carried on in a mixture of German, French, English, Latin and gesticulations ... swapping was naturally indulged in and many black German caps are now reposing on unfamiliar Rydal heads. 'A jolly good crowd of chaps,' was the verdict of one Rydal boy. The party left by charabanc for Snowdon, being given a rousing send-off by their hosts. After climbing Snowdon the party proposed to hike to Cardiff.[10]

A Hitler Youth group off on a **Fahrradtour** *(bicycle tour), 1937.*

The problem occurred after 24 May 1937 when the *Daily Herald* ran the story *Nazis Must be Spyclists* in which it was claimed that German cycle tourists *'will be expected to carry out the duties of amateur spies as well,'* quoting the German cyclist magazine *Der Deutsche Radfahrer* (*The German Cyclist*) one of the official organs of the German National Union for Physical Culture, or as the article described them 'The Nazi Cyclist Association' as giving the following instructions to German sportsmen when travelling abroad:

> *On your journey pay attention to and memorise all the country you pass through, plains, mountains, villages, towns, roads and railways. Get into your head all landmarks like steeples and towers and all fords and bridges and acquaint yourself with them in such a way that you will be able to recognise them at night. The time may come when you will be able to serve your country by this knowledge.*[11]

'Spyclists' caught the imagination of the public and was repeated in the next edition of the British magazine *The Cyclist*, but when MI5 investigated and tracked down the *Herald*'s 'special correspondent' he turned out to be Richard

Bernstein, a German living in exile in Prague who found it in a German language newspaper. The article claimed to be from *Der Deutsche Radfahrer* could not be traced in previous editions of the paper.

The 'Spyclists' article in the *Daily Herald* did, however, cause far more members of the British public to view the Hitler Youth visits as having a darker intent when they saw or read about the uniformed Hitler Youth groups riding through the British countryside. Nonetheless, very much in the spirit of appeasement which pervaded at the time, there was no ban on Hitler Youth group visits to Britain and they continued with the boys having their photographs taken at well-known tourist destinations such as York, Oxford, Windsor Castle, the

Cover of **Der Leichtathlet** *showing German runner Rudolf Harbig competing at White City Stadium, London 1937.*

Houses of Parliament and with Beefeaters at the Tower of London[12] right up to the month before the Munich Crisis in 1938.

Sport was also used as a useful tool to make contact with potential British recruits for the German intelligence services. Any international sports meeting attended by German teams would have a few intelligence men tagged on as diplomatic officials or support staff. The 1936 Summer Olympics in Berlin had provided a major opportunity for Nazis to make useful contacts among the visiting British sportsmen, their entourage, visiting dignitaries and spectators. The German intelligence services knew the British have a habit of saying 'do drop by if you happen to be passing' when departing from holiday acquaintances; it's often given as a nicety and not really expected to be taken up, but rest assured, if German intelligence considered you useful further contact would ensue.

Even some of the smaller international meetings would frequently be supported by senior members of the *Deutscher Reichsbund für Leibesübungen* (DRL), (the Nazi governing body for sport), naturally bringing a small

41

entourage with them. For example in July 1937 the Hitler Youth swimming section that had been raised from the German nationals community in London were visited by DRL Leader Herr Hans von Tschammer und Osten at the Porchester Swimming Baths, before he attended the England v Germany swimming gala at Wembley pool a few days later.[13] The following month some fifty German sportsmen were brought over and entertained, with help from the Anglo German Association and our old friend *Unterbannführer* Joachim Benemann, for the International Athletics Meeting at the *White City* Stadium. It was all grist for the mill to show the world the

England Full-back and astute political commentator Bert Sproston, 1938.

The infamous image of the England team giving the Nazi salute at the England v Germany match in Berlin on 14 May 1938.

sporting prowess of Aryan man and every visit was an opportunity for more espionage and intelligence gathering, if they could get away with it.

There has been much discomfort and debate over the England Football Team giving the Nazi salute during the playing of the German national anthem ever since the England v Germany match on 14 May 1938. It is generally accepted that when the team first heard the salute would be expected from them, the request was met by a flat refusal from the players and representations were made on their behalf by the Football Association representatives with them to Nevile Henderson, the British Ambassador in Berlin. Henderson was desperately keen to avoid a diplomatic incident, it was just two months after the *Anschluss* and the FA officials conveyed to the team how Henderson had explained to them that the diplomatic situation at the time was so precarious it would '*only need a spark to set Europe alight*'. Only then did the team agree to comply. The England players made the salute but Germany lost the match 3–6.

The legendary England and Stoke City player, Sir Stanley Matthews recalled the incident well and would tell of how he and his team mate Bert Sproston had gone for a stroll the day before the match. The pair saw the streets and buildings decked with swastika flags and Hitler was driven by in his motor car with a cavalcade of escorts. As he passed by the crowds of onlookers suddenly became animated and, filled with some strange adulation, flung their right arms skyward in salute to *der Führer*. Sproston turned to Matthews and uttered one of the most incisive comments in twentieth century political analysis:

> *Stan, I'm just a working lad from Leeds. I know nowt about politics and the like. All I know is football. But t'way I see it, yon 'itler feller is an evil little twat.*[14]

43

Chapter 4

Spies Among Us

When there is no enemy within, the enemy outside cannot hurt you.

Winston Churchill

Both refugees fleeing Nazi Germany and those who came to Britain to study, live and work from the mid-1930s suffered a growing fear they were being watched. MI5 and Special Branch certainly kept a weather eye on the community, especially Otto Bene and the *Auslandsorganisation*, MI5 Director Vernon Kell wrote to Russell Scott at the Home Office in April 1936:

> *What I feel is that it is the organisation* [Auslandsorganisation] *rather than the individual at the head of it which is definitely dangerous ... He* [Bene] *works in close touch with the* Hafendienstamt *which is in liaison with the Gestapo for the purpose of supervising the activities of German nationals in this country and for maintaining Party discipline ... There is evidence that the* Landesgruppe *is used as an instrument of German foreign policy to the extent that Otto Bene has played a prominent part in working for the creation of a pro-German feeling in Great Britain. That is, of course, unexceptional in itself, but it is difficult to resist the inference on general grounds that this is done as part of a policy whose ultimate object is to neutralize Great Britain and separate her from France ...*[1]

Kell continues and points out:

> *A special organisation subordinate to the* Landesgruppe *exists with the sole and express object of Natzifying these 'old Germans' ... The name of this organisation is the* Deutsche Vereinigung, *we have recently heard that the British Embassy in Berlin has obtained information that proves conclusively that the party organisation in Berlin and its leaders are particularly pleased with the progress which has been made in the* Landesgruppe *under Otto Bene in London in winning back these old Germans to their allegiance to the Swastika. In the event of war between Great Britain and Germany after all German subjects had been deported the 'old Germans' – British subjects*

– of the Deutsche Vereingung *would remain in this country as ready-made machinery for the organisation of sabotage and espionage work.*[2]

There were numerous instances of suspicions and incidents that confirmed the fears that Germans were being observed while they were in Britain. The deaths of Fabian and Wurms (see chapter 2) rocked the German community and some of the characters involved attracted the attention of Special Branch, notably Heinz-Alex Nathan whom they continued to watch long after the verdict of the inquest was returned. A Special Branch report of 20 February 1936 recorded:

The German refugees here still consider him to be an agent but there is no evidence in possession of the Metropolitan Police to show that he is working for the Nazis. It seems clear however, that someone is working for the Gestapo at the London School of Economics for many students who returned to Germany after having completed their studies there found, when interrogated, that the Secret State Police were in possession of full details concerning their activities and sympathies whilst in London. At least two students, on their return to Berlin were shown photographs of themselves reading the Pariser Tageblatt *in London and these, with others, who whilst at the London School of Economics did not always express full agreement with the Nazi regime, were sent to a special school of training in Germany to be re-educated in the Nazi ideals and aims. Nathan is suspected of being the man who supplied the information regarding students and in consequence is shunned by them.*[3]

In March 1937 the *Evening Telegraph* ran a report entitled *The Men Who Listen* that claimed:

Reliable estimates place the number [of German spies] *operating in Britain at 1,000. This number includes only professional spies and there are many more who are either amateurs or free-lancers seeking to turn a dishonest penny by selling information in the highest market'.*[4]

The article goes on to mention the types of information being sought such as secret weapons, military secrets and industrial espionage but also points out:

Major secrets of this type are the special concerns of a few master spies who work in various and devious ways to secure the details. Hosts of lesser spies are employed in gleaning items of information that reveal the existence of major secrets. Hints and references in the casual conversations of civil servants, soldiers, sailors and dockyard workers are overheard in restaurants, tea shops and public houses by waiters, waitresses and barmaids whose employment in those capacities is merely a cloak to cover their real activities.[5]

Despite being stifled by appeasers in senior government offices, MI5 wanted to act and a large swathe of the British public expected something to be done. As a result, three supposed journalists working for Nazi organisations did not have their journalistic permits for the UK renewed in August 1937; they took the hint and returned to Germany without a fuss. The three, Werner Bonaventura Crome, Wolf Dietrich von Langen and Franz Otto Wrede had all been subjects of MI5 and Special Branch interest for some time and were strongly suspected of espionage activities.

Wrede had drawn particular attention. Although claiming not to be a member of the Nazi Party, he had already published pro-Nazi booklets aimed at young people in Germany, was employed by the Bureau Ribbentrop in Berlin and was in fact on a mission to disseminate Nazi propaganda to the German community in Britain, especially those of suitable age to join the Hitler Youth. His wife was also found to be actively organising a branch of the BDM in London and, as anticipated by British intelligence, when Wrede was expelled his wife went with him. The German reprisal was swift and Norman Ebbutt, the veteran Berlin Correspondent for *The Times* was ordered to leave.

Despite no official reason for the refusal to renew the press permits to the Germans being given by the Foreign Office (FO), it was clear to the British and world press it was an expulsion in everything but name. Most of the British press toed the FO line, but that did not mean they all had to like it. *The Evening Standard* reflected a number of calls for greater light on the affair stating:

If the men have been guilty of espionage it is better that the public should be told so than the present atmosphere of uneasy speculation should exist ... wide publicity is being given to theories of an alarming character.[6]

The world press, however, felt no need to be quite so coy. In New York *The Jewish Telegraph* did not mince its words in its report:

The real reason for the ousting of three German newspapermen from England this week was that they had been spying on German refugees [in London]... The German journalists' ousting was entirely due to their activities among fellow Germans and had nothing to do with what they wrote for the papers at home or with military espionage. For some time, British authorities have been observing the tactics of Nazi agents who keep watch on their countrymen to be sure they remain loyal to the Nazi regime. Any who were hostile or even wavered slightly in their support of Hitler were warned their attitude would bring trouble either for themselves or relatives remaining in Germany.[7]

The article goes on to explain the three expelled Germans were:

… connected with an inner ring of Nazi agents which has been watched by a special division of Scotland Yard detectives. The Nazi secret bureau was in daily touch with Berlin … in a great new building operating under control of the German Foreign Office there is an index file giving the name, address, occupation, friends, acquaintances and social and political activities of every German resident abroad, whether refugee or a Nazi sympathiser.

John Baker-White, one of the founders of the independent 'Section D' who had sought out and exposed Nazi infiltrators in the 1930s, identified another card index, this one detailing '*thousands of British men and women with notes on their political opinions and reactions to Nazi propaganda*'[8] held and maintained by the Anglo-German Information Service whose headquarters were within the shadow of Big Ben at 38–39 and 45 Parliament Street, London. The director of the service, Dr Rudolph Gottfried Rösel, a man whose primary reason for being in Britain was officially recorded as a journalist, was in reality, one of the leading Nazi propagandists in Britain and it was he who ensured duplicates of each card created were sent back to Berlin by diplomatic bag.

When he was finally expelled from Britain in the summer of 1939 the originals went with him.[9] The Nazis did get careless and not every index got away. In September 1939 MI5 obtained a Nazi Party card index of members up to 1934 from a second-hand furniture dealer who had handed them into the police. Apparently, the cards had been left in cabinets cleared out from the Germany Embassy during Ribbentropp's refit.[10]

*　*　*

Concerns were further compounded when Nazi German authorities issued a decree on 3 February 1938 requiring all German citizens who had been abroad for more than three months to register with their nearest German consulate. Once registered each person would be expected to keep the consulate updated of any subsequent change of address. It was the responsibility of the heads of households to ensure all those residing with them were registered, failure to do so could result in a fine of up to 500RM. Anyone who knowingly or persistently failed to register would be declared to have lost their German nationality.[11]

The official reason given was that this act would unite German nationals abroad and maintain their relationship with the Fatherland, but few were under any illusions – the act was created to enable the Nazis to impose tighter regime control over Germans living abroad. With fear and coercion, threats of reprisals against family, seizure of money or property back in Germany all at their disposal, this decree gave Nazi authorities the ability, at will, to apply pressure on any German national abroad, to spy on neighbours and/or spy for the Reich. The fear that soon emerged was that this could potentially create the greatest spy network of all time.

The *Western Mail* special correspondent reflected the tone and content of a number of newspapers in being in no doubt whatsoever of the objectives of the registration scheme, listing them as: dissemination of pro-Nazi propaganda in Britain; military, political and industrial espionage and gathering confidential information of value in expanding Germany's overseas trade. Quoting a Nazi Party official: '*Of every 100 German propagandists we send to England 90 return here with half their National-Socialist training undone and full of all kinds of democratic ideas. The Germans in Britain swallow too much English air.*'

The article continued with the ominous news:

In future there will be no lukewarm Nazis in this country. Germans over here will have to show 100 per cent active support of the cause or lose their German nationality. The 25,000 German servant girls in this country will form the nucleus of a great new information gathering chain. They are employed for the most part by well-to-do people, businessmen, Civil Servants, Army, Navy and Air Force officers ... Two special training schools have already been established in Germany for training women to collect information. The first batch, consisting of 22 girls is already working in this country under the immediate control of Gestapo (secret police) officials living here ostensibly as commercial travellers.

Germans who have dared to disapprove of the Nazi regime have either been arrested on their return to Germany, had their passports cancelled, or found that reprisals have been taken against their families. The mere knowledge of the presence of Gestapo agents is sufficient to make the majority of Germans comply immediately with any demands the authorities in Berlin may make of them.[12]

It did not take long for the matter to be brought before the House of Commons. On 29 March 1938 Wolverhampton Labour MP Mr Geoffrey Mander asked the Home Secretary, Sir Samuel Hoare if he was aware of the:

... activities of the German secret police, the Gestapo, in England and whether he is aware that German residents in London are continually watched and reported on to Berlin by this organisation? Hoare replied: '*It would not be in the public interest to say more on this subject than that foreigners while*

resident in this country are entitled to the freedom which is enjoyed by all persons who are subject to the protection of our laws and the position is being closely watched by the responsible authorities.'

Mander replied by pressing: *Is the Home Secretary aware that the Gestapo put pressure on Germans in this country who desire to obtain naturalisation and who in other ways do not toe the line, through their families in Germany and will take steps to put a stop to that kind of thing?*

Hoare remained obdurate replying: '*If I have any evidence that unlawful acts are being committed, I will certainly take action.*'

However, when Mr Bellinger asked: '*In order to allay any uneasiness in the public mind, will the Right Honourable Gentleman give a categorical assurance that no agents of the German secret police are working in this country.*' Hoare simply referred him to his previous answers.[13]

Mander revisited the subject in the House of Commons on 6 April 1939 when he asked Sir Samuel Hoare*: 'In the interests of national security, will* [the Home Secretary] *consider the advisability of cancelling permits to reside in this country of members of the German secret police, the Gestapo, and other Nazi organisations?*'

Hoare assured him: '*… careful attention is given to the activities in this country of these organisations, with a view to appropriate action when such action is called for, and within recent weeks steps have been taken with a view to terminating the residence in this country of three persons connected with these organisations.*'

But when Mander's Labour colleague 'Manny' Shinwell enquired: '*If there was any reason to believe that there are still members of the Gestapo residing in Britain?*' Hoare refused to answer, stating he had: '*answered the question on the paper.*'

Fred Bellenger then asked if the Gestapo agents were given diplomatic immunity and he was given the straight answer of 'No', but when William Gallacher the long serving Honourable Member for Fife Western asked of Hoare: '*Will the Right Honourable Gentleman be willing to close down the headquarters of the Gestapo in Belgrave Square?*' he received no reply at all.[14]

Nothing more is mentioned of Belgrave Square as headquarters of the Gestapo in London in parliamentary debates. A few newspapers picked up on the statement[15] but the exact location of the headquarters was not revealed, although it was likely the honourable member was alluding to the former Austrian Legation at No 18 Belgrave Square that had been used as a consular department of the German Embassy after the *Anschluss* in March 1938.

However, the Square, situated in the heart of Belgravia just around the corner from Buckingham Palace, was certainly an intriguing place for here were also located the Portuguese and the Spanish embassies and in the magnificent Georgian mansions and buildings of the square resided some of London's social and political elite, including a number of peers of the realm, highly successful Jewish businessmen and George, Duke of Kent, the fourth son of HM King George V and brother of the reigning monarch King George VI. The Duke of Kent had remained close to his brother the Duke of Windsor after the abdication and their extended German family and there were concerns, especially after the Duke of Windsor's tour of Germany and meeting with Hitler in 1937, that the Duke of Kent also had pro-Nazi sympathies. His cousin Prince Ludwig von Hesse wrote of him in 1938: '*Duke of Kent. Very German-friendly. Clearly against France. Not especially clever, but well informed. Entirely for strengthening German-English ties.*'[16]

Among those who also had residences there were the renowned authority on international affairs Victor Cazalet MP at No 33; one of America's sharpest critics, the Conservative politician Henry 'Chips' Channon at No 5; there was Earl Bathurst at No 12; the Duke of Norfolk at No 14 but at No 15 was the Duke of Bedford (Marquis of Tavistock), chairman and financial backer of the far right British People's Party. At No 48 was Hamilton House, renowned as the setting for some of London's biggest and most exclusive society events, home of Sarah Winter, a British Nazi supporter and member of the British Union of Fascists who had used her swish gatherings to raise funds for the Anglo-German Fellowship. She drew controversy when she ordered her staff to fly the Nazi flag from her house after the *Anschluss* in 1938. Winter was only persuaded to take the flag down after a personal telephone call from Lord Halifax.

German domestic servants working in the households of the wealthy and influential in Britain were also the subject of concern. German servants maintained a reputation for efficiency and smartness, were popular among the German *émigré* community, were often cheaper and were believed to be less indiscreet than British domestics. The problem was those who were acting as spies were not listening for gossip.

There were a number of agencies active in London that specifically marketed German servants. One that became infamous was The Anglo-German Agency for Domestic Servants that had offices in the Haymarket, London. Headed by Mrs Alexander Raven Thomson (before marriage she was Elisbeth Roentgen, the daughter of Wilhelm Roentgen, who discovered the X-rays), it was not surprising the agency drew suspicion because her husband Alexander Raven Thompson was the high-profile director of policy in the British Union of Fascists. Their disinclination towards supplying German girls to work for Jewish families did not go unnoticed either.[17]

The German Embassy and Nazi Party in Britain were never comfortable working with the BUF; they much preferred a more discreet approach and direct control. Consequently, in 1936, when German born widow Mrs Margaret Newitt approached Otto Bene, the leader of the Nazi *Auslandsorganisation* in Britain, at a dance at the German Embassy with the idea of creating a new agency for unemployed German girls, a further meeting was arranged to discuss the proposal and it was given the green light. The plan was that this new agency would be a creature of the Nazi Party and the German Embassy which would place compliant German domestic staff in the households of those who were of particular interest to the Nazis. For doing this Mrs Newitt was assured by Bene personally that she *'would be doing the German government a great service.'*[18]

Thus, the International Employment Agency was first established in offices on Moray Road, Finsbury Park. The facade of these premises, however, was down at heel and the area in Mrs Newitt's estimation was less than salubrious – no place to welcome the girls or clients of the calibre they were trying to attract – so smart new offices were found for the business on Victoria Street, London SW1 and she was good to go.[19]

Newitt went on to join the BUF in 1938 and was finally arrested after she moved to Droitwich to get away from the air raids on London in October 1940. Her house was searched and a mass of incriminating material was found which revealed her connection, not only to British Nazi leader Bene, but to Jerome Becker, an infamous American-German spy in Holland in the First World War; Baron Livonius who had worked with Baroness von Einem who had been sentenced to death for spying by the French shortly before the Germans invaded France and thus evaded execution and a Kurt Burlin, a known German agent in Iceland.[20] It also appeared Mrs Newitt had been attempting to obtain a position with the Censor Department and later the RAF before her arrest. She was removed to Holloway Prison and a case was prepared against her.[21] Ultimately, with the DPP and intelligence services already stretched to the limit, she was simply interned for the duration of the war.

Servants seeking positions, and for that matter intelligence services wishing to place servants in households of interest, would not just be reliant on their tame agencies. Every national and provincial newspaper regularly contained adverts offering positions for servants and there were other agencies that innocently obtained positions for both male and female German staff, some of them working with absolutely no other intent than to earn a living while others were undoubtedly working to a Nazi espionage agenda.

Just days after the outbreak of hostilities in September 1939 Guy Liddell recorded:

The question of domestic servants has once again been raised. Sir Alexander Maxwell [Permanent Under Secretary at the Home Office] *is averse to any steps being taken to instruct people in the services to lay off their alien domestics and he wants them to be dealt with by the tribunals in due course. My feeling is that we should press the three armed services to get rid of enemy alien servants whether employed in or outside barracks and that any other alien servants should be vetted. At present the army and air force will not allow enemy alien servants in barracks and alien servants only after being vetted. The navy seems to have them everywhere.*[22]

The situation was only properly tackled by the arrest and internment of 'enemy aliens' from May 1940. Finally on 21 June 1940 it became forbidden for officers of the armed forces to employ 'enemy aliens' as domestic servants or in any other capacity. However, it had not escaped the notice of the intelligence services just how many male and female 'enemy aliens' in customer-facing service industries, notably, those who had worked in the West End and at some of London's best known luxury hotels, returned to Germany shortly after the outbreak of war. Some would reflect on this being confirmation of their long-held suspicions and it is intriguing when searching through the KV2 file series of released MI5 files at The National Archives just how many former servants and hotel staff who had been employed in Britain before the war were exposed as a result of their activities during the war as confirmed agents of the Third Reich.

A case in point, is that of Josephine Fillipine Emilie 'My' Eriksson (née Karp). German born, Swedish by marriage and by the 1930s a divorcee, Eriksson had been employed in the households of several notable British families since her first arrival in the UK in April 1930. She occasionally caught a ferry over to the continent and during one of these visits she was recruited by the man she claimed to know as 'Dr Rantzau' (Nikolas Ritter) and became his message courier and paymaster for spies operating in the London area. Over the years 1934 to 1938 she made six recorded trips to the continent, returning having been debriefed and given new instructions with 50–100RM in her pocket each time.

Eriksson first came to the attention of the British Security Services following a chain of events that began in late 1937 when MI5 had received a tip-off that Mrs Else Duncombe of Broadhurst Gardens, Hampstead had been *'acting as a post box for the German Secret Service'*.[23] A Home Office Warrant was obtained and Duncombe's post was soon being intercepted. MI5 were particularly interested in the communications and apparent movements of a certain Hermann Simon; he too was subject of a HOW and his correspondence was also intercepted which showed he had required cash for expenses during his time in the UK obtained from a number of sub-agents of the *Abwehr*. 'My' Erikssen was investigated after Simon wrote to her requesting money in January 1938.

Further letters suggested the pair had met and Erikssen became Simon's main link with Ritter. Detective officers put on Simon found they could have grounds to arrest him for failing to sign one of the hotel registers where he had stayed. They tracked Simon to room 315, Liverpool House in the Minories, East London where he was arrested; his baggage was searched which revealed a series of notebooks and sketches relating to British airfields he had spied on.[24]

It remains unclear from the files released to date, why despite being caught with his sketches of airfields, a notebook of contacts and equipment for secret writing in his baggage, Simon was not prosecuted as a spy. Instead he was arrested for failing to sign the aliens' register when he was staying at The Chequers Inn, Tonbridge, Kent and was sent to prison for six months for the offence. Hermann Walter Christian Simon (aka Carl Petter, Wilhelm Andersson) would be deported but re-emerged in June 1940 when he landed on the west coast of Ireland equipped with a wireless transmitter. He was later arrested and interned for the duration of the war.[25]

Eriksson also evaded prosecution, perhaps because she was seen as more the messenger than an active agent. She remained subject to a Home Office Warrant where her letters were intercepted and it seems MI5 were happy to wait and watch to see who she would lead them to. She always seems to have been plausible and inoffensive and was fortunate to have nerves of steel, whereas Mrs Else Duncombe, the woman who previously couriered the messages and money from Ritter to Simon and vice versa had committed suicide. Erikssen subsequently served in a number of notable households including Viscount and Lady Elveden at Gloucester Lodge, Regent's Park where she spoke openly about her acquaintance with the Görings. She then found a placement through Mrs Hunt's Agency on Marylebone Road with the Duchesse Château-Thierry.[26]

Anna Sonia de Rais-Bouillon, Duchesse Château-Thierry.

Anna Sonia de Rais-Bouillon (née Salamonska), Duchesse Château-Thierry (aka Uhlig), was born in Nijmegen, Holland in 1877 and had lived in Britain since before the First World War. Divorced from her first husband (Oscar Uhlig) and widowed by her second husband in 1936, by the late 1930s she was a fading socialite who was nearly bankrupt. However, never one to let standards drop, the duchess still retained a cook and maid but was very particular and her maid servants often did not stay for long. 'My' Erikssen, however, got closer to the duchess than any other servant.

Duchesse Thierry, as ever in dire financial straits, had a piece of land in Germany and wished to get the funds out to her UK account without serious loss and 'My' Erikssen suggested she might just know the man to help her. Erikssen's contact in Germany was *Abwehr* middle-man Fritz Gallus who in turn passed the contact on to Ritter, who contacted Thierry under the name of Dr Reinhardt stating he was happy to help. In July 1938 Ritter sent funds for the duchess to travel to Munich to meet with him. Shortly after her return she wrote to 'My' Erikssen:

> *You'd better not write anything about these negotiations to your friend or your relatives, as it may not be wise to write about it … I also very much hope that I shall be able to show my appreciation to your friends in getting results in the various things he wishes, but nothing can be done without funds … I only hope I may be of some use to him, only you must let him know that whatever I do in commercial and business transactions he must officially keep my name out of it.* [27]

Thierry had the idea that she could be of great value to the German intelligence service through her influence and many London society contacts. Ritter was much enamoured with the idea and the plan was hatched that Thierry should built a social salon where she would host parties and dinners, create contacts and recruits for espionage work. To fund this Ritter agreed to pay sums of money under the guise of payments for machinery that did not exist or 'beauty products' for the duchess's 'business projects'. [28]

In late January 1939 the duchess met with Ritter again, this time in Hamburg and on 4 February 1939, less than a week after her return, she placed an advertisement in *The Times* for a companion au pair at her apartment at 102, Dorset House, Gloucester Place, Marylebone NW1, literally just around the corner from Baker Street. Ritter had promised the duchess a young hostess to assist in the operation and instructed *Abwehr* agent Vera Schalburg to reply to the advert and advised the duchess to accept her application when she received it.

Vera took up her 'position' at Dorset House in March 1939. The instructions given to her by Ritter before she left for her stay with the duchess were:

1. Not to mention his name to the duchess.
2. To report what the officers who were supposed to come to the duchess's flat and other people said about the possibility of war.
3. To get hold of any documents belonging to officers visiting the duchess and photograph them. The films were not to be developed in England and were not to be sent by post but were to be taken personally to Ritter by Vera.
4. To find people who would be prepared to work for Ritter, preferably people who were financially embarrassed or in trouble.
5. Air matters were to be given first place.

Vera was given the names of various persons in London whom German intelligence believed would be helpful to her and members of the duchess's circle who could, potentially, be of value to German intelligence.[29]

The set-up in the flat was described by Winifred Morrish, the duchess's cook resident in the flat at 102 Dorset House from June to October 1939 in an interview conducted by Richard Butler:

Mrs Kaplan was living at the flat when Morrish arrived ... Vera Schalberg was also there when she arrived but left shortly after the beginning of the war ... The Duchesse told Morrish that she received an allowance for Vera. She said that Vera received the money and paid it over to the Duchesse herself. Vera was known as the Duchesse's companion. Vera slept in a room downstairs ... Many people called at the flat ... very often the Duchesse opened the door to her visitors herself. Morrish said that the Duchesse drank very heavily each evening, usually whiskey. She never heard the Duchesse express anti-English views. After war was declared the Duchesse kept Morrish waiting for about two weeks for her wages. She said she was waiting for Vera's money. The Duchesse was very often hard up but matters usually came right when Mrs Kaplan paid her each month when Vera's money arrived. The Duchesse went to Holland in July 1939 and when she came back appeared to have a fresh supply of money.'[30]

'My' Eriksson was arrested for a breach of the Aliens Order 1920 when she attempted to leave Britain in December 1939 and after release she was interned for the remainder of the war. Even experienced MI5 officers, 'TAR' Robertson and John Marriott, were taken in when they interviewed Eriksson at Aylesbury Prison in October 1940. In their report they noted they had 'pressed her strongly' regarding the payment they could prove she had made to Simon: ... *but she maintained that she knew nothing about him when he wrote and were satisfied that on learning that he was connected with her Uncle Fritz's friend, Dr Rantzau* [Ritter], *she made the loan out of pure kindness.*

Explaining further that '*Uncle Fritz is Fritz Gallus, an old friend of her family and not in fact any relation of hers. He wanted to marry her,*' Robertson and Marriott concluded:

> *We were very much impressed with Erikkson's* [sic] *demeanour who struck us as an honest woman who had fallen under suspicion through the misfortune of having an old family friend, in the shape of Gallus, a man who was associated with Rantzau and who is himself probably in the Secret Service.*

In his annotated note on the file copy of the report Helenus 'Buster' Milmo (later a High Court Judge) was more incisive: '*Well! Well! This is not borne out by her letters. She must be a most impressive liar!*'[31]

In a later interview Vera claimed her visit to London achieved nothing. None of the officers whom she was supposed to meet ever turned up at the duchess's house. There never were any documents to photograph and she had no camera and no money to buy one.[32] She may have been speaking the truth about the documents, but the intelligence gathered by her and the Chateâu-Thierry circle could have been responsible for providing information that led to one of the greatest tragedies of the early war years. What is certain is that Vera fled to the continent shortly after the outbreak of war, but it would not be the last time Vera Schalberg would cross the shores of Britain.

* * *

Espionage was far from restricted to female domestic servants in private homes. The very best hotels in London held considerable numbers of German and Italian staff in the 1930s. They too were smart and added a certain *je ne sais quoi* to the ambience of the halls of marble, chandeliers, mirrors and palms of the receptions that greeted guests, who were served in luxurious lounges and smart silver service restaurants. The Savoy, The Ritz, The Dorchester, The Waldorf and Claridge's, these were the favoured venues for civil servants

Abwehr *Agent Vera Schalburg.*

56

LONDON
SAVOY HOTEL

Unter allen Hotels in London bietet das Savoy Hotel allein ein wunderbares Panorama des historischen Themse-Flusses, von der berühmten St. Paul's Kathedrale bis zur altehrwürdigen Westminster Abbey. Seine feine Küche, die gebotenen Unterhaltungen und vornehm-ruhevolle Stimmung ziehen die Aristokratie der Welt an.

DAS IN LUXURIÖSESTEM STIL EINGERICHTETE HOTEL IN EUROPA.

Pre-war German magazine advert for The Savoy Hotel, London 'The most luxuriously furnished hotel in Europe.'

from all manner of ministries, senior army officers and doyens of the secret services to dine, hold some of their meetings, and even hire rooms for soft interrogations.

The Savoy was a particular favourite of the British intelligence services; Claude Dansey, Assistant Chief of the SIS (Secret Intelligence Service) would take his lunch there most days and would often find a quiet table to interview potential recruits. MI5's Guy Liddell would conduct lunchtime meetings over cocktails at the American Bar.[33] In fact, members of the intelligence services from an array of countries frequented the same notable hotels, the bedrooms and suites of which provided the height of luxury for visiting diplomats to ingratiate them with their hosts who would be footing the bill and hopefully grease the wheels of diplomacy.

Nazi officials showed a preference for staying at Claridge's in the early 1930s. They held press conferences there and in later years some of the dinners for visiting Nazi dignitaries hosted by the Anglo-German Fellowship were staged within its opulent function rooms. But Ribbentrop, subtle as ever, raised hotel occupancy to another level when he took over two floors of the Carlton Hotel on the corner of Pall Mall and The Haymarket for himself and his forty-strong entourage, parked five gleaming jet black Mercedes Benz limousines outside and flew a swastika flag over the hotel's entrance on The Haymarket during the Anglo-German Naval Agreement negotiations in 1935.

As the winds of war gathered in the late 1930s mistrust and inter-personal issues between staff – and even between staff and customers – were known to flare up on occasions, especially when strong opinions were expressed about the leaders of their home nations or the pros and cons of the war. Such an outburst

Benjamin Sumner Welles, American Under-Secretary of State, 1940.

or even coming to blows with a customer would mean instant dismissal, but the damage to the reputation of a good hotel could not be risked and excuses began to be made to terminate the employment of a number of foreign nationals in London hotels. A few clung on to their German and Italian staff into the early war years when issues over who was or was not a Fascist became an ever-present problem and suspicions and rumours were rife.

One tip-off based on a rumour nearly led to a major diplomatic incident in March 1940. Benjamin Sumner Welles, the American Under-Secretary of State and major policy advisor to President Roosevelt, was staying at an apartment in Claridge's during a diplomatic trip to London. The US Embassy's Head of Intelligence Herschel Johnson had received information from a former American diplomat who had met Count Carlo Sforza (an Italian anti-Fascist politician) when on holiday in Italy before the war and had apparently been told '*the Italians had fitted Claridge's up with microphones*'.[34] The rumour was that they had been put there with the collaboration of Italian Fascist sympathisers on the hotel staff.

The matter was taken seriously and MI5 B Division Director Guy Liddell went to investigate personally with Johnson, taking an expert from the GPO along with them. They were met by Miles Thornewill, one of the directors of the Savoy, who obtained a master key and let them into Welles' room. After conducting a thorough search the investigators could see no microphones had been installed, unless they had been built-in and plastered over in such a way they could only be revealed if the walls were pulled to pieces. Thornewill offered his full co-operation and profuse apologies and, in stereotypical obsequious hotelier manner when a problem lands squarely in their court, he told the MI5 officers he was '*prepared to sack the whole staff rather than lose American custom*'.[35] Johnson spoke with the American ambassador who made the decision that it was best not to take any chances and reserved rooms for Welles at The Dorchester. Liddell suggested the hotel wait until Welles had left the country to take action and seven weeks later the general manager of Claridge's was given his notice.

The problem was Welles could have jumped out of the frying pan and into the fire with the move. Many members of the intelligence community had their concerns about The Dorchester. The managing director, Anton Bon, was probably one of the best known hoteliers in the world, however he was also known to be a personal friend of a number of senior German officers including General von Reichenau, General Udet and General Milch, from his time as chairman of the Esplanade Hotel in Berlin in the 1930s. Discreet enquiries by MI5 revealed:

> *Bon was exceedingly unpopular with the British members of staff at the Dorchester Hotel and exhaustive investigation along this line revealed that he was definitely sympathetic to Germany and German methods and contemptuous of the British.*'[36]

There were also stories of Bon tapping telephone lines and obtaining the services of a French polisher to open a locked desk to obtain access to confidential papers. Special Branch Head Norman Kendal concurred with MI5s' findings and was very much of the opinion Bon was a Nazi sympathiser. The MI5 report on the Dorchester continues:

> *At this stage* [October/November 1940] *nearly everybody in London seems to have started harbouring suspicions about the Dorchester in general and Bon in particular and our daily post bag became a kind of race with Bon first and the rest nowhere. From investigation of the various pieces of information*

which reached us we established that the Dorchester has a shocking reputation in the hotel world where it is referred to as a 'nest of spies', that is a meeting place for almost every person of internationally questionable reputation.[37]

The problem was that Bon was a Swiss national and as a non-enemy alien from a neutral country he could not be interned under 18B, nor was he known to be a member of any right-wing organisation, nor was there any concrete proof he was engaging in espionage. So, the man known to his staff as 'The Major' remained at the helm of the Dorchester with a weather eye on him from the intelligence services.

Germans visited London just as they visited any other European tourist destination in the 1930s and many of the notable London hotels courted guests by advertising in German magazines – all pretty innocuous stuff – but the guise of tourist, travel agent and businessman all provided easy cover for German agents to come and go pretty much as they pleased. One of a number of Nazi agents operating in the London hotels throughout the 1930s was Otto Hans Felix Weil. Born in Munich in 1911, he had worked as *maitre d'hotel* at the Palace Hotel, Mannheim in Baden-Württemberg, but fancying some travel and adventure he came to London under an Anglo-German work arrangement as a hotel clerk at the Waldorf Hotel in 1932.

Weil's native tongue was German and he was fluent in French and English. He was an ideal recruit for espionage because he was young and impressionable. Weil could see the way the political wind was blowing in Germany and was eager to please the Nazis as they came to power, especially as he had dark hair and brown eyes and a slightly hooked nose. Indeed, he was said to resemble a Frenchman, and because his surname was known as a German Jewish name as well as a German name, he did not wish to give the impression he was anything other than Aryan. For this same reason Weil had joined the Nazi Party in the 1920s and he would have been one of the very first Nazi agents in London, being in place before and from the moment they assumed full power in 1933. It was not long before he progressed from hotel clerk to work for European travel organizers, tourist agents of the Grafton Hotel, as a guide and interpreter for parties touring the country.[38]

Despite applications by John Kugi, the Waldorf's general manager, Weil's visas were not extended in 1934 and he was ordered to return to Germany in May 1935. No specific reason for this is stated on Weil's MI5 file, but clearly he had become a person of interest and a Mr Chester at the Ministry of Labour candidly commented in a telephone conversation with an MI5 officer that he thought Weil was 'a wrong 'un'.[39] Chester's suspicions were justified. In May 1935 MI5 intercepted a letter from Weil in Mannheim to Otto Bene leader of the Nazi *Auslandsorganisation* in London, in which Weil revealed that on his

The Waldorf Hotel, Aldwych c1939.

return to Germany he had been employed by Nazi intelligence service during the recent Saar Plebicite.[40]

Weil then received a letter from Bene reminding him that he has not paid his subscription to the Nazi Party since 1928. Whether he had or not is another matter. Paperwork that provided long standing 'proof' of non-membership of the Nazi Party, which implied disaffection with the Nazi regime, was something German intelligence hoped would cause other countries to step back from scrutinising the non-party Germans when they arrived in their countries. However, to the trained eye this was one of the tell-tale signs that Weil was or would soon be engaged in espionage. Weil entered Britain again on 3 July 1937 (the year of the Hitler Youth 'spyclists' tours) as a 'tourist agent' and took up residence at 22 Mecklenburg Square, Bloomsbury WC1.[41] He was just a few doors away from *Unterbannführer* Joachim Benemann, the organiser of the Hitler Youth tours who was at 27, Mecklenburg Square. Weil leaves a few days later taking a party from London to Hamburg and then returns to London via the Hook of Holland.

Mecklenburg Square, Bloomsbury, home and office to Otto Bene leader of the Nazi Auslandsorganisation in Britain and London base for Nazi agent Otto Weil in the late 1930s.

And so it went on, with Weil based for his 'business' a five minute walk from Mecklenburg Square at the Bonnington Hotel on Southampton Row, London WC1. He was regularly in and out of Britain 'on business visits' and with tour parties. Weil's travel index cards in his own name record journeys to and from Germany, France and Holland. It is also likely he was making additional journeys on at least one other passport under an assumed name. On reflection there is little doubt he was constantly couriering letters and escorting agents, providing a significant conduit for the *Abwehr* in and out of Britain right up to his last recorded visit in June 1939.

Weil would carry on his espionage work on the continent. He was unfortunate to be caught spying when he was Paris where he was tried, found guilty of espionage and sentenced to death. He was only saved from execution by the entry of German forces into France in 1940. Weil was then deployed to recruit agents for *Ast Wiesbaden* in Bordeaux. (An *Ast* was a subordinate station of the *Abwher*.) In September 1941 he was assigned to *Referat III F Ast Bruxelles* where he had notable successes working in counter-espionage, in the detection of clandestine radio transmissions and 'turning' agents sent from England to 'double-cross'. In 1944 he was assistant to Hauptmann

Schellewald, Leiter of *Abwehrtrupp 363* at Liège where his MI5 file comments Weil was '*concerned with interrogations and is reported to have authorised torture on occasions*'.[42]

The problem for any spy operating in foreign territory has always been getting the information they discover out of the country and back to his or her masters. There were undoubtedly more like Weil who couriered mail to and from abroad in their baggage or by using dupes and collaborators. To avoid detection, it was a tricky balance of recruiting reliable, discreet individuals willing to act as 'postboxes' to provide cover addresses for mail to and from enemy agents. Officially, mail could only be opened if the address it was being sent to or from was subject to a Home Office Warrant (HOW). Too much mail from abroad to one address would draw suspicion; spreading the post boxes over many people increases the risk of one of them giving the game away or losing their nerve and reporting their actions to the authorities to avoid serious punishment. As we saw with the case of Mrs Else Duncombe it would only take one of them to get caught or buckle and the whole ring and agents could be compromised.

* * *

Then there was the high profile case of Mrs Jessie Jordan in 1938. Born Jessie Wallace in Glasgow in 1887, she had married a German waiter in 1912 and returned with him to Germany therefore becoming a German citizen by marriage. Herr Jordan was killed while serving in the Germany Army in 1918. After a brief return to Perth, Scotland in 1919 Mrs Jordan returned to Germany and married again but it did not last and ended in divorce in 1937. Soon afterwards it appeared Jessie returned to Scotland to reconnect to her roots. In reality she had been recruited by the *Abwehr* who had paid for her to have this 'fresh start'.

Jessie initially lodged in Perth and began sending sketches of military installations to her handler at an address in Hamburg. The Hamburg address had been the subject of a HOW obtained by MI5 in 1936 and Jessie's mail with the incriminating sketches had been intercepted, but being of such low quality they posed minimal threat to security and were allowed to be sent on. A later letter bore the partial impression of the sender's address and it was traced to the rooms occupied by Jordan. The problem for MI5 was that Jessie had moved on by the time a HOW had been granted for the address.[43]

Jordan had set up a small hairdressing business on Kinloch Street, Dundee but suspicions were aroused at her paying over the odds to purchase the premises and laying out a small fortune in renovating the building and fitting it with fancy equipment in such a deprived area. She had in fact received the money for the refurbishment from a relative, but Jordan carried on sending sketches and information about key military sites. She also acted as an *Abwehr* post box receiving parcels from German agents in America and sending them to addresses in Amsterdam from whence they would then be sent to the *Abwehr*.

The problem came about when maps, notably one marked by Jordan with the positions of coastal defences between Montrose and Kirkcaldy, were discovered by her cleaner, Mary Curran, who reported her concerns to Dundee Police. Initially her claims were dismissed, but Mrs Curran and her husband John pressed the issue and MI5 were informed. They were granted a HOW on Jordan's Kinloch Street address in December 1937. It did not take long before incriminating mail addressed to Jordan from America from the German agent 'Crown' (Guenther Rumrich who was supplying details of fleet dispositions and ship–to–shore signalling systems to the *Abwehr* and a member of what would be exposed as a major spy ring in the USA)[44] led to her arrest and trial at the High Court in Edinburgh in May 1938. Jordan pleaded guilty to the charges of espionage and after proceeds lasting less than half an hour she was sentenced to four years imprisonment. Newspapers recorded she showed little or no reaction and she walked 'unconcernedly' out of the dock after the sentence was passed.[45]

* * *

The German intelligence services knew international operations would become far more difficult if a state of war existed and redoubled efforts to re-establish their intelligence network in Britain when the storm clouds of war closed in. British military intelligence agents were almost exclusively recruited from the 'old boy network' of friends of friends from similar privileged backgrounds and education being the usual recruiting ground. The *Abwehr*, however, knew they stood a good chance of recruiting agents from British collaborators sympathetic to their cause or from those who could be duped by agents to carry out the work for love, money or the excitement of being a spy. If someone was approached in a British provincial hotel or pub with the suggestion of working in espionage it would almost certainly have been on behalf of the Germans, but they chose their marks and cloaked their activities well, up to a point.

The problem for the British intelligence services was they were badly understaffed and were confronted with the huge challenge of monitoring the activities of the Nazi *Auslandsorganisation* and other sympathetic groups in

Britain. These included far right organisations such as the British Union of Fascists (BUF), The Link, Nordic League, the Communist Party of Great Britain and extremist off-shoot groups and 'fronts' organisations of the left or right. There was also the Peace Pledge Union, which wished to sabotage weapons and hinder the war effort which had also been infiltrated by the BUF for their own ends. There were also many persons of interest considered potentially or actively 'subversive'.

Consider, investigations into hundreds of suspicious persons were running at any one time; it was before the age of modern computers and heavily relied on card indexes, files on persons of interest being updated and hopefully not lost among a pile of others on an officer's desk. The circulation of photographs, printed notices, bulletins and correspondence between all the appropriate authorities was conducted by post. Add to this the massive workload for passport control officers over the months before Britain's declaration of war and even into the early war years, when political refugees and those fleeing the Nazi heel were flooding into Britain. The individual business traveller without overt connections to or known communication with members of Nazi organisations in Germany or abroad were far harder to detect and undoubtedly passed in and out of the UK undetected and unchallenged, although some of them were revealed at a later date.

A typical case among these was Gerrit Schut aka Johann Schutt, Johann Peulen or Peuylen who claimed to have been born in Rotterdam in 1917 (both his true name and origins are not established beyond question). Schut was recruited by German intelligence in the late 1930s and made the first known of a number of trips to Britain in January 1939. On his travel documents to enter and depart from Great Britain over his visits, passport control noted Schut described himself variously as a ship's chandler, a ship buying agent for Holland, a bulb grower and a diamond merchant.[46] Schut's first mission to Britain was to gather intelligence about shipbuilding on the Clyde. He took a room at Bain's Hotel, India Street, Glasgow for three weeks. In her statement to the police, hotel manager Elizabeth Annovazzi recalled Schut spoke openly of how his father had a shipping business and after his death he had taken over the business and had come to this country to buy ships. He seemed an agreeable enough person and encouraged Annovazzi to write to his sister in Holland, which she did a few times and received replies.

On several occasions Schut was found out telling lies; once in particular he stated that he had bought a particular ship on the Clyde but unbeknown to Schut a ship's captain was residing in the hotel where he was staying at the time. Schut was standing drinks all round that night, celebrating the alleged purchase of the ship. The captain enquired about the purchase the following day

The Rex Hotel, Whitley Bay, Northumberland, one of the recruiting grounds of Nazi agent Gerrit Schut in 1939.

and learned that it had not been sold. Schut returned again in March 1939 and this time he suggested he would write a letter in Dutch to his sister, Annovazzi should copy it and send it to her. Understandably uncomfortable about writing something she did not understand, Annovazzi declined his request. She also noted there was a German couple staying at the hotel at the same time and they were all seen leaving the hotel together on at least two occasions.[47]

Schut left soon after and did not return to the Clyde; it was then he removed his operations to the Whitley Bay area of Northumberland. His methods changed little, he represented himself as Dutch and that he was broker for a Rotterdam shipping company. He often had money to buy drinks for others to celebrate the success of his business deals in the bars where he had become known, specifically at the Rex Hotel and the Esplanade Hotel in Whitley Bay and the Park Hotel, Tynemouth.

It seems Schut made a lot of contacts but few bore fruit. He was known to have made the acquaintance of two of the beach photographers, but they were not willing to comply with his requests for photographs of the guns at

Tynemouth Castle. It was also noted when he was at Whitley Bay that Schut had been seen with an expensive Leica camera with a special lens. On another occasion while at the Rex his cover was almost blown when a well-meaning member of the hotel staff introduced Schut to a Dutch lady, Miss Geraldine Franken, who was left with the impression Schut was not Dutch at all because he spoke so badly and she thought he was more like a German. The police and MI5 were aware of Schut and some of those he was trying to recruit from late 1939, but having been highly delighted to have successfully uncovered a spy operating in the North they had been very disappointed that he had already left and did not follow up on his known associates.

There the case of Gerrit Schut may have been left, but in May 1940 Schut was arrested in Holland as a suspected enemy agent. A search of his room revealed maps of gun emplacements from the North-East coast of England and his papers revealed he was in touch with two individuals in particular. MI5 was contacted at 'Box 500', Newcastle where the case was assigned to Major C.P. Hope to liaise with local police and look into the matter further. One of those named was a 33-year-old Sunderland widow, Eileen Child, whom Schut met at a dance at the Park Hotel in Tynemouth in May 1939. The general impression among their known associates at Whitley Bay was that Schut and the widow were to marry.

Investigations revealed she worked at a Sunderland radio retailers and was known to go out every Tuesday and return late each time. It was also known that she received occasional post from Holland and Norway. One day she was followed by a Special Branch officer, the people she visited were checked and all were found to be of good standing and not known to have any connections to pro-German organisations. The police, however, left a note on her file that they considered her 'a loose woman'.[48] On 14 May 1940 Child's house was searched and when she was brought in for an interview conducted by Sunderland Police, she was asked whether she had any correspondence in her possession regarding friendships with foreign seamen. Without hesitation she stated that she had various letters and telegrams from a Dutchman named Gerrit Schut who she believed to be a ship's broker from Rotterdam.[49]

Mrs Child stated that she had met him at a dance held in the Queen's Hotel, Whitley Bay about May 1939. Since that time she had corresponded with him on various occasions and had spent the week prior to the outbreak of war in 1939 with him at the Zuid-Hollandsch Hotel, Rotterdam, returning to England on the day war was declared. Whilst there she had met a woman who was introduced as his sister. Schut had proposed marriage to her but she had not treated the matter seriously. She stated that he had never at any time asked any questions regarding shipping, nor had she supplied him with any information of this nature. Between May and August 1939 she met him about four times in Whitley Bay, once in Hull and once in Sunderland on the occasion when he came to take her to Holland.

*   *   *

The other person revealed in Schut's papers was Fred Ibbotson from Whitley Bay. He was a former Territorial soldier who had served in the First World War. After the war he had returned to his old employment in the GPO SC & T (Sorting, Counting, Telegraphs and Telephones) and worked there for years, but having hit hard times and with a family to support he sought to alleviate his situation by turning to theft. He was caught stealing postal packets and had been given a custodial sentence with hard labour in 1932. Dismissed from his former job, Ibbotson had found it very hard to find regular employment and had taken occasional work as a bookie's runner and had become a salaried ARP warden on the outbreak of war.

Brought in for interview by Northumberland CID, Ibbotson confirmed he had paid regular visits to the Esplanade Hotel, Whitley Bay when he was working as a bookie's runner, having asked the manager if he had any work going there on a number of occasions, the manager introduced him to Gerrit Schut. Schut claimed he was Dutch but Ibbotson recalled his first impression was that Schut did not speak English particularly well '*passable like but not perfect by any means*'. He had his suspicions about the man but he desperately needed money and asked Schut if he could get him a job. Schut invited him over to Rotterdam to see if they could find him some work. While in Holland Ibbotson stated: '*He* [Schut] *was so evasive in many ways, and never told me what the job was going to be until just on our return journey … he told me he wanted some information on shipbuilding and things like that. He said it was because it was in his line and that I would help him in his work. I honestly did not really believe him.*'[50]

Schut gave him £40, £20 for his travelling expenses for the Holland trip and he was left with about £20 in pocket. Ibbotson admitted that he had been sure that Schut was a German agent, but claimed he knew very little about his activities and that what information he had supplied was obtained from a book which was available to the general public across Europe. The visits occurred twice more, on the next he even met a man Schut claimed was his boss, a man introduced as Captain Johnson at the Hotel Atlantic. His English was also very poor. Ibbotson's last visit was in August 1939 and he returned eight days before war broke out. Each time he carried letters through Customs back to England where he bought stamps and posted them from South Shields, possibly to other duped individuals who could then pass them to their contacts who they may or may not have realised were spies, all in an effort to avoid interception while they were being handled by the GPO.

By the time Child and Ibbotson were interviewed Schut was long gone and was released from custody after the German occupation of Holland. According to his MI5 file he was believed to be resident in Paris and was thought to have been involved in plots to get individuals to plant explosives on allied merchant shipping.[51] He was not spotted again until 1943 when he was seen in Spain with Rudolf Kellerman, another Nazi businessman cum agent, and was seen entering Spain on a number of subsequent occasions.[52] Schut stayed in Grenada with Kellermann when it was noted he had been travelling from Malaga, via Algeciras and appeared to have recently been in Gibraltar. At that time Gibraltar was a highly sensitive place, key to allied shipping in the Mediterranean and also for intelligence. Under no circumstances should Schut have been allowed through British Passport Control, he was after all an enemy alien, but it is intriguing to note that the man responsible for counter-intelligence in the area at the time and whose name appears in Schut's folder was Harold 'Kim' Philby,[53] who was revealed as a double agent before defecting to the Soviet Union in 1963.

The fates of those who had been co-opted by Schut while he was at Whitley Bay were that Eileen Child had a weather eye kept on her by CID and a local informer. Fred Ibbotson, who had supplied information and carried letters was not prosecuted, but was arrested under article 18B and was detained until November 1943 when he was released under restrictions, it being then felt that the German intelligence service would not approach him again.

Tantalisingly, it seems there is more to the story. In October 1940 MI5 Regional Officer co-ordinator Captain Derek Tangye wrote in reply to an enquiry from Major the Hon. Kenneth Younger at Newcastle Box 500: '*Indeed I wish I had never heard the name of Schut. As soon as I have time I will write you a book on him and all his associates, together with a description of his relations with Miss Eileen Child. At the moment the files are 'lost'* ...[54]

Chapter 5

Fatalities of Spy Mania?

Falsehood flies, and truth comes limping after it, so that when men come to be undeceived, it is too late; the jest is over, and the tale hath had its effect.

Jonathan Swift

Within a handful of years, the deaths of Fabian and Wurm were all but forgotten; among their friends the deaths were consigned to a sad episode in the past. But consider this, suicide pacts are rare, most coroners in the 1930s would preside over only a handful of such deaths in their careers, but the deaths would be chillingly echoed as a result of an alleged spy ring in Birmingham in the autumn of 1939. The war was just days old when a letter was received by the Chief Constable of Birmingham on 8 September 1939 in which Wilfred Ronald Ward (27) of Handsworth, made allegations about five people, denouncing them as members of a 'spy ring'. But this time it appears the Home Office were keen to bury it from the word go.

The persons involved in the allegations were described in the newspaper reportage as Mr X, Miss B, Mr C, Dr A and Mr D. All strenuously denied the allegations and the matter was brought to court when the man known as Mr X countered the allegations with accusations of attempted blackmail by Ward who had threatened to expose him as a spy unless he paid him £500. Ward was brought before Birmingham Police Court on charges of demanding money with menaces from Mr X.[1]

Mr M.P. Pugh, solicitor for the prosecution, stated there were five charges of criminal libel that arose from a letter sent to the chief constable of Birmingham in which he had claimed Mr X: '*was very actively engaged in this spy ring, a German possibly naturalised English … whose services (at night) for Germany included entry of shadow factories, stealing and copying plans of new and secret aircraft etc and members of the organisation were getting same to Germany.*'

Of Miss B, the letter claimed she was '*also engaged in minor degree by this spy ring … Check up on her father and brother who I believe operate on cargo boats between Tyneside and Germany and transport secret information and plans to that country.*' In court Miss B said there was no truth in the allegations made against her. She had had nothing to do with spies or espionage and neither had her father or brother who were in the Merchant Service, nor had she ever given any impression they were involved in espionage. Miss B said that she had been employed at the same institution along with one of the few witnesses in the case to be named, 'Treasure' Muffett (real name Mabel Nellie Muffett) who was then posing as a German. She claimed at that time, Muffett always spoke with broken English and was claiming she belonged to Nuremberg but was educated in a French convent.

Mr C was described in the letter from Ward as: '*Young, small fellow, worked into partnership of metal company. Possibly brass foundry in ---- I believe some years ago prior to becoming associated in espionage. Believe he was blackmailed into it.*' Mr C stated he had been a porter at the hospital where Miss B worked along with Treasure Muffett. He stated he had never been in the metal business but had taken Treasure out a number of times.

Dr A was mentioned in the letter as '*Have only vaguely heard of Dr --- mentioned as an associate of the group. There is a surgeon of the same name in the Birmingham telephone book.*' In court Dr A claimed he had never met Muffett.

And finally, there was Mr D, described as of: '*half Greek nationality, I understand he operates in a big way from his own business, a garage in ----Check up on his car sales. I believe he supplies all big cars to most of the many houses in many parts of England and Scotland where these spy groups have their headquarters and need cars for their operations.*'

Mr D testified he was indeed the proprietor of a garage but was now serving as an aircraftsman in the RAF. He denied all the allegations and swore he had never supplied cars in Scotland. He had met Muffett but claimed he had never met Ward nor any of the others named. The only way Ward could have learned anything about him would have been from Muffett whom he had known in 1935 as Treasure Street when she was a nurse at the County Mental Hospital, Gloucester.[2]

Treasure Muffett (24) and Maire Williams (22) who originated from Treforest, South Wales were both key witnesses in the case. They were described in newspaper reports as young women who were '*very attractive but very short of money*'. They had shared a flat at Acocks Green, Birmingham. Muffett told the court she was a nurse and that she had always led Mr X to believe she was German, but her parents were English. She admitted to the court that she had told thousands of lies. Maire Williams was described as Ward's girlfriend. Little was known of the pair in Birmingham, newspaper reports went so far as claiming '*they seemed to have been surrounded by an air of mystery*' but they were understood to have worked as nurses in the district.

It would later be revealed that 'Treasure' Muffett had left her husband in 1938 after a marriage that lasted just eleven weeks. Maire Williams had not seen her parents in over a year. Both Williams and Muffett had been training as nurses, but neither had passed their exams. The last time Miss Williams's family had heard from her was a letter stating she was in London and was going over to France with Muffett to serve as nurses. Muffett had visited her mother more recently with Williams; they needed to borrow some money, but they did not appear depressed, let alone suicidal.

The girls had rented a furnished flat in an apartment house on Alexandra Road, Maida Vale. Their landlady Mrs Lily Abbot recalled that when they arrived they were wearing steel helmets with nurses' uniforms under their overcoats; both were members of the Civilian Nursing Reserve. They had no luggage but said it was being sent on. They also said they had met at a nursing home in Birmingham and came to London to escape from a man. Mrs Abbot had also been tapped for money adding: '*They talked to me about the Mr X case in Birmingham. They were both very depressed and sad and worried about it.*' The girls had returned to London for a few days before returning to Birmingham to continue giving evidence at the trial.[3]

Mrs Abbot last saw Muffett and Williams on the morning of Friday 27 October just before she went away for the weekend and she got back on Tuesday night. The sound of constantly running water by day and night from a tap that had been left running in the girls' flat attracted the attention of the occupants of other flats in the building and they reported the matter to the landlady who went to the flat to inquire on Wednesday 1 November. Outside stood several milk bottles and loaves of bread. Looking through the glass panel of the kitchen door the landlady saw a girl's arm outstretched on the floor. Police forced their way into the flat and Muffett and Williams were found dead, lying side by side on the floor of their lounge on a mattress wearing their night clothes.

Newspapers reported: '*When the girls died they had only sixpence halfpenny between them. The money laid beside the key of the flat on the sitting room table when they were found...Death was believed to have occurred several days previously.*'[4]

An inquest was held at St Pancras before Coroner Mr W. Bentley Purchase. The police constable who had been summoned to the flat and forced the entry stated: '*All the taps of the gas stove were turned on and there was a slight smell of gas. The window of the room was closed and there was a handkerchief in the keyhole of the door, which was jammed.*' Home Office pathologist Sir Bernard Spilsbury, who had examined the bodies declared both women had died of coal gas poisoning. Miss Williams had also been found to be in the early stages of pregnancy.[5]

Just as you may think the matter was cut and dried there is an intriguing postscript. Inspector Culliss of the Metropolitan Police gave evidence at the inquest that he had seen both the women recently and he described Mrs Muffett as appearing to be '*quite jolly in a general manner but a little worried*'. Apparently, she was concerned that they were being followed. Culliss had put them on a bus and gave them certain instructions in case anyone should be following them.

Detective Sergeant Brown of Scotland Yard also stated that on the night of October 27 the women had telephoned him to say they were being followed by two men. Mrs Muffett had wondered whether anyone was following her in connection with the case. With their knowledge Detective Brown had kept them under observation but he claimed he saw no-one following them.[6]

The question does arise of how could he be so sure? Even MI5 B Division head Guy Liddell commented on the general situation in late 1939:

There is very little attempt to use imagination or make a real drive to collect agents provocateurs. We are of course up against many difficulties, not least of which is trying to follow people in the black-out and the present means for investigation which are at our disposal seem to be very meagre.[7]

A verdict was returned that both women had taken their lives while of unsound mind. Wilfred Ward was found guilty of blackmail at Manchester Assizes on 8 November 1939. He swore that everything he had learned of the spy ring he had ascertained from 'Treasure' Muffett adding: '*I have done it in the interests of the country. Every word I believed to be true. I have made notes from time to time about what she told me.*'[8] His downfall had been demanding £500 from Mr X to keep his mouth shut. He was sent to prison for three years.

Was 'Treasure' Muffett just a delusional woman and her frightened, pregnant friend Maire Williams driven to suicide through money worries and the blackmail case, or was the long arm of the Gestapo involved? Witting or unwitting, had 'Treasure' Muffett become involved with the intrigue she always sought, got in too deep and dragged her friend in with her? Having discussed the case from the published accounts with legal professionals it does seem there were channels of enquiry that could and should have been followed up. One of the big problems was that the apparently authoritative pronouncements of Home Office pathologist Bernard Spilsbury were often taken as law in courts and hearings and went unchallenged. Re-examination of his cases in recent years reveal he often treated the presentation of evidence with an unshakable belief in his own infallibility and was not as thorough as he was thought to have been at the time.[9]

Tragically there are no files released or noted as retained by the Metropolitan Police and there are no files apparent to indicate the case of Muffett and Williams brought to the attention nor investigated in any way by Special Branch or MI5.

Chapter 6

The Venlo Incident

Then I, and you, and all of us fell down,
Whilst bloody treason flourish'd over us,

William Shakespeare

In the weeks and months immediately after Britain's declaration of war, appeasement was far from forgotten by Prime Minister Chamberlain, nor the senior members of his War Cabinet like Lord Halifax. They continued to believe a bloodless peace settlement could be achieved with Nazi Germany.

Chamberlain remained optimistic that Germany would come to its senses and realise they could not win the war. Shortly before the outbreak of hostilities overtures had been made by members of parties in opposition to the Nazis to see if a peace agreement could be reached. It was known that there was dissatisfaction with Hitler among some elements of German high command and there were even rumours of plots to remove him from power. The senior officers of the British intelligence community, privy to this information, were keen to keep their cards close to their chest and a trusted officer of the SIS was despatched to investigate further. Even to those in the highest positions he remained a 'mystery man' but MI5 Director of Counter Espionage Guy Liddell, would record in his diary on 18 September 1940 SIS Section V head Valentine Vivian had told him David Boyle, personal assistant to Stewart Menzies, who was soon to be appointed Chief of SIS, had been 'the Mystery Man' who went to Germany just before the outbreak of war and *that his purpose was to contact a certain German General whom it was thought might lead a revolt in the Germany Army'.*[1]

The Supreme War Council held their second meeting in secret at Hove Town Hall, Sussex on 22 September 1939. The British group consisted of Prime Minister Neville Chamberlain, Foreign Secretary Lord Halifax, Sir Alexander Cadogan, the Permanent Under-Secretary at the Foreign Office, and Cabinet Secretary Edward Bridges; and for France, Prime Minister Édouard Daladier, French senior military commanders General Gamelin, Admiral Darlan, Munitions Minister Raoul Dautry and Jean Monnet, the Chair of the Franco-British Economic Co-ordination Committee.

The Supreme War Council including British Prime Minister Neville Chamberlain (centre) and French Prime Minister Édouard Daladier (far right) leaving their secret meeting at Hove Town Hall, Sussex on 22 September 1939.

By this time the French army had been mobilized and the British Expeditionary Force had been despatched to France and had deployed to defences along the border with Belgium. Both forces were now ready and impatient for action, but Chamberlain urged caution and would not give his assent to any suggestion of offensive operations against the Germans.[2]

Nothing appears to have developed beyond Boyle's mission, but the suggestion there could be co-operation between German rebels and British intelligence to remove Hitler from executive power and enter into peace negotiations was clearly a tempting prospect. Chamberlain and Halifax were not going to give up and they would bring secret peace agreement offers before the war cabinet for consideration. Winston Churchill, at that time First Lord of the Admiralty, was also a member of the war cabinet and firmly held the opinion that it was both dangerous and duplicitous to entertain any secret peace discussions with Germany. In a private note to Lord Halifax on 1 November 1939 he warned: '*There is a great danger in these secret communications ... the Germans could use it to undermine French confidence in us with possibly fatal effects.*'[3]

The entertainment of secret peace negotiations at the highest echelons of power in Britain had not escaped the attention of German intelligence and presented them with a golden opportunity to exploit such exchanges to their own advantage. Despite the scheme of enticing persons of interest and threat to locations on European borders with the Fatherland so that they could be abducted being a known, tried and tested method of the German Secret Service, the sting operations to entice those into such a situation would continue to achieve the desired effect. They would result in what was probably the most significant failure of the Secret Intelligence Service (SIS) during the Second World War.

After the declaration of war Holland attempted to remain neutral but had become a hotbed for German espionage agents who saw the country as an ideal location for running intelligence operations and meeting potential spies recruited around Europe. Wolfgang zu Putlitz, the man who had been British intelligence's best insider source at the German embassy in the mid-1930s, had been at the German legation in The Hague for over a year before the outbreak of war and noted the number of intelligence operatives attached to the legation increased dramatically. Indeed, there were so many they took over a hotel with nearly a hundred rooms to accommodate their new departments.[4]

Sigismund Payne Best, 1939.

Major Richard Henry Stevens, 1939.

However, government intelligence often plays a long game; other countries also had intelligence agents in Holland, indeed Putlitz commented: '*It was common knowledge at The Hague that British Intelligence was directed from the Passport Office of the British Consulate at Scheveningen by a certain Captain Stevens.*'[5]

The man in charge was in fact Major Richard Stevens, a former British Army officer who had served as intelligence officer in India and who had been put in charge of the SIS station in The Hague in 1939. There had been problems with the station managers and Stevens was sent in as 'a safe pair of hands' in far more of an administrative and management role than that of a field agent. Although experienced in intelligence work out in India, he simply did not possess the experience and skill set he needed to deal with the likes of the *Abwehr* or the *Sicherheitsdienst* (SD), Nazi Germany's elite intelligence agency of the SS in Europe. Indeed, Stevens had inherited a station that had already been penetrated by several *Abwehr* agents who were relaying information back to German intelligence about operatives, informers, operations and the information the station was receiving from its sources and its London bosses.

Armed with such information it had been quite simple for a false flag operation to be created, aimed at the vulnerable agents of the British station at The Hague by the Foreign Intelligence section of the SD. *Sturmbannführer* Walter Schellenberg, Deputy Chief of the Reich Main Security Office was called to a meeting with his immediate superior Reinhard Heydrich at SD Headquarters in Berlin in September 1939. Schellenberg wrote that Heydrich had told him:

> *For several months now we have maintained a very interesting contact with British Intelligence. By placing misleading material in their hands, we have succeeded in penetrating their organization. The point has now arrived when we must decide whether we want to continue this game or break it off and be satisfied with what we have learned.*[6]

Drawing the relevant files, Schellenberg got himself up to speed with the operation to date. A German agent Schellenberg names only as F479 had established himself in Holland under cover as a political refugee with connections to a strong opposition group in the *Wehrmacht*. All Schellenberg had to do was create a suitable high-ranking German officer with a convincing back story and join the meetings.[7]

Agent F479 was 53-year-old businessman Dr Franz Fischer who had fled Germany in 1935 claiming it was for political reasons, but in reality it was because he faced charges of embezzlement.[8] After a few months in Sweden he went to Paris where he met with German Freedom Party founder Dr Carl Spieker and through him began contact with SIS agents. The problem was they did not realise Fischer had been recruited as an agent for the SD in the spring of 1937 and was reporting back to them information about German émigrés in Paris. After having to leave Paris along with many other German nationals expelled in the light of the machinations of Nazi Germany in 1938, he moved to Holland and there he carried on spying on his refugee neighbours in Amsterdam. In the spring of 1939 he moved to lodge with a refugee couple in The Hague.[9]

Fischer also visited London on a number of occasions where he was brought into contact with Wickham Steed and, like Berthold Jakob (see Chapter 2), provided him with information; but of course in the case of Fischer it was information that had been provided by the SD specifically to earn the trust of both Steed and Spieker. Fischer warned them of both Hitler's planned annexation of the Sudetenland and his attack on Poland days before they took place. Both Steed and Spieker passed this invaluable information on to their SIS intelligence contacts. It earned Fischer enormous credibility as a source and SIS agent Sigismund Best was told by his London controller to make contact.

Best was an agent of considerable experience who operated under cover as the managing director of the pharmaceutical firm 'Pharmisan' and was living with his Dutch wife in The Hague. The meeting was arranged and it was then Fischer revealed that he could arrange a meeting with a credible and significant group of German officers wishing to remove the *Führer* from power and enter into discussions for peace with British authorities in anticipation of a successful coup. After a further meeting with Fischer and one of the supposed group, Best was not entirely convinced and voiced his concerns to his superiors in London via SIS station commander Major Richard Stevens. Both were reassured that Fischer had previously provided valuable information and that they were to press on with the meetings.[10]

Stevens and Best needed co-operation from Dutch military authorities to help them navigate through the Dutch zones

Walter Schellenberg in the uniform of SS-Oberführer.

that had become militarised near the borders since the outbreak of war. Major General Jan van Oorschot, head of the Dutch Army Intelligence Division, provided them with one of his own men, Lieutenant Colonel Dirk Klop, under the strict understanding he was only to act as an observer at the meetings. Fischer would join them again for another meeting with other German officers from the rebel group and this time one of the new rebel officers they would meet would be Schellenberg posing as rebel spokesman Major Schämmel, adjutant to a rebel German general.

The meeting appeared to go well, common ground was soon established between the British agents and the German officers. Even years later Stevens would recall in a television interview for a CBS documentary, with a smile and tone akin to a gentleman reminiscing about meeting a new member at his club, that Schellenberg was '*a very polite fellow with charming manners*' and that their conversation not only dealt with the intentions of the rebel group, interpersonal bridges were built through a shared appreciation of classical music. The apparently cautious but cordial discussions had been carefully planned and the terms they offered were calculated to be appealing to Chamberlain and his remaining supporters for secret peace negotiations.

Stevens sent reports of the meetings to date to Admiral Hugh 'Quex' Sinclair, Chief of SIS which were, in turn reported by Quex to Lord Maurice Hankey (the Minister without Portfolio who had special responsibility for intelligence services in the Chamberlain war cabinet) and further up the chain of command it went. Prime Minister Chamberlain was under pressure, there was already criticism for his lack of aggression in the pursuit of the war, but he would arrogantly show his teeth if there was any suggestion of his resignation as Prime Minister. The credible suggestion of achieving the overthrow of warmonger Hitler and a peace agreement with Germany without bloodshed saw Hankey reply to Sinclair in up-beat tones reporting Chamberlain had declared, having read the report, '*It was one of the most cheering documents I have read.*'[11] Praised for his efforts to date and with full support of his masters in Britain, Stevens was given the green light to take the meetings forward.

Clearly high hopes were being invested in these negotiations, the kudos for those involved if this proved successful was so great, they would throw caution to the wind rather than listen to the warnings of those who suggested the talks may not be all they seemed. Wolf Putlitz had realised he had been compromised when *Oberstleutnant* Walter Schultze-Bernett, head of KO-Niederlande in den Haag (the *Abwehr* war organisation in the Hague) visited Putlitz in his office and laid before him a list of German agents in the Netherlands – a list of names Putlitz recognised as agents he had recently passed to a trusted intermediary who had passed it to the Passport Control

Office. When confronted about the list Putlitz flatly denied any knowledge of it nor those named being spies, but he did not feel he was believed when the intelligence officer replied haughtily:

My dear Putlitz, I would not be Schultze-Bernett if I did not have an agent with Stevens. I know everything that goes on in his set-up. Where could he have got hold of these names except from here? Answer me that ... I can assure you I intend to get to the bottom of this.[12]

Putlitz was left in no doubt that the SIS station at The Hague had been penetrated by at least one enemy agent, but under the threat of further investigation he fled to England on 15 September. Tragically, his warning went unheeded, the reason being that the general impression in SIS, as understood by Guy Liddell at least, was Putlitz was not taken seriously because he had become jittery about his own situation and lost his nerve to stay any longer.[13] Concerns were also raised by Sigismund Best that the German rebels may be double agents, but these too were passed up the line and responded to with the advice that the British agents should simply stay away from the border with Germany for any meeting.

It seemed impossible to meet anywhere that was secure and discreet for both sides other than the border, so a meeting was set up to be held at the Cafe Backus on the outskirts of Venlo, just a few metres away from the border with Germany. It was here Stevens, Best, Klop and his Dutch Army driver Jan Lemmens arrived to meet with their rebel German contacts on Tuesday, 7 November 1939. They met with two German officers, Major Schämmel and Lieutnant Grosh (in reality Schellenberg and SD Officer, SS-*Hauptsturmführer* Walter Christian). If all went well, they were due to meet a German rebel general the following day.

Arriving at the meet the next day they found only Schämmel, he explained the general had been called away to discuss an appeal for peace made by the Queen of the Netherlands and the King of the Belgians. He then informed them that an attempt was to be made to assassinate Hitler on Saturday so the next day, Thursday, would be their last chance to stage the meeting.

On 9 November 1939 Stevens and Best knew the stakes were high and so was the pressure. They armed themselves with Browning automatic pistols for the meeting set for 4pm, just in case something went badly wrong. What they had not anticipated, nor had Schellenberg expected, was that Heydrich's superior Himmler, who had been kept up to date with the progress of the meetings, gave orders that the two British intelligence officers should be arrested so they could be removed to Germany for interrogation. In his account of the incident Walter Schulze-Bernett stated the reason behind Himmler's decision was that an unsuccessful attempt had been made on Hitler's life on 8 November when a bomb had detonated at the *Burgerbräukeller*, Munich shortly after the *Führer* and entourage left the building.

It is highly likely the bomb incident was actually engineered by the Hitler regime to increase his popularity at home and seek sympathy from neutral powers. Himmler claimed he was convinced that the English intelligence service had instigated the assassination attempt and that Stevens, Best and Klop may have either been informed of it or might have been involved. He ordered their arrest in a telephone call direct to Schellenberg in his apartment in Düsseldorf and sent a team of SS *Sonderkommandos* to carry out the task under *Sturmbannführer* Alfred Naujoks and SD member Hermann Goetsch.[14]

On the day of the meeting the group drove over in Best's car, a Ford Lincoln-Zephyr. The car was kept maintained at a garage owned by Jan Lemmens who had acted as their driver for the previous meetings and this time he came along again. As the car passed outside Cafe Backus, Schellenberg was waiting for them on the veranda and Stevens saw him tip his hat in what he believed was greeting to them. In fact, it was a signal for the *Sonderkommandos* that this was the car containing their targets and this was the moment to act. As the car pulled up to park in front of the cafe a burst of fire rang out and, after a brief exchange during which Klop was mortally wounded, the snatch squad swooped on the agent's car and Stevens, Best and Lemmens were dragged out of the vehicle. Bundled the last few metres over the German border to the customs house where they were lined up against a wall at gun point, they were searched and handcuffed, then thrown into the SD officer's car and driven at high speed to Gestapo Headquarters, Düsseldorf.

Despite the stooge for the Hitler bombing, Georg Elser, being 'captured' soon afterwards and insisting he had acted alone, the propaganda opportunity to claim that the recently captured British agents were involved was too great to ignore and on 22 November 1939 the *Deutsche-Allgemeine-Zeitung* was one of numerous German newspapers showing portrait photographs of each man and named Elser, Stevens and Best as conspirators.

The greatest concern among British intelligence was how much the captured agents would reveal to their captors. Guy Liddell noted on 12 November: '*The danger is that Stevens generally carried a list of his agents in his vest pocket.*'[15] After preliminary questioning at Düsseldorf, Stevens and Best were removed to Berlin and there began a lengthy series of interrogations for both men. They were kept apart and their interrogators interviewed each separately, giving the impression the other was co-operating without revealing the true source of the information. Held in concentration camps until released after the end of the war, each blamed the other for disclosing too much sensitive

81

The 1948 reconstruction of the 'Venlo Incident' where it happened at Cafe Backus, Venlo, on the borders of Holland and Germany.

information. In *A History of British Secret Service*, the standard work on the subject between its first publication in 1969 with revised editions up to the 1980s, Richard Deacon stated:

> *Thus in a single day the British Secret Service on the continent of Europe was almost totally destroyed ... The Germans obtained from Best and Stevens a massive and detailed picture of the whole SIS set up in Europe, even to some extent covering the counter-espionage department of MI5 ... The* Abwehr *had names of senior personnel and addresses of nearly all the Intelligence Officers in Britain as well as agents in the Low Countries. All this information was set out in a confidential report* Der Britische Nachrichtendienst [The British Intelligence Service] *made early in 1940. By the time the Germans had invaded the low countries and France in the spring of 1940 Britain was left with practically no effective intelligence service in Europe.*[16]

In more recent books and articles historian Nigel West contends Stevens and Best were in fact only used to validate information that had already been supplied to German intelligence before the war by their moles in SIS.[17] Although there is some debate over the names of those West and others have suggested as responsible for this betrayal, the amount of detailed material the Germans claim to have obtained from Stevens and Best begs the question of how these two men could have known so much without being captured carrying extensive folders of documents and not just a list of agents in Stevens' vest pocket.

MI5 files released in 2012 shed more light on the matter, naming four agents that had penetrated the SIS station at The Hague. Kapitän Richard Protze (aka Wagner, Petersen, Paarman and Onkle Richard) was a former German Navy officer, Head of *Abwehr* III and a friend of *Abwehr* chief Admiral Wilhelm Canaris. After his retirement Protze carried on with his intelligence work running an independent intelligence bureau on behalf of Canaris in Holland from 1938 known as 'Stelle P' which reported direct to Berlin.[18] Schulze-Bernett described him as having *'a great reputation and clever man at his job'.*[19] In his interrogation after capture by the Allies Protze named a number of those he believed had acted as agents at the PCO in 1939. One was a German 'V-man' named Friedrich Gunter who was working for *Abwehr Ast* Hamburg, who Protze said *'insinuated himself with great success in Steven's office.'*[20] Protze continues:

> *A man named Gordon Perry was recruited. He must have occupied a peculiar position in the Passport Control Office. He had a psychological weakness which was exploited. Perry worked for us for as long as was possible. Through some accident which we have never discovered, he was sacked from the PCO. After that he spent a great deal of his time in the Horse Bar in the Hague and here he was one day beaten up by members of the PCO. This accident was a signal to the* Abwehr *to exfiltrate Perry to Germany. In view of his intimate knowledge of past events, he was then employed in the German Foreign Office.*[21]

There were also PCO employees William John 'Bill' Hooper (aka John Cooper) and Frank Taylor 'a consular officer' attached to the PCO. When talking about the German-counter espionage effort against PCO agent Adruanus Vrinten, who was becoming a real threat to the operations of the German intelligence service in Holland, Protze recalled an order was given to supply him with misleading, forged and falsified material in an attempt to bring Vrinten's sub-agents to light so that action could be taken against them should they ever cross the German frontier. Protze stated:

The success of this work was thanks to the PCO employee Hooper who turned traitor to the English Intelligence Service and in particular to his own office, namely the PCO in the Hague. Hooper had met representatives of Ast Hamburg *in South Germany where, in return for payment, he handed over files which he had removed from the PCO. These files contained agents' reports and accounts of the payments of these agents. The papers comprised a fairly large volume. They are pencil notes representing the assessment of the chief official of the PCO* [Stevens]. *Apart from these papers Hooper delivered during his period of activity other reports which I personally can no longer remember.*

A further role was played by Taylor. Taylor and Hooper belong together, Hooper was also in Berlin, but I am not sure whether he was at that time in the company of Taylor. However, a further meeting took place in Switzerland where representatives of the Abwehr *met both Hooper and Taylor. The information which was supplied at this meeting was well paid for by the Germans.*[22]

* * *

Then there was Folkert Arie Van Koutrik who had started working for the PCO early in 1938 and was 'turned' later that same year by the *Abwehr.* He was soon conveying all the secrets of the PCO that he could obtain for them under the codename of WALBACH. Evacuated with his wife to England in May 1940, he was taken on by MI5 to assist in the interrogation of refugees. Koutrik was revealed by Protze as the worst offender by far. When contracted to observe enemy agents on behalf of the PCO, he was so bad at concealing himself he was approached, a discussion ensued and it soon became clear that Koutrik would

Folkert Arie Van Koutrik, the first German agent to penetrate MI5.

be perfectly happy to work for the other side if they paid him more money. Protze continued that Koutrik was informed by his handler that he:

… would be remunerated according to the value of his reports. The first rendezvous took place in a little cafe on the viaduct in The Hague at the

Wassenaar fork. The success of this was quite staggering. It was quite clear that the Abwehrdienst *had never before been so well supplied with names of foreign intelligence service as through Koutrik.*[23]

Christopher Andrew points out in *Defence of the Realm* that for the first time in its history MI5 had been penetrated by a German agent.[24] After his own extensive research intelligence, historian F.A.C. Kluiters also commented on Koutrik: '*It looks like he caused more damage than Stevens and Best after their arrest.*'[25] One of the final notes on his MI5 file dated 5 November 1948 provides the summary:

Koutrik acted as a double agent on behalf of the German intelligence service from the end of October 1938 to the date of his evacuation from Holland in May 1940. After his arrival in this country he proved thoroughly unsatisfactory when in British service and disloyal to the Dutch Government in the UK when employed by them.[26]

Colonel Valentine Vivian, SIS was blunt in his comments in his concluding note in the Koutrik file: '*The man has blood on his hands.*'[27]

As a result of what became known as the 'Venlo Incident' critical damage was inflicted on Britain's intelligence network in Holland and its repercussions were felt across Europe. Britain had been exposed as conducting espionage operations in what was still officially a neutral country. In intelligence circles it was known that the Dutch were so fearful of the event getting blown out of proportion they did not wish to make any protest.[28] Guy Liddell recorded his conversation on the situation with Stewart Menzies in his diary:

SIS is going through a very difficult time owing to the liquidation of Stevens' organisation. General van Oorschot of the Dutch General Staff, who was party to Stevens's activities, has been dismissed and Sir Nevile Bland [the British envoy] has been asked by the Dutch government to instruct the Passport Control Office to cease all illegal activities. Similar difficulties are being experienced in Sweden where the government has set up an organisation under one Martin Lundquist to go into the foreign agencies. As Lundquist is thoroughly pro-German and served in the German Army during the last war, he is confining himself to enquiries into SIS activities under Passport Control. Menzies says that in a number of cases his agents are being arrested and that it is easier now to operate in Germany than in neutral countries.[29]

Chamberlain had also suffered the embarrassment of being exposed as still open to negotiations for a peace deal with Germany. The aftershock of the incident was felt yet again when it was used in the German declaration of war on the Netherlands on 10 May 1940 when it was cited as evidence of the breach of neutrality by the Dutch government.

Vindicated by the Venlo incident, Churchill never wavered in his stance and remained against British support for German groups opposed to Hitler for the remainder of the war. SIS would need to be rebuilt and would become better known as MI6. Soon after Churchill became Prime Minister in 1940 he would instigate the amalgamation of selected MI departments to create the Special Operations Executive (SOE) specifically to conduct espionage, sabotage and reconnaissance against the forces of Nazi Germany in what would, by that time, be occupied Europe.

Chapter 7

Operation Lena

Let him depart; his passport shall be made,
And crowns for convoy put into his purse

William Shakespeare

Parachutist scares began after the invasion of the low countries and intensified after the Fall of France in June 1940 with the now imminent, threat of invasion and because airfields in France made it easier for enemy aircraft to fly operations against Great Britain. Even after internment scares over enemy agents, the Fifth Column remained and false alarms were

Soldiers of Panzer Regiment 8 on a visit to Hamburg in 1938, the group includes new recruits and some of the 'V-men' from **Ast Hamburg** *(in civilian clothes).*

KLOPSTOCK-PENSION — HAMBURG

Vornehm eingerichtetes Pensionat
Hochherrschaftliche Zimmer in ruhiger Lage

Klopstock-Strasse No. 2   □□□   1., 2. u. 3. Etage

Ecke Alsterglacis, Zwei Minuten vom Dammtorbahnhof
:: :: Bei der Esplanade, Binnen- und Aussenalster :: ::
Telephon: Gruppe 4, 9579

Zimmer mit u. ohne Pension :: Vorzügliche Küche :: Prima Referenzen

The Klopstock Pension (Guest House), Hamburg where many of the Operation Lena agents stayed during their **Abwehr** *training.*

rife. The police and Home Guard were kept on their toes with mistaken sightings and suspicious characters. Clouds in the moonlight, puffs of smoke discharged from the barrels of AA guns and the reflected light of a searchlight off a barrage balloon were some of the causes of supposed sightings of enemy parachutists. In June 1940 the *Abwehr* was making plans that would make these fears a reality.

In June 1940 Admiral Canaris entrusted Colonel Erwin von Lahousen, Head of *Abwehr II* with the commencement of espionage operations against Great Britain. Just days before the Fall of France, the war diary of *Abwehr II* recorded:

> *On the direction of the Head of Division* [Lahousen] *Abwehr II's work has in the main been switched over to the war with England. In addition, preparations are being made for work overseas. The only work in the east now concerns*

Colonel Erwin von Lahousen, Head of Abwehr II.

88

looking after the Ukranian minority and transferring old contacts to Abwehr III.

Codenamed Operation Lena, the plan was to send *Abwehr* agents to Britain. They were to scout ahead gathering information about military defences, emplacements, troop concentrations, minefields in specific coastal areas, to observe the morale of the British people (especially during air raids) and to get amongst the population at the moment of invasion. Findings were to be regularly transmitted back using agreed codes and during specific windows of time, all of which was to be carried out to assist the planning for, and imminent arrival of, German invasion forces.[1]

Hauptmann *Nikolaus Ritter (aka Dr Rantzau).*

Ast Hamburg, under the overall command of *Korvettenkapitän* Herbert Wichmann, was given responsibility for the operation with Section I-L (Air Intelligence, the 'L' was for Luft) under *Hauptmann* Nikolaus Ritter (aka Dr Rantzau) to oversee agents parachuted into Britain. Section I-M ('M' for Marine) under veteran *Abwehr* officer Hilmar Dierks (aka Van Dongen, Miller and Sanders) was for agents delivered via seaborne landings codenamed *Hummer Süd* (Lobster South) for landings in the south of Britain and *Hummer Nord* (Lobster North) for landings in the north. Both Ritter and Dierks took a great personal interest in the recruitment and training of their agents over the years immediately before the outbreak of the war, travelling between Germany, Belgium and Holland and using various cover names and addresses as they did so.[2]

Operations began with marine landings and, before the release of the relevant MI5 files, there has been some debate in books and articles over details and locations. The following account is a transcription of the MI5 report based on interviews with those involved:

In the early afternoon of the 2 September 1940, two single-masted diesel-engined fishing boats named La Mascott and Rose du Carmel, left Le Touquet for Boulogne where they waited for a favourable tide to cross to England. On leaving Boulogne each boat was taken by a German mine-sweeper and conducted across the Channel to within a mile or so of the English coast south of Dungeness. After sailing some distance in a westerly direction two rowing boats were put out and into these climbed Jose Rudolf Waldberg [25] and Karl Heinrich Cornelis Ernst Meier [24] from La Mascotte and Sjoerd Pons [28] and Charles Albert Van Den Kieboom [26] from the Rose du Carmel.

Poor visibility enabled the rowing boats to approach the shore without being seen. As they drew near the land, Waldberg and Meier sighted a patrol boat in the distance and fearing trouble immediately threw overboard, as previously instructed, a weighted package containing a circular code and two maps. With no further mishap the occupants of the first boat landed in the early morning of Tuesday 3 September, on the beach between Dungeness and Rye and those of the second boat between Rye and Dymchurch.

Each pair was equipped with a wireless set, a revolver and magazine, two pairs of binoculars, two compasses, British currency to the value of £60 each in £5 notes and a small bottle containing a liquid for making secret writing visible.

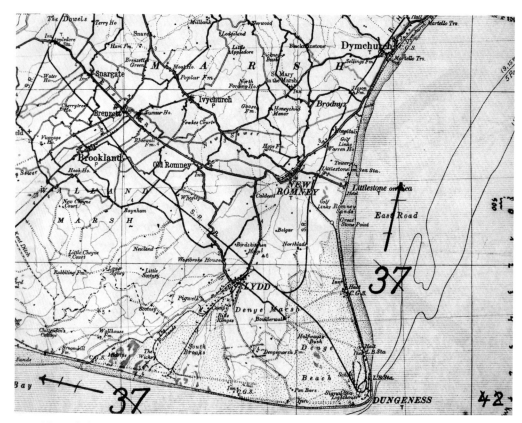

Map of the Dungeness peninsula, Kent carried by the Operation Lena agents who landed there on 3 September 1940.

They carried toiletries, some spare clothes and underwear and a sack of rations, the following being the remaining contents of these bags as recovered after capture:

Food sack of Meier and Waldberg

1. 10 tins of pork and beans packed in Belgium
2. 18 tins (1lb) corned beef, American
3. 2 tins condensed milk, British made
4. 14 packets eating chocolate approx. 1lb each, all Belgian made
5. 12 2oz round packets of biscuits in bag
6. 23 2oz square packet of biscuits in bag
7. 1 packet Jacobs Cream Crackers
8. 5 packets of Belgian cigarettes
9. 3 loaves bread
10. Bottle of brandy
11. Empty bottle of grapefruit juice
12. About 1lb sugar

Food sack of Pons and Kieboom

1. 10 tins pork and beans packed in Belgium
2. 18 tins (1lb) corned beef, American
3. 5 tins condensed milk British made
4. 13 packets eating chocolate, approx. 1lb each, all Belgian made
5. 10 packets Belgian cigarettes
6. 38 2oz flat packets biscuits
7. 1 bottle of brandy
8. 1 length of rope

The contents were supposed to last the agents around ten to fourteen days.[3] The group seemed doomed from the outset. They had not had extensive training and, rather than being hard-line volunteers, they had been coerced into the role of agents. The way they were dressed and the handsome young Aryan features of three members of the group would be noted, making them stand out. The obvious oriental mixed-race features of half Dutch, half Japanese, Kieboom was certainly going to draw attention in this sensitive area of the British coastline.[4] As it was Kieboom and Pons did not even get to interact with any members of the public after they made dry land.

At approximately 4.45am on the same morning Private Sidney Charles Tollervey, D Company, 6th Battalion, Somerset Light Infantry was on patrol at Romney Marsh. It was still dark when he was near the road at the Grand

Charles Albert Van Den Kieboom.

Sjoerd Pons.

Redoubt at Dymchurch, a few yards from the beach, when he heard rustling from a ditch filled with bull rushes and suddenly he saw a figure of a man silhouetted against the sky as he ran across the road towards the sea wall and flung himself onto it. Private Tollervey challenged the man, 'Halt! Who goes there?' and ran down some nearby steps and, despite not asking for a password, he heard a voice call out 'I do not know your code word.'

Tollervey asked if he had any means of identification to which the man replied he did not understand what he meant. Tollervey told him to advance and be recognised, this the man did with his hands up. He was dressed in civilian clothes wearing white shoes with another pair of shoes slung around his neck along with a pair of binoculars. The man appeared very keen to point out he was a Dutch refugee and asked to see one of Tollervey's officers to whom he would explain his case. He did not know it at the time but Private Sidney Tollervey had the distinction of capturing the first Operation Lena spy to land in Britain.

Private Tollervey returned to his platoon HQ with the suspicious individual. Second Lieutenant Eric Arnold Batten was there and asked the as yet unidentified man who he was, to which he was given the reply 'a Dutch refugee'; the man then produced a Dutch passport that revealed his name as Charles Albert Van Den Kieboom. Batten asked him if he was armed, Kieboom admitted he was and produced a Belgian pistol containing a clip of nine cartridges. Kieboom was handed over to the police a short while later, but as he awaited the police Kieboom found an opportunity to destroy his code, map and reagent for secret ink by pushing them down a lavatory.[5]

The sea front and wall at West Hythe, just below the Grand redoubt, where Pte Sidney Tollervey captured Operation Lena agent Charles Van Den Kieboom, 3 September 1940.

Boat used by Kieboom and Pons to row ashore making landfall between West Hythe and Dymchurch on 3 September 1940.

Lieutenant Batten also sent parties of soldiers out to search the area where Kieboom had been discovered. One pair of soldiers found a small rowing boat floating close to shore and a sack containing the provisions that had been brought over by the spies on the steps to the beach. A further search party was sent out and Private James McDonnell found a black leather equipment case containing a Morse key and batteries that had been placed in a ditch and hidden by rushes on Romney Marsh. A short while later Lance Corporal Reginald Goody discovered another black leather case containing a radio that been hidden under grass in the corner of a field near the road, about 75 yards away from the ditch where Private McConnell had found his case.

Lance Corporal Robert North was one of the 'Stevedore Battalion' Royal Engineers stationed at Morle Tower, Hythe. At approximately 5.25am on Tuesday, 3 September 1940, he was on guard duty at No 1 Support Post, West Hythe, near Romney Marsh. He was facing seawards about 500 yards from the Grand Redoubt when he spotted a figure moving in the field about 150 yards away. It was dark and as he could not recognise the figure so he challenged, 'What are you doing there?' to which the man replied: 'I am a Dutchman.'

North commanded him to stand still and at the same time directed other guards to assist by surrounding the suspicious person. He then arrested the man and removed him to a hut where they could have some light and question him. He noticed that the man's clothes were very wet and that his shoes gave the appearance of having been in the sea. North asked 'How did you come

View of the dyke with bull rushes, a short distance from the sea wall, near the Grand Redoubt and Beach Holiday Camp, Dymchurch where Kieboom had been hiding and sprung from when he was spotted by Pte Tollervey on 3 September 1940.

A Somerset Light Infantry Colour Sergeant shows Kieboom's radio, Morse key, batteries and equipment cases to the press.

to be here?' and the man replied, 'I have a companion and we crossed from Brest in a fishing boat and when a few miles from the shore we were cast off in a small boat.'

Lance Corporal North said, 'Who is your companion and why hasn't he come with you?' and the reply was, 'He left the boat before me and perhaps he has been shot.' The man was then searched and a Dutch passport was found in the name of Sjord Pons. North then conveyed Pons under guard to Seabrook Police Station near Hythe.[6]

Meanwhile on the Lydd side of the Dungeness peninsula, the MI5 report picks up the narrative:

Waldberg and Meier fastened their boat and unloaded their hand luggage, unpacked a wireless transmitter and transferred a sack of food, which was too heavy to carry far, to a small empty motorboat higher up the beach. They had been told that their own rowing boat would be washed out by the receding tide and leave no trace of their arrival. Meier partly hid the wireless transmitting set in the sand as it was still early morning; both went to sleep for a couple of hours against the wall of a house. As dawn came they crept across an open stretch of land to a ditch and found suitable hiding for themselves and their possessions near a shrub. About 9am Meier, who spoke English well, set off in the direction of Lydd to find a drink.[7]

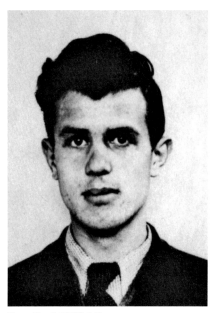

Jose Rudolf Waldberg.

Karl Meier.

In the case file for the prosecution of Waldberg and Meier it states the agents decided against burying the radio set hiding it instead under an old advertising hoarding and hid themselves, initially, in an old boat on the beach.[8]

Meier walked to Lydd and entered the Rising Sun pub. Having seen an old sign outside for cider champagne, he asked the landlady, Mrs Mabel Cole, for

The beach at Lydd where Waldberg and Meier landed on 3 September 1940.

The boat used by Waldberg and Meier to row ashore at Lydd on 3 September 1940.

a glass of it. The alarm bells started to ring immediately because the brand of cider had been discontinued for a number of years and surely every adult had some idea of the licensing laws that would not have permitted her to sell an alcoholic beverage so early in the day? She suggested to Meier that he should go and buy cigarettes at the shop across the road, then visit the local church and return again at 10am, which he did.

It was a warm sunny day and Horace Rendal 'Rennie' Mansfield, an inspector of the Aeronautical Inspection Directorate (AID) and his friend, insurance adviser Ronald Silvester, who had been staying with Mansfield and his wife on Ness Road had called in the pub for a drink where both were immediately struck by the agitation of the landlady. Sylvester recalled:

> *The reason for this was soon made clear to us. In a whisper she told us 'There is a strange man in the next bar and he has been hanging about outside since 9 o'clock this morning; I'm sure he's up to no good; he came in as soon as we opened and ordered a champagne cider and some biscuits and has been here about an hour, do please go in the private bar and see what you think of him.' Our curiosity being aroused we at once entered the next bar. His appearance and unusual style of clothing struck us immediately as he sat at a small table sipping his drink and munching his biscuits. His clothes had touched the sea*

and contrasted strangely with his rather refined appearance. We were perhaps too obvious in our scrutiny of him as he looked decidedly ill at ease and gulping down his drink called the landlord's wife to pay for what he had consumed.[9]

Mrs Cole told him, 'That'll be one and a tanner' – slang for one shilling and sixpence. The money parlance threw Meier so he pulled some money out of his pocket, but it seemed to puzzle him so he held it out for her to take the sum she required. This was also noticed by Mansfield and Sylvester, as well as his accent. Sylvester continued:

Strangely enough his accent was distinctly American and we were expecting to hear broken English as he had a most Teutonic caste of features. Pocketing his change and with a gruff, 'Good morning gentlemen,' he made his way to the street, crossed the road and entered a small general store opposite. 'Come on,' said my friend, 'Let's follow him.'[10]

Seeing seen Meier emerge from the shop having purchased more biscuits and lemonade and set off down the Dungeness Road towards the sea, the pair rushed to Mansfield's car and after about 400 yards, passed Meier and alighted. Producing his AID photo identification Mansfield pointed out that Meier was in a restricted area and asked to see his permit to travel so near the coast. Meier offered a Dutch passport for inspection but, as he did not have any other paperwork, he agreed to accompany Mansfield and Silvester to Lydd police station. Silvester recalled, 'As he entered the car he said: '*You've caught me I guess and I don't mind what happens to me but I refuse to go back to Germany.*'[11]

Police Sergeant Tye at Lydd police station had already been alerted by telephone of the suspicious character.[12] Meier was given a good meal and washing facilities and Mansfield and Silvester were asked to wait while contact was made with Seabrook police station near Hythe for further instructions. Mansfield and Silvester were asked to take Sergeant Tye and Meier there.

When questioned Meier was quick to point out he was a Dutch subject and explained he had no permit because he was a refugee who had landed on the beach in a boat from France the previous night, the MI5 report continues:

'By mistake,' he said, 'We arrived last night,' thus disclosing the arrival of the other members of the party. Meier was immediately taken into custody and was the first of the four spies to be interrogated. After three and a half hours of prevarication, he told briefly the true story of his journey and mission and gave the police directions as to where they could find Waldberg.

Meanwhile Waldberg, who could speak very little English, found some bushes to hide in with a large shrub where he attached his aerial and remained there awaiting Meier's return. At 8.30pm he decided to send out his first wireless

The bushes near Boulderwall Farm, Lydd, where Jose Waldberg hid and sent his radio messages from 3–4 September 1940. The large shrub on the right is where he strung out the aerial of his radio.

message, using an emergency code which he had written in his notebook, the first stated:

> *Arrived safely document destroyed English patrol two hundred metres from coast beach with brown nets and railway sleepers at a distance of fifty metres no mines few soldiers unfinished blockhouse new road Waldberg.*

His second message on 4 September reported:

> *Meier prisoner English police searching for me am concerned situation difficult I can resist thirst until Saturday if I am to resist send aeroplanes Wednesday evening eleven o'clock am three km north of arrival* [the point where they had landed] *long live Germany Waldberg*

A third message was ready for despatch when Waldberg was tracked down and arrested. It stated:

> *This is exact position yesterday evening six o'clock three Messerschmitt fired machine guns in my direction three hundred metres south water reservoir* [water tower] *painted red Meier prisoner*

All three messages were found written out in his pocket book with the code when he was searched.[13] The four spies were soon in custody at Seabrook police station. The MI5 report noted Pons was the last to be questioned, but the first to give a straightforward statement; it would appear that this may just have saved him from the gallows. Remarks on the intelligence learned from the interviews were recorded:

> *The demeanour of the spies was such that they were convinced invasion would take place before the middle of September. The spies work in pairs and were provided with food and £60 in British currency for expenses to last fourteen days. There was no German contact in England. The spies gave the information that the contact was unnecessary as the Germans would be here within two weeks. Each spy had been given instructions of how to signal to the advancing armies in order to cross over and give further instructions.[14]*

The signal would be given by handkerchief to approaching German forces. He was then to contact an officer and say *'Ich bin hier mit einem Sonderfrag für deutschen Wehrmann'* [literally translates as 'I'm here with a special question for German Man-at-Arms,' it was intended for and to be understood by field intelligence officers] followed by the password 'Elizabeth'.[15]

When interrogated further in London by officers of MI5 on 5–6 September, Waldberg, the most experienced of the agents, provided corroboration and detail to the accounts provided by the others. Apparently absolutely convinced that the invasion was imminent and would be successful, he was willing to work for England 'loyally' giving his *parole d'honneur* until the German forces arrived. All agents had been carefully primed with details of the planned invasion, Waldberg's interrogation report records:

> *Asked what false message would induce the Germans to invade in this quarter, the reply was 'weak coastal dispositions'. Strong forces on the canal [the Channel, in German der Kanal] would not affect the issue. On the other hand, a report that the coast was strongly held would result in an abandonment of an attack in this area but would not prevent the proposed landing on the East Coast of England from Aldborough as far as, but not including, the Wash, as the German intelligence believes the Wash was to be heavily mined ... The general German plan is to take London simultaneously from Rye/Hythe and Aldborough/The Wash.[16]*

Guy Liddell summed up the doom of the four agents in his diary entry for 6 September 1940: *'They were given no contacts in this country and in fact they were singularly badly directed and to anybody with any knowledge of the conditions in this country should have been apparent that none of these could hope to succeed.'[17]*

The British press were kept at a distance from reporting the landings of enemy spies and the trials of these men were held in camera before Mr Justice Wrottesley at the Central Criminal Court at The Old Bailey between 19–22 November 1940. The jury found Kieboom, Meier and Waldberg guilty as charged under Section 1 of the Treachery Act, 1940 and they were sentenced to death. Waldberg and Meier were hanged by Stanley Cross, assisted by Albert Pierrepoint and Henry Critchell, at Pentonville on 10 December 1940.

Kieboom appealed against his sentence but subsequently withdrew the appeal. This caused a delay and consequently he was hanged a week later on 17 December at Pentonville by Stanley Cross, assisted by Herbert Morris. Only a scripted press announcement of the executions was issued by the Home Office press office on 10 December 1940:

Two enemy agents, acting on behalf of Germany, were executed at Pentonville Prison today, following their conviction under the Treachery Act, 1940, at the Criminal Court on 22 November. Their names are Jose WALDBERG, a German born on 15.7.15 at Mainz and Karl MEIER, a Dutch subject of German origin, born at Koblenz on 19.10.1916.

Declarations of the Sheriff displayed on the doors of Pentonville Prison announcing the execution of German agents Waldberg and Meier, 10 December 1940.

These agents were apprehended shortly after their surreptitious arrival in this country. They were in possession of a wireless transmitting set which they were to erect in the field at night and of considerable sums of money in £1 notes. They had instructions to pose as refugees from enemy occupied territory and to move about amongst the population obtaining as much information of a military kind as possible. They had been made to believe that they would shortly be relieved by German invading forces.

Editors were however asked: '...*not to press for any additional facts or to institute enquiries. Editorial comment might profitably take the form of drawing public attention to loose talk of all kinds, particularly in the presence of strangers.*'[18]

The broadcast talk on the BBC on the night of 10 December '*by an officer intimately concerned with protecting the leakage of information to the enemy,*' scripted by the Ministry of Information, also spoke of the executions and expanded on the theme of careless talk:

However successful our intelligence services and police may be at detecting enemy agents, we must never rely on the dangerous assumption that this menace has been completely eradicated from our midst. Modern methods of transport – the aeroplane, the submarine and the speed boat and the modern method of communication, such as wireless, all facilitate the work of the spy. We have been glad to welcome to our country many thousands of genuine refugees from Nazi oppression, [but] the presence of so many foreign subjects in our midst can only make the detection of the spy difficult. Whereas an English accent, heard in the streets of Berlin, might immediately betray the presence of a British agent, a foreign tongue spoken in Britain today does not even call for comment. It is therefore a most important duty for us all to make the work of the enemy spy, who may be present in this country, as difficult as possible. We can do this quite easily if we make an absolute rule never to discuss any subject likely to be of interest to the enemy in a public space.

Do you discuss such subjects in the bus, in your club, or on your way home in the train? You may look round quickly and say to yourself 'Oh, it's alright, we're all friends here, because everybody here knows about it. But are you quite sure there is no stranger present? Are you sure that of all the people round you, there is not one man who might be an enemy agent and ignorant of the things you are discussing? In a few hours, he may be sending this information back to the enemy, causing inestimable damage, and maybe the loss of valuable lives and property. Do not think for a moment that the enemy is only interested in what appears to you to be highly secret and important information. The main work of all intelligence services is piecing together scraps of information, perhaps from hundreds of sources, the net result of which may be the disclosure of vital operational information...[19]

Despite doing very much the same as his fellow agents that landed on 3 September, and despite all of them having grounds to argue they had been coerced, Pons was the only one of the agents that was deemed by the jury to have been forced to work as an agent against his will. Although he was acquitted of the charges, it was decided by the security services that he should not walk free so he was made the subject of a detention order under 12 (5) (a) of Aliens Order 1920 and was interned at Camp 020 (Latchmere House).

Clearly there had been hopes Pons would help with further investigations, he had probably offered a deal in exchange for his life, but once he was off the hook over the weeks and months after the trial he became increasingly uncooperative and unreliable when interrogated. Pons was described in a letter from 'Tin Eye' Stephens the commandant of Camp 020 to Dick White in May 1941 as a *'difficult, dangerous and surly customer'*.[20] Pons was finally released and deported in July 1945 and a note attached to his file that '*He should not be allowed to land again in the United Kingdom.*'[21]

In its final analysis of these landings the MI5 report compiled by M.H. Clegg at Camp 020 concluded:

The manner in which the expedition was planned shed light on the German position at the time. An element of blackmail entered into the recruiting of three of the spies. The training of all was extremely sketchy and instructions at times contradictory. Equipment was inadequate; they were, for instance, landed in a Defence Area without any civilian papers. Detailed instructions for their behaviour on landing were completely omitted, a fact which assisted in their speedy arrest. Invasion spies need not all be highly trained and equipped but the lack of organisation on this expedition seems rather to indicate a state of unpreparedness on the part of the Germans. The Fall of France had come unexpectedly soon and the rapid and enormous adjustments of plan for a further invasion led to confusion and failure in technique at some points.

The speedy arrest of these four spies brought invaluable information into British hands, among which were names and descriptions of potential agents, names of English contacts and information on the GSS [German Secret Service]. The British Secret Service was thus provided at a crucial moment in the war with a skeleton plan of enemy espionage activities near our shores.[22]

In Germany 13 August 1940 was planned to be *Adlertag*, Eagle Day when a mighty offensive by the Luftwaffe would destroy Royal Air Force Fighter Command and pave the way for the invasion and conquest of Great Britain. The day did not go as anticipated for the Germans and foreign correspondents observed knots of Germans gather in hotel foyers, restaurants, squares and the Reich Chancellery in Berlin to read newspapers and hear the latest news of the air battle over Britain relayed over speakers. The Luftwaffe failed to achieve a decisive victory over the RAF, but a news report released on the afternoon of 14 August offered some salve to the situation for the enemy. It announced a small number of German parachutists landing in Manchester and Birmingham specifically to carry out acts of sabotage as a precursor to invasion.[23]

The New British Broadcasting Service (NBBS), a German propaganda radio station that could be received in Britain and that had become infamous for the haughty voice of one of its presenters dubbed 'Lord Haw-Haw' (actually voiced by a number of presenters including William Joyce) had acquired some following as the 'true' news of the war. It also attempted to up the fear factor in Britain by running reports in tandem with the dropped parachutes, scaremongering about the landing of German paratroops on Britain.

The British evening papers of 14 August were quick to scotch rumour and panic by reporting the 'Mystery of Parachutes in England'[24] and the 'Hunt

German paratroopers in training c1939.

Troops practising anti-parachutist drill on the Norfolk coast, 1940.

for Phantom Parachutists'.[25] As more details became available, the dailies of 15 August stamped on any concerns, making clear the fact that the parachutes had just been dropped with empty harness and the military authorities were making doubly sure by containing the areas where parachutes had landed. Reports told of about eighty German white silk parachutes having been found in various places in different parts of Yorkshire, Derbyshire and South-West Scotland. At the time the parachutes descended church bells were rung in some of the areas, the Home Guard, local military personnel and police were mobilized, roadblocks set up and parties sent out to search for parachutists.

In the North Midlands a 'parachute invasion area' of 600 miles was described as 'surrounded by a ring of steel' consisting of soldiers and roadblocks across main roads. Parties of troops undertook searches of garages, factories, public air raid shelters, haystacks, barns and outbuildings carried out through the night by military and civilian authorities; some of the searches were even assisted by bloodhounds. Anyone outside during the night on foot or in vehicles was challenged, and in some cases where they were found not to be carrying their identity cards, they were detained until their identity was definitely established.[26]

Most of the parachutes were found on the ground with the harness beside them. Some were on the tops of trees, some on the roofs of houses and others in the middle of cornfields without any tracks leading from them. In each area the parachutes were dropped one set of panniers such as those used for mules carrying ammunition were also discovered, these had been filled with maps of the areas where they were found, operational orders and instructions.

Veteran aviation correspondent William Courtenay raised the question in his article of whether the parachutes had actually been planted by members of the Fifth Column,[27] but over the days that followed newspapers were quick to relay the findings of the military and government experts who examined the recovered parachutes and panniers:

The harness attached to the parachutes also seemed well worn. In one case the cords, which would be attached to a parachutist, had been cut; an expert expressed the view that this must have been done weeks before … The parachutes were examined where they fell and the evidence was fairly conclusive that most of them came down without anything attached to them. There was no evidence whatever that any of them had been used by a parachutist.

On closer examination the panniers were dirty with rusty pieces of steel and were badly worn … They were made of canvas with steel frames … but they were not the kind of things that would be used by a parachutist as they were much too heavy. One comprehensive document purported to be an order addressed to a parachute regiment to carry out certain operations, but when you came to look at the whole thing it was soon obvious to the expert eye that the document was just a spoof. It had a secret number, but they made one bad mistake in one case by dropping in a file copy. There were maps of the area in which the bags and parachutes were found. They were the usual survey maps copied from British maps and printed in German. There were also more detailed instructions in German to the parachute troops, but these did not ring true.[28]

Despite the 'phantom parachutes' being a clumsy effort to create panic and alarm and add to the pressure around *Adlertag*, in the hope that Britain would capitulate, (British intelligence had received information that just such a stunt was due to be attempted back on 20 July),[29] the dropped parachutes did raise the question in the minds of the British general public of what exactly should the public do if an enemy parachutist dropped in their neighbourhood? A number of papers and magazines were happy to oblige and offered their readers helpful hints on what to do:

Should you be in doubt whether the man is friend or foe report his presence immediately to the nearest police officer or Home Guard and then keep your lips sealed.

If you are a Home Guard or an armed soldier insist that the stranger puts his hands up and accompanies you to the nearest police station.

Generally, parachutists drop in small groups and if you see them do not let them out of your sight. Let somebody else warn the authorities.

It is vitally important not to say anything to anyone after the proper authorities have been informed: shouting the news would only spread rumours and alarm people.

Home Guards and others on patrol would do well to have some pre-arranged signal so that if parachutists are observed they can warn their comrades without the enemy being aware of what is happening.

It is quite safe as a rule to approach within 500 yards of a parachutist, for if he is carrying an automatic weapon the range is small – 200 yards at most.

Familiarise yourself with your own district so that if you do see suspicious persons drop by parachute you can describe precisely the field or open space in which you believe them to have dropped. Don't be afraid, the parachutists are probably a lot more scared than you could ever be.

If you spot an enemy make sure he does not know you are watching him. Learn to take cover.

Don't waste time. Every minute is precious, two or three parachutists may be the vanguard of airborne troops.

If you are in a country area make sure you know where the nearest public and private telephones are situated.

Suspect any man who calls at your house and asks for maps, means of transport or anything like that. Refuse any information and as soon as he is gone get in touch with the police.[30]

*   *   *

Around 3am on the morning of 6 September 1940, just three days after the landing of the spies by boat at Lydd and Dymchurch and as SIS were receiving a number of reports regarding the imminence of invasion, Lena agent Gösta Caroli landed by parachute in a field at Denton, Northamptonshire. His mission was to report on the area of Oxford, Northampton and Birmingham with particular interest in the air raid damage to Birmingham.[31] He had bailed out at 15,000 feet but had been stunned by a blow to his head by his wireless set and had been discovered lying in a ditch and was rapidly in the hands of the authorities. In 1940 there was a news blackout of the story, but like so many tales that were bracketed 'now it can be told' after the end of the war in Europe, in May 1945 the *Northampton Mercury* ran the story of the 'Parachute Spy' caught at Cliff Beechener's farm, 'The Elms' at Denton:

At about 5pm Mr Beechener was told that there was a man with a suitcase lying in a ditch in one of the fields. He had been seen lying there by an Irish farm worker, Patrick Daly. Mr Beechener decided to go and investigate and took his gun 'just in case'.

He could just see the feet of a man protruding from a bush. As Mr Beechener passed, the man tried to draw himself farther behind the bush but his boots were yellow. Mr Beechener turned sharply and ordered the man out. Mr Beechener found he was carrying a loaded automatic. He forced him to march to the house, which he did in a rapid goose step, and there Mr Beechener set a guard upon him while he summoned the police and Home Guard.

The guard had strict instructions to shoot in the event of an attempt to escape and it was sufficiently heavy to be effective – two farm workers armed with Mr Beechener's Home Guard rifle and a .22 rifle and Pat Daly with a shotgun. When police arrived the whole company with their arms and the prisoner went to the spot and searched the kit left in the ditch.

They found a portable radio set in the suitcase, chocolate and whiskey, extra clothing, the parachute on which had been lying a compass, maps, clock and other odds and ends. Mr Beechener's opinion is that he might have made a getaway but for the amount of equipment. It took three men to carry it. When searched the spy was found to have about £300 in his possession and an identity card with a Birmingham address, but there was a mistake which would have given him away later had he escaped, the address was in continental style, street name first then the number and in addition the date was wrong.[32]

The following day Guy Liddell wrote:

He [Caroli] had been dropped by a Heinkel plane and had embarked at Brussels. He had intended to land at Birmingham and thought that on landing he was somewhere near Stratford-upon-Avon. It transpired he had been in England as late as December 1939 when he stayed with friends at Boughton. He was in possession of a National Registration Certificate. He had been trained at Hamburg. Colonel Hinchley-Cooke took down a statement from him at Cannon Row police station and he was sent on to Latchmere House [Camp 020].[33]

After a few days in captivity Caroli opened up, as Liddell recorded:

[Caroli] is not apparently interested in his own life but merely that of his friend [Wulf Schmidt]. He himself is quite prepared to be shot as a spy and is apparently a student of philosophy. Owing to his German parentage and his admiration of the German regime he joined the German army but was, however, reluctant to become a spy, so having taken the job was prepared to

HOME OFFICE,

WHITEHALL, S.W.

6th September, 1940.

IMMEDIATE AND MOST SECRET

Sir,

LANDING OF ENEMY AGENTS.

1. I am directed by the Secretary of State to inform you that a case has recently occurred in which persons believed to be enemy agents landed on the coast from boats. It is considered probable that further attempts of the same kind may be made shortly, and also that attempts may be made to land agents from the air.

2. In the case in question some of the persons concerned represented themselves to be former members of the Dutch Army who had succeeded in escaping from the Continent to take refuge in this country. There is reason to believe that similar tactics may be adopted by other persons attempting to land.

3. I am to ask that you will immediately review your existing arrangements for detecting surreptitious landings both from the sea and from the air, and warn all members of your force to exercise the utmost vigilance in this direction. Any persons found in suspicious circumstances who cannot give a satisfactory account of themselves should be detained for enquiries.

4. If any person thought to have landed surreptitiously is arrested or detained the procedure set out in paragraph 6 of the memorandum enclosed with the Home Office circular (700,170/116) of the 12th July last will apply, subject to the following modifications:-

(i) the Duty Officer, W Section, M.I.5. should be informed immediately by telephone, and asked for directions as to further action, including the disposal of the prisoner. The Regional representative of M.I.5. should be informed by telephone as soon as possible afterwards.

(ii) all articles in the possession of each prisoner should be carefully preserved and kept separate; and any articles found in the neighbourhood which are at all likely to be connected with the case but cannot definitely be assigned to a particular prisoner should also be kept separate.

/(iii)

(iii) special care should be taken to search the immediate neighbourhood of the arrest, and of the place where the prisoner is thought to have landed, for any wireless apparatus, or object likely to be such apparatus, and batteries, and for blank paper. (Wireless apparatus may be quite small - possibly no larger than a hand camera - and may be concealed).

(iv) special care should be taken to see that the prisoner does not make away with any article in his possession while relieving, or feigning to relieve, the calls of nature.

(v) a thorough search should be made in the vicinity of the arrest both for suspicious persons and suspicious articles, and in the case of landings from the sea the Coast Watchers in the police district should be asked to give special attention to the possibility of other landings being attempted.

5. A description of any missing person thought to be connected with a prisoner should be circulated to neighbouring forces as quickly as possible, e.g. by Express Message, but the message should be confined to essential information and should not give more details of the case than are necessary to enable the missing person to be identified.

I am,
Sir,
Your obedient Servant,

R. J. Wells.

The 'Immediate and Most Secret' instructions for dealing with enemy agents issued to chief constables, 6 September 1940.

see it through and determined not to give away his friends. Malcolm Frost and Max Knight seem to have succeeded in persuading him that the Germans had given him a very raw deal and had sent him over here ill equipped and under somewhat false pretences. He came round eventually to this view and agreed to work his wireless set, which he had up to then refused to do.[34]

Caroli and Wulf Schmidt had trained together and had agreed to meet up when they had both landed in England, so a deal had been reached between MI5 and Caroli. In exchange for a guarantee that Schmidt's life would be spared, Caroli would inform them of when and where they should expect him to land. Curiously, if Schmidt had no idea that he was going to be picked up shortly after landing, his training had been such that he was supremely confident or naive of what to do when he landed.

Liddell also spoke with Colonel Kenneth Strong the then head of the German Section at MI14 (later Major General Sir Kenneth Strong, the first Director of the Joint Intelligence Bureau 1948–1964) after he had spoken with Kieboom, Meier, Waldberg, Pon and the newly landed Caroli:

What puzzled him was that the Germans, should have given their agents details of their plan of attack. The details they had given more or less agreed with what we had received from other sources and from aerial reconnaissance etc. of the dispositions of enemy forces. This made it difficult to believe that the spies had been sent over here to mislead us. Strong has a great regard for German efficiency and cannot bring himself to believe that they could have been so stupid as to send these men over here without having schooled them properly and worked out plans by which they could be really effective.[35]

Wulf Schmidt landed by parachute on Fen Field, Glebe Farm, Willingham, Cambridgeshire around midnight on the night of 19/20 September 1940. He believed he had been dropped from 3,500 feet and had even been briefly caught in the beam of an anti-aircraft searchlight battery on the way down. Instead of hitting the ground, Schmidt had become entangled on telegraph wires, he managed to extricate himself but sprained his ankle on landing.[36] He then set about hiding his parachute and radio under cover of darkness and then he limped off to find the nearest village, Willingham, where he bought some aspirin to relieve the pain in his ankle and bathed it under the village pump. He had also smashed his watch when bailing out so he bought a cheap replacement at a barber's shop, and a paper at the newsagents and had some breakfast at a local tea room.

A stranger in a rural village would always attract attention, but especially so in war time when his dress, demeanour and foreign accent raised concerns. Schmidt was asked to show his identity card by Home Guard Tom Cousins. He produced a Danish passport and a forged British Identity Card, but when he could not easily explain his presence in the village he was taken to the Three Tuns pub kept by Willingham Home Guard Platoon Commander Major John Langton who questioned Schmidt, but not being satisfied with the answers he received he called the police. By lunchtime Schmidt was at Cambridge police station under the personal charge of the chief constable with Captain Dixon the Regional Security Liaison Officer.[37]

Caroli had been co-operating with MI5; he and Schmidt had trained together and had made a pact to meet up after both of them had landed in Britain. In exchange for a guarantee Schmidt's life would be spared, Caroli advised MI5 when Schmidt would be landing and he had been expected.

Of course, his safety on landing could not be entirely guaranteed. After a few incidents where Home Guard and farmers had been over zealous in the use of the weaponry they had to hand when dealing with enemy pilots, and some foreign allied pilots that were harshly dealt with because of their strange accents, appeals from the Air Ministry appearing in newspapers grew in frequency and prominence. They urged members of the public and home forces 'to exercise great care and discretion' emphasising:

> … *only if a parachutist adopts a threatening attitude or attempts to commit a hostile act should force be used. If he is identified as a German or if his identity cannot be established at once e.g. by production of his RAF identity card, he should be made prisoner and handed over to the police or military authorities.*[38]

Cambridgeshire Home Guard had done exactly as they should have, so after a night in the cells Schmidt was transported to Camp 020 at Latchmere House on 21 September 1940.

The microphones hidden all over Latchmere House were already yielding useful information intercepted from casual conversations between the German officers and agents held there. At the same time, under the guidance of Dr Harold Dearden, the psychological and often gentle touch employed when attempting to turn agents to double-cross appeared to be working well too. Indeed, in the spirit of one volunteer being worth ten pressed men, it was apparent from the agents being sent to the UK by the *Abwehr* that any agent working under duress would soon prove to be a liability to their German masters.

The problem was there were still some old-school interrogators and one incident in particular was brought to the attention of Guy Liddell the day after Schmidt's arrival at Latchmere. Schmidt was already being co-operative, he had said he would help them find his hidden wireless set, but the following day the interrogation had broken for lunch and, noticing Colonel Alexander Scotland (the commandant of the MI19 prisoner of war facility, known as 'The London Cage') had left where they were eating, Malcolm Frost followed him and as recorded by Liddell:

> … *eventually discovered him in the prisoner's cell. He was hitting Schmidt in the jaw and I think he got one back himself. Frost stopped the incident without making a scene and later told me what happened. It was quite clear to me that we cannot have this sort of thing going on in our establishment. Apart from the moral aspect of the whole thing, I am quite convinced the Gestapo methods do not pay in the long run … I am told that Scotland turned up this morning with a syringe containing some drug or other, which is thought would induce the prisoner to speak.*'[39]

An excuse was made up, Scotland was told Schmidt was too ill to be interrogated and was not allowed to see him. Liddell brought the matter to the attention of Major General Frederick 'Paddy' Beaumont-Nesbitt, Director

Wulf Schmidt, aka double agent TATE and his transceiver radio.

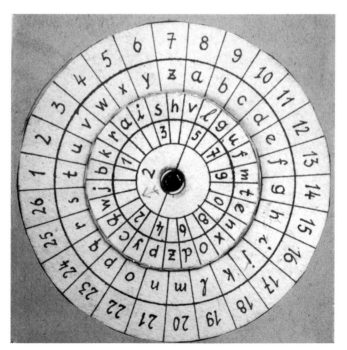

Schmidt's code wheel.

of Military Intelligence and said they did not wish to have Scotland on the premises again.[40] There were fears for Schmidt's frame of mind to co-operate in a double-cross following the assault after the little ground they had made, but it was felt he should be worked if possible.[41]

Schmidt did come round and was willing to reveal the location of his wireless transmitter that he had hidden near where he had landed and was transported by car back to the site to recover it. The problem was that in their excitement and haste B Branch did not inform Cambridgeshire police nor the Regional Security Officer (RSO) that they were doing this. The local constabulary and Home Guard had been searching for the set for the previous forty-eight hours and encountered members of the public who alerted them to 'some mysterious diggers' that had come down in a car and had removed what appeared to be a wireless set. It was only after urgent further investigation that they had been informed that these people were officers of MI5. Cambridgeshire Constabulary were less than pleased, MI5 Deputy Director Jasper Harker had ended up having to make a frank apology over the telephone and Charles Butler (Harker's deputy) kindly offered to go over personally to smooth things over the following day.[42]

Both Schmidt and Caroli were initially held at Camp 020 but were removed to 'safe houses' from which they sent regular messages back to their controllers. Caroli was given the MI5 code name SUMMER and Schmidt was dubbed TATE, because he bore a likeness to the popular music hall comedian Harry Tate. The situation, however, did not sit well with Caroli and on 11 October he attempted to commit suicide.[43] After recovery he was released to MI5's 'Home for Incurables' (those who would not be turned to become double-cross agents or were no longer trustworthy or able to carry on in the double agent system) at The Old Parsonage, Hinxton in Cambridgeshire.

On 13 January 1941 he was left with only one guard whom he knocked down and tried to strangle. Then, having tied him up he got hold of a motorbike that belonged to one of the other guards and, lashing a 12ft canvas canoe from a nearby barn on one side and a suitcase on the other, he sped off in the direction of Newmarket. After a number of falls from the bike and when it spluttered to a halt Caroli handed himself in to the authorities at Newmarket Police Station.[44] If Caroli had got away the risk was that he could expose the fact we were turning agents and could have destroyed the whole double-cross system.

Liddell was clear about his future after the incident: '*Clearly SUMMER can never be allowed to use his wireless transmitter again and will have to remain under lock and key.*'[45]

A course of action was decided upon:

We had a long discussion this morning about SUMMER's future and that of the other people with whom he has been associated. We have all come to the conclusion that somehow or other SUMMER must be eliminated ... If therefore we report that he has been captured, the Germans may think that the whole organisation has been compromised. Various ingenious suggestions have been made. The best, I think, is that BISCUIT should report that SUMMER is on the run, that he has put his wireless into the cloakroom at Cambridge station, and sent the key to BISCUIT. Later we could say that he has been picked up by the police for failing to register.[46]

Caroli was left to sit out the war incarcerated and in radio silence; he was repatriated to Sweden in August 1945.[47] Before recent releases of previously classified files and further research, it had been suggested Caroli had been discreetly but summarily given an appointment with the hangman. However, the reason why this did not happen and the reason why Pons was acquitted and at least one agent from every group that landed, even if they were uncooperative or had come to the end of their time as effective double-cross agents, were not sent to the gallows or firing squad was provided by Masterman in his book *The Double-Cross System in the War of 1939–1945* originally compiled and written in 1945:

... the Security Service always opposed execution except when no other course was possible. A live spy, even if he cannot transmit messages, is always of some use as a book of reference; a dead spy is of no sort of use. But some had to perish, both to satisfy the public that the security of the country was being maintained and also to convince the Germans that the others were working properly and were not under control. It would have taxed German credulity if all their agents had apparently overcome the hazards of their landing.[48]

TATE was a very different matter; he became one of the longest running double-cross agents. In October 1940 Liddell wrote:

It has been decided that TATE is to pose to the other side as Harry Williamson, a British subject educated in Denmark. As a result of failing to establish contact he had almost given up hope and had resigned himself to living here for the rest of the war and had accordingly not gone to the trouble of obtaining information for which he had been sent over. Now he has established contact he will set out his job and is awaiting instructions.[49]

TATE continued communications with Germany throughout the war and participated in the Operation Bodyguard deception that misled the Germans about the date and time of the Normandy landings. He was never found out, indeed he was considered a valuable agent to the very end, and was even awarded

The Hotel Reichshof, Hamburg where Vera and her fellow agents shared a meal together before embarking on their mission to Britain.

an Iron Cross. After the end of the war TATE continued to live in Britain and kept a low profile working as a photographer in Watford under his cover name of Harry Williamson which he retained until his death aged 80 in 1992.[50]

* * *

The German agents kept on coming; this time under *Hummer Nord* I three agents were flown in an X. Fliegerkorps He 115 seaplane from Stavanger, Norway and were set down between Buckie and Portgordon on the Moray Firth coast off what was then known as Banffshire, Scotland around dawn on 30 September 1940.

The party consisted of Karl Drüke, who was supplied with false documents and a cover story under the name of François de Deeker, a French refugee from Belgium; Robert Petter who was given the name Werner Heinrich Wälti, a Swiss subject living in London and, for the first time, a female agent was to be deployed in these operations.

Karl Drücke who landed in Britain under the name of Francois de Deeker.

She had been one of the pre-war agents active in England, Vera Schalburg (probably known at the time as Vera von Wedel) who, for this mission, would have the cover identity of Vera Eriksen, a Dane living in London. All three of them were experienced espionage operatives and they were not deployed under any coercion.

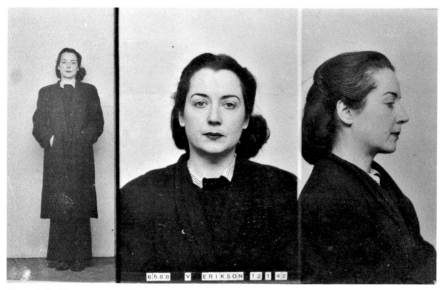

Vera Schalberg aka Erikson during her captivity in Britain, January 1942.

116

They had practised launching their 4ft x 10ft rubber dinghy from a seaplane, getting into it and rowing ashore in a fjord in Norway before they departed. Indeed, they had become accustomed to the flights in the seaplane, having prepared themselves mentally and had actually set off to begin their mission on two previous occasions, but the aircraft carrying them had to turn back due to adverse weather conditions. Still, it's quite a leap between training and becoming operational and they disembarked onto a choppy sea rather than a calm fjord. The bicycles they had been sent with were soon ditched over the side to prevent the boat filling with water and the two male agents rowed for three and a half hours before they came to the shallows at the mouth of the Burn of Gollachy.[51] The three then found they had to get out of the boat and wade some distance through the sea in order to come ashore.[52]

According to Vera, Wälti wanted to go by himself and stayed behind to sink the boat while she and Drücke made their way to a nearby village where they found a station. However, since the sign boards and place names of Britain had been removed in the face of the invasion threat, they had no success in discovering where they were, so they walked on and rested under a hedge until daylight.[53]

Portgordon railway station, Moray, Scotland where Vera and Drücke were captured as they waited for a train just hours after they landed on 30 September 1940.

About 7.30am they returned to the station and found Stationmaster John Donald in the booking hall. He was approached by Drüke who enquired of him 'What station is this?' to which Donald replied, 'Portgordon'. Vera said 'What?' and the name of the station was repeated to her. Drüke claimed he did not attempt to speak to anyone owing to his ignorance of English. In the hope of avoiding suspicion and to not give away their final destination Vera purchased two single tickets to Forres.[54]

Stationmaster Donald recalled how odd it had struck him that someone should be at the station and ask where the station was at such a time in the morning and he watched Drüke running his finger down the list of stations from Portgordon to Elgin and on to Forres. The stationmaster also could not help but notice that the bottom of Drüke's trousers, his shoes and the bottom of his overcoat were soaking wet, as were Vera's shoes and there was a slight deposit of hoar frost on the shoulders of her coat. This and the fact that the man also appeared to be trying to hide his face, aroused such suspicion that Donald told porter John Geddes to keep them talking as he rang the police. He then opened the ticket window of the booking office and Vera purchased the two tickets to Forres for which she paid 5/2d.[55]

PC Robert Grieve of Banffshire Constabulary who was stationed at Portgordon was despatched to the station as a result of the call. He arrived shortly after 8am and found Drüke and Vera in the waiting room and asked them to produce their identity cards. Grieve asked them their nationality, it was Vera who replied, 'He is Belgian, I am Danish.' PC Grieve then asked to see their passports, Vera claimed she had left hers in London, Drüke did not reply but produced his Belgian passport. On examining the document the constable found there was no Immigration Officer's stamp authorising the holder to land.

The summary account of what happened next is in the MI5 file collated for the prosecution of the agents:

They were asked where they came from and the woman said, 'We came from London.' The man did not speak. Asked where they had stayed the previous night the woman said, 'We stayed in a hotel at Banff.' Again, the man did not answer. When asked the name of the hotel in Banff in which they stayed the woman shrugged her shoulders but neither made a reply.

The constable then asked how they had got to Portgordon from Banff. They replied, 'We hired a taxi to within a mile of Portgordon and then walked'. The constable, being dissatisfied with their explanations then told them he would take them to the police station pending enquiries.

The woman then repeated what the officer had said to the man and he took hold of a small dark blue suitcase with nickel fittings. After arrival at

118

the police station, Grieve communicated with Inspector Simpson at Buckie Police Station and, after a hearing the constable's conversations, she said, 'I told you lies at the Railway Station,' and continued 'we landed from a small boat about a mile along the coast, the boat was in charge of a man named Sanderson.' When asked where the boat was, she replied, 'It has gone back to Bergen.'

They were subsequently taken into custody and escorted to Portgordon police station where they were questioned further by Inspector John Simpson:

He asked the man who he was and the woman said, 'He cannot speak English.' The woman gave her name as Vera Erikson and said she was 27 years of age, a widow and had no occupation. She added that she was a Danish subject born in Siberia. They again produced their Identity Cards and the man his passport. Inspector Simpson observed that Continental figures were on both Identity Cards. When asked how they had arrived at Portgordon the woman said, 'We came from Bergen on a small boat called "Nor Star", the name of the captain was Anderson.'

Inspector Simpson then searched the man and in his overcoat pocket found a box containing nineteen rounds of revolver ammunition and when asked if he had a revolver the man replied, 'No'. In addition the Inspector found an electric torch with a blue bulb, bearing the name 'Hawe' and 'made in Bohemia' on the bottom, a watch with the initials 'H.W.D' engraved on the back, a pocket knife, a leather wallet, a Traveller's Ration Book bearing the number C.A. 568263; a piece of flexible material sewn into a piece of blue cloth; a single third class railway ticket from Portgordon to Forres dated 30th September, 1940; £327 in Bank of England notes; a piece of German sausage and other foodstuffs.

Later in the man's presence the small suitcase was forced open and the Inspector found a small 'Mauser' pistol containing six rounds of ammunition in the magazine; two circular cardboard discs fastened together with a brass split pin; a sheet of paper bearing a number of place names; a sheet of graph paper; a wireless set …'[56]

A transmitter was also found; the game was up and Vera admitted that her National Registration Card was false. After communication with an MI5 regional officer who reported to headquarters, instructions were given for the urgent dispatch of the two persons with all the equipment and other possessions found with them. Their statements of landing by boat were also brought into question when Coastguard James Addison spotted an object in the sea drifting from Portgordon to Buckie at around 11.45am. The Buckie harbourmaster was put out in his boat to recover the object. As he proceeded

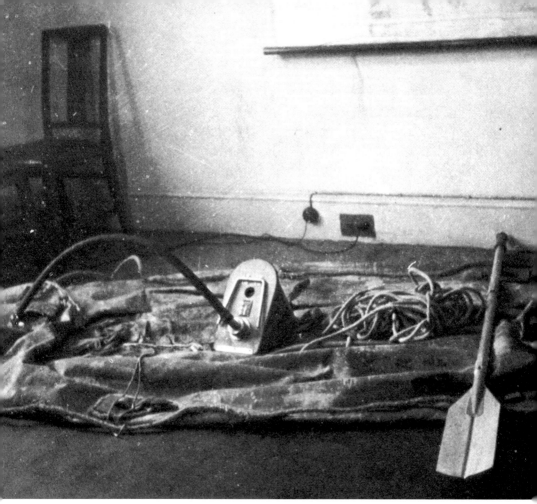

The rubber dinghy used by Drücke, Vera and Wälti after its recovery from the sea.

there, he picked up a pair of bellows suitable for the inflation of a rubber boat that were floating on the sea and, upon reaching the object spotted by Addison, discovered it to be a rubber dinghy that had been rolled up.[57]

After the detention of Vera and Drüke enquiries were instituted by Banffshire Police to ascertain if any other suspicious individuals had been encountered on the coast that morning in similar circumstances. This dragnet received information from James Smith, a porter at Buckpool, who had encountered a man at 6.50am who was not sure of where he needed to travel to and spoke with a foreign accent. Smith had directed the man to Buckie Station and there he turned up around 8am.

Alexander Paterson, a porter at Buckie Station encountered a man looking at the timetable outside the station and asked him if he had lost his train. The man, without speaking, produced a third-class single ticket to Edinburgh from his wallet and was told that his train was at 10am. Paterson suspected the man to be a foreigner and remembered that he had with him a suitcase and a dark coloured briefcase. He was advised to put the luggage into the booking office, which he did. At 10.04am Paterson saw the man board the Aberdeen train with his luggage.[58]

Lieutenant Mair of the Scottish Regional Security Office was informed of the arrival of two suspicious persons believed to be foreign agents on the Buckie coast and he instigated enquiries conducted by local CID and police at all railway stations, hotels, boarding houses and other likely places. Thomas Cameron, a porter at Waverley Station, Edinburgh had attended a man he believed to be the owner of this case,

Abwehr agent Robert Petter aka Werner Wälti.

whom he said came off the Aberdeen train at about 4.30pm and spoke with a foreign accent. Cameron was able to identify the case and to say that the owner was returning about 9pm to collect it, prior to departing for London. About 6pm a case was traced in the left luggage office at the east end of the station. This case was damp and had particles of sand adhering to it.

A report of what happened next is recorded in the MI5 case folder:

Detective Inspector Alexander Sutherland, Detective Alexander McCowan and Police War Reserve James Fair made a search of the case and found that it contained a complete transmitting set contained in a leather case. Also in the suitcase were articles of clothing which were wet. At 6.50pm Lieut Mair telephoned a description of the suspected foreign agent and this tallied with the description of the man who had deposited the suitcase ... In consequence of the find in the left luggage office a watch was kept on Waverley Station.

At 8.58pm that night the suspected agent came from the vicinity of Waverley Steps and after hesitating at the left luggage office he continued to the book stall, some 20 yards distant. A minute or so after he had taken up his stance at the book stall, keeping his eye on the left luggage office, Detective Superintendent Merrilees [who had borrowed a railway porter's uniform so he would blend in] *was joined by Thomas Cameron.*

Just then the prisoner approached Cameron who asked if he wanted his case. The prisoner replied 'Yes' and handed Cameron his cloakroom ticket.

Detective Superintendent Merrilees was immediately joined by Detective Lieutenant [sic] Cormack, Detective Inspector Sutherland and Detective Sergeant Swan and the prisoner was held. He, however, made an effort to resist, but was overpowered while in the act of trying to put his hand in his left-hand trouser pocket. He was searched and a Mauser automatic pistol was found in his left-hand trouser pocket. He was taken into the left luggage office where Detective Constable McCowan and Police War Reserve Fair were on watch ... His articles of wearing apparel were soaking wet. On being arrested, without being spoken to, Walti exclaimed, 'I am not German, I am Swiss.'[59]

Drüke, Vera and Wälti were brought to London under escort and interviewed at Latchmere House. The MI5 report on the interrogations dated 2 October 1940 revealed all three had tried to stick to their cover stories. Vera was first to divulge useful information, but the two men remained uncooperative and more had to be derived from the physical evidence of the items found in their possession, deduction and the few scraps of information they were prepared to divulge:

It is, however, quite clear that both Erikson and de Deeker are skilled and practised German SS Agents who have been involved in such work for a long time. The exact nature of their mission to this country is not yet clear. It is just possible that Erikson was instructed to proceed to London and it is also just possible that she was to be contacted here by a local German agent. A further interesting fact regarding Erikson is that she has been in this country before, staying with the Duchess de Chateau Thierry at Dorset House, Gloucester Place. The Duchess is well known to this office and Erikson's stay with her confirms previous suspicions that she has been mixed up in German espionage.

From Walti's background story it would appear that he was recruited for the German SS in Brussels. Though younger than the other two (24), Walti had obviously had experience with the German SS and in his possession were found maps detailing the area of the eastern Highlands of Scotland, Elgin, Aberdeen, Sutherland, Caithness, Ross and Cromarty, as well as areas in England which included Norwich and the greater part of Norfolk, Wisbech, King's Lynn, Peterborough and the surrounding country, Bedford and the surrounding country, Cambridge and the surrounding country, Bury St Edmunds and the greater part of Suffolk.

It is difficult to account for such a wide area of patrol, but it is possible that Walti had to hand some of the maps over to other agents ... while varying somewhat in form from the cases of the other six spies recently arrested, the three new ones are clearly directed by the same organisation belonging particularly to the Hamburg end of it.

... It is reasonable to suppose that the two men were intended to carry out espionage similar to that of the previous six on defence works in Scotland and on the East Coast. The woman Erikson may have had a mission of an entirely different order and it is just possible that she was really intended for London. The wireless sets in possession of the spies are of a similar type to those previously discovered in the case of the first six. They are capable of transmitting and receiving. The codes are of the type supplied to those parachutists, that is, they are in the form of circular discs. As all three have so far shown considerable composure under interrogation and appear to be reconciled to the inevitable fate meted out to spies, their interrogation presented considerable problems. It is probable that several days more will be necessary before the whole truth can be extracted from them.'[60]

The problem for Drüke and Wälti was they had already been 'burned' after national newspapers published the story of a male Nazi spy being caught on Edinburgh station[61] and the whole operation could have been viewed as compromised by their *Abwehr* masters. Drüke and Wälti refused to co-operate with MI5, even after frustrated interrogation officers overstepped their authority and offered Wälti the chance to evade the gallows in return for a full confession, he did not accept the offer.[62]

Drüke and Wälti were tried in camera before Mr Justice Asquith at the Central Criminal Court, The Old Bailey on 12–13 June 1941. Like the previous spies they were represented by legal counsel but were convicted under the Treachery Act 1940. Their appeals against the sentence of death were heard by the Court of Criminal Appeal but were dismissed on 21 July. Still arrogant enough to believe they had been betrayed by an informant rather than their own incompetence and misfortune as agents,[63] and undoubtedly bitter at having been convinced they were to be part of a vanguard for an invasion that had still not arrived, Drüke was left feeling he and his fellow agents were just 'a cargo of meat'.[64]

Jona 'Klop' Ustinov, (the father of the affectionately remembered actor and raconteur Peter Ustinov) was an MI5 operative whose perception and genial hospitality was key to 'turning' a number of informants and agents. He concluded in his report based on conversations with Vera during a brief interlude of soft interrogation when she was allowed out of Holloway Prison: *'The truth seems to be that she and her companions were no more important than the other operational spies who arrived at roughly the same time. They were obviously thrown to the wolves.*'[65]

It was a view echoed by Dick White (who went on to become Director General of MI5) when he concluded: *'Doubtless the only satisfaction which the directors of the German intelligence ... obtained from the venture was their ability to report to the High Command that they were dispatching spies to the United Kingdom in preparation for the invasion.*[66]

Wälti and Drüke were hanged at Wandsworth Prison by Thomas Pierrepoint, assisted by Albert Pierrepoint, Harry Kirk and Stanley Cross on 6 August 1941.

* * *

Vera, however, never faced trial. There are a number of possible suggestions for this – one is that she was, or at least claimed to be, pregnant. Another is what may seem an old fashioned view now, that the British authorities simply did not want to hang a pretty young woman, especially after the backlash they had received for the execution of Edith Thompson in 1923. She was hanged for collusion in the murder of her husband by her lover Freddie Bywaters – even after Bywaters made a written confession exonerating Edith of any involvement. Vera could easily have become a *cause célèbre* too, especially when the outrage over the execution of Nurse Edith Cavell by the Germans for 'war treason' had been used to such great effect by the Allies during the First World War. The last thing British authorities wanted was to hand the Germans the propaganda opportunity of the execution of a beautiful woman agent in this war.

With all of those possibilities borne in mind the overriding reason was far more prosaic in that she presented the best prospect of being of use as a double-cross agent and infiltrator than the agents that landed with her. However, that did not mean Vera did not present her own problems.

Within days of arrival at Latchmere House Vera was 'showing signs of going on hunger strike' and was removed to Holloway Prison.[67] MI5 seem satisfied with Vera's account of her mission being to reprise her role as hostess at the duchess's salon and she gave up the names of a number of those she came into contact with but, very much as Ritter had complained that the duchess's contacts had been of little use back in 1939, when MI5 investigated them the trails ran cold or had already left the UK. Those they could trace were mostly already interned or proved to be more Nazi sympathisers in words rather than dirtying their hands getting involved in actual espionage operations.[68] But there were significant exceptions. Vera did identify 'My' Eriksson as a courier and scouting agent for Ritter. Already interned, Eriksson was questioned on the matter and as usual proved both convincing and as slippery as ever.

Richard Butler's take on 'My' Eriksson after interviewing her was: '*I am more than ever certain that My is an extremely clever woman, a brilliant actress and a consummate liar.*' (He held a similar view of Vera.) [69]

Others who it would have been far more worthwhile to have identified are described by Vera with vague recollections such as 'Wilkinson' or 'Wilkins'. She mentioned this name in her earliest interviews when she claimed she was a courier for the radio she and Drüke had been found with and that Wilkinson, who she described as tall and thin with fair hair, would be calling on her at the Dorchester Hotel within the next five days.[70] Vera would alter the claim that Wilkinson was Ritter's paymaster and principal agent in London and enlarged on her description of the man to detail that he was: '*tall and slim, with fair hair and moustache aged thirty or just under, English or half English and of ordinary undistinctive type*'.[71]

It is intriguing that this description echoes Elizabeth Allworth's description of the tall, fair haired man seen at the flat of Fabian and Wurms on Great Ormond Street before their deaths by poisoning under mysterious circumstances in March 1935. There is a possibility Vera actually slipped up and named a proficient German agent believed to have been in London at the time named Werner Uhlm and tried to cover the slip by claiming it was the phonetically similar Wilkinson.

Uhlm is a good match for her description too, it was recorded in the MI5 file compiled from captured agent testimonies as:

Age 31, looks 27, Height 6ft, athletic build. Blue eyes no glasses … Dark blonde hair plastered back, Very determined looking. Speaks fluent English, French, Italian, Spanish and Malay. Uses various cover for his spying activities (Commercial Traveller, Doctor, Engineer etc).[72]

The problem with Vera was that it was always difficult to know when she was telling the truth. Colonel Robin Stephens interrogated Vera on several occasions and summed her up well in a report on 6 January 1941: '*… she prefers to lie and in order to get rid of us, she not infrequently gives an answer which is calculated to please.*'[73] In a later memo he had clearly lost patience with her dishonest claims and simply described her as 'a prize liar'.[74] Richard Butler believed Vera and 'My' Erikssen should be taken out of Holloway and spend some time at Latchmere House on Ham Common, stating: '*If it is not possible to have these women at Ham, I do not know how they can be "broken". I am convinced, however, that some real effort should be made.*'[75]

In his report to Liddle on his interrogations of Vera dated 24 October 1940 Stephens made his opinion on the matter of Wilkinson clear:

A main, if not the primary object, of the investigation to my mind was to establish the existence and identity of Wilkinson, the reputed right hand man of Rantzau [Ritter] in this country. In my judgement, the existence of this enemy agent in England has been established, but further investigation is necessary conclusively to connect his identity with that of Paymaster Lieutenant A.P. Wilkinson of HMS Ganges, *Ipswich. On the one hand I so distrust Chateau-Thierry,* Vera Erichsen [sic] *and* Costenza [the beautiful young Austrian Countess Edeltrude Claudette Von Costenza], *that I naturally suspect connivance to lead us away from an agent indiscreetly revealed by Erichsen.*

On the other hand, the search of Costenza's property in B.8, dating back to her arrest ten months ago, provides outside and independent corroboration. Again independent descriptions are uncannily close, while lastly, there is evidence of overspending at places such as the Dorchester and the Kit Kat Club by a junior officer in the Paymaster branch of the Navy ... I have already ventured to suggest that a main objective is the arrest of Wilkinson and it may well be considered that the investigations in the subsidiary cases might be held in abeyance until this object is achieved.[76]

Known associates of the duchess and her circle were identified; photographs of these people were assembled and shown to those who worked both in Dorset House and for the duchess. None of the photographs were named, they were just identified as 'A', 'B', 'C' etc. One of those shown the photographs was Miss Dorothy Morrish who had been employed as the duchess's cook from June to October 1939.[77] Morrish said she was 'absolutely certain' she recognised one of the men on the photographs as the man who had called for Vera fairly early one morning a short time previously when she was out. Explaining Vera was expecting him, he proceeded to wait and it was noted by Morrish how he '*seemed to know his way around the flat*'. He returned again on another occasion; both he and the event stuck in her memory because it was '*the only occasion in her recollection that the Duchesse and Vera had one man alone for lunch in the flat.*'[78]

This man was indeed named Wilkinson and on further investigation he was found to be a serving officer in the Royal Navy. Traced to the Royal Navy shore establishment HMS *Ganges* at Shotley in Suffolk, MI5's Richard Butler joined with Commander Mallett, the Harwich SOI and the pair interviewed 23-year-old Paymaster Lieutenant Anthony Peter Wilkinson [generally known as Peter Wilkinson] on 16 December 1940. Wilkinson admitted attending a cocktail party at the Normandie Hotel in Kensington on Christmas Day 1939.

He claimed he had attended the event with friends and remembered meeting both the Duchesse Thierry and Lady Mayo at the party and that one or other had hosted the event. But when he was informed that MI5 had independent evidence that he had visited 102, Dorset House on several occasions prior to the cocktail party, Wilkinson claimed he could not recall ever having been there and suggested he didn't even know where it was. He also appeared unphased by the suggestion he may have to come to London so that the servants could identify him.

Wilkinson had been an officer aboard HMS *Royal Oak* when she was torpedoed and sunk at Scapa Flow with the loss of over 800 men on 14 October 1939. As a result of the shock he had then suffered Wilkinson had been appointed to the shore job of secretary to the captain of HMS *Ganges*. He had a brother who was '*remarkably tall and very fair*' who was also a Royal Navy officer based at Scapa. He also admitted to having dated the Countess Costenza who, like Duchesse Thierry, had subsequently been interned. Wilkinson claimed he had financed these extravagances with money from an inheritance he had received at the time.[79]

It seems very unlikely that Paymaster Lieutenant Wilkinson was the man named by Vera as the 'Wilkinson' who was supplying information to Ritter and the *Abwehr*. It seems far more likely she latched on to him as an acquaintance who could fit the bill in an attempt to kick the dust over the tracks of Ritter's real 'right hand man' in London after her own careless disclosure of his existence during her interrogation. However, by perhaps some casual slip, had Wilkinson said too much to the duchess or one of her confidantes and sealed the fate of the *Royal Oak*? Or perhaps, especially as he was facing interrogation, he *thought* he had let some indiscretion slip to Thierry, Costenza or Vera that had ultimately resulted in the sinking. The interviewing officers, Butler and Mallett, shared the opinion that they were '*fairly confident that this young Royal Navy Officer was not being used as a German agent. We are however also equally confident that he is concealing something.*'[80]

Whether or not there were plans to use Vera for double-cross work these would have been scuppered in March 1941 after British SIS received intelligence from German espionage centres in Norway that they were aware all three agents had been captured. Despite the reservations of Stephens, Butler and MI5 officer Helenus Milmo in a letter stating the Director of Public Prosecutions had decided against taking proceedings against Vera under the Treachery Act, in which he recorded: '*So far as her continued sojourn in Holloway is concerned it is felt that since this woman is an experienced and dangerous spy there is no more suitable place for her to be lodged.*'[81]

After a return to prison, however, an experimental method of soft interrogation was devised by which Vera was taken out of prison, bought new clothes in the shops on Oxford Street and went for a sojourn with the Ustinovs at Barrow Elm, Gloucestershire. There she was entertained and shown kindness over a period of a few days during which, while in conversation, she opened up and spoke freely providing valuable insights of a number of her fellow inmates in Holloway.[82] Vera much appreciated the stay and wrote a letter of appreciation:

Dear Klop!
I have been very happy staying with you both and I hope the time will come when we shall meet again under more normal circumstances.
Vera

The note was written in ink in her own hand and it inspired Ustinov to consider using another new means of gaining an insight into the psyche of Vera. He contacted the friend of a colleague who was a graphologist. The comments of the graphologist based on the sample supplied were remarkable, to the degree 'Klop' described them as 'amazingly good' and they are recorded on a sheet attached to Vera's the MI5 file:

I have an unpleasant feeling with this handwriting
The writer (woman) is a cold and calculating person.
Easy, youth, good upbringing, education (culture) medium.
Certain doubtless existing talents were never developed because of too little energy and diligence.
Very selfish, a hard person, who feels lost (lonely) and not happy in her present situation.
She has great worries about a person close to her.
A great many social lies, even during the writing of the note in front of me there were some mental reservations. Has a great deal of interest, perhaps too much, in other people's affairs and often judges strangers too harshly.
Very easily offended pride, sufficient vanity.
Has a great erotic disappointment.
On the whole very indolent and lazy in spite of occasional flickering of energy.
Cool, calculation, as mentioned above.[83]

Vera's candid revelations and participation in what MI5 Director General David Petrie described to Sir Alexander Maxwell, Permanent Under-Secretary of State to the Home Office as a '*somewhat unorthodox course of action, which has been fully justified by the results which have been obtained*'[84] proved to be her ticket out of Holloway. MI5 was not keen for her to return there because those to whom she would be returning in prison were '*the very people whom we least desire to know anything of what had taken place*'.[85] So Vera was sent to Aylesbury Prison and was soon transferred to Camp W internment camp on the Isle of Man where she proved useful as a stool pigeon reporting on her fellow prisoners for the rest of the war.

Sometimes events happen in the world of espionage that would be viewed as too incredible to be included in a spy thriller book, one such event took place on 23 September 1940 when the cutter *La Parte Bien* entered Plymouth harbour. Captained by Hugo Jonasonn with two crew, Belgians Gerald Libot and another simply recorded as de Lille, all of whom had been recruited by Otto Voight of the German Secret Service as saboteurs. During their crossing from Brest to Le Touquet to collect more agents they had become so drunk they put into Plymouth by mistake.[86] They too were given a warm welcome at Latchmere House for the rest of the war.

In a similar incident the fishing smack *Josephine* under Dutch captain Cornelius Ebertsen landed at Milford Haven on 12 November 1940. When asked their business at the port by a naval patrol Ebertsen claimed he was en route from Brest bound for Dublin and one of his passengers, Nicolas Pasoz-Diaz had developed an abscess and required medical treatment. The boat crew and passengers were landed as refugees but sent for further interrogation during which it was soon revealed the vessel had four crew and three passengers, Cubans named Silvio Ruiz Robles, Pedro Hechevarria and Pasos-Diaz. The crew revealed the three passengers had been recruited by the *Abwehr* as saboteurs and were to have been landed in the Bristol Channel to carry out acts of sabotage around the Bristol area. Reciprocally the Cuban passengers claimed the captain and two of the crew (Arie van Dam and Peter Krag) were German or in the pay of the *Abwehr*. A search of the boat revealed a hidden Browning automatic pistol and materials for sabotage including explosives hidden in cans labeled 'Green Peas'. Removed to and interrogated at Camp 020, the entire crew were imprisoned and deported after the end of the war (with the exception of Pasoz-Diaz who died while in Liverpool prison in April 1942.[87]

* * *

The third of Ritter's parachutists landed on fields near Easton Maudit, south-west of Wellingborough, Northamptonshire on the evening of 3 October 1940. He was not spotted on his way down and did all he should have done as per his espionage training – cutting up his harness and parachute and stuffing them down rabbit holes, stowing his equipment under bushes and changing into civilian clothes. However, the weather was inclement and he took shelter in farm buildings on the Grendon Road, Yardley Hastings where he was discovered by market gardener, Thomas Leonard 'Len' Smith.

The problem for the lurking stranger was that the area was particularly alive to the reality of German spy parachutists; Caroli had landed only a short distance away at Denton less than a month earlier. It had not made the newspapers but news travels fast in the countryside and the Civil Defence, Home Guard and Observer Corps in the area had been briefed to be extra vigilant.

When Smith challenged the stranger about what he was doing he tried to make the excuse he had been sheltering and said, '*It is a bit finer now, I think I will be going.*' When Smith asked where he had come from the stranger could not tell him but in good English, explained he was staying at a nearby farmhouse, although he could not remember its name. Smith asked to see his identity card and the stranger obliged. The card, in the name of Philips, A. with the address of 20, Grange Road, Southampton looked genuine, but something was not right and it struck Smith that it looked too new to be genuine, so Smith said he would walk with the man back to where he was staying to establish his identity.

Smith was at his gateway when neighbouring farmer Percy Keggin was driving along the road in his car and Smith signalled him to stop. Smith didn't know what to do with the stranger so Keggin also checked his identity card and suggested they drive up the road together to see if they could find the farm where the stranger was staying, and they could sort the matter out there. Failing to find the farm, the three went to Keggin's home where they talked over the names of local farmers to see if they could jog the stranger's memory of where he was staying. He seemed to recognise the name of Mr Penn so Keggin telephoned him.

Walter Penn just happened to be head air raid warden and section leader of the Easton Maudit Home Guard. Taking Robert Ingram with him, the two men went to Mr Keggin's home where Penn asked to see the stranger's identity card. The newness of the card also aroused Penn's suspicions as did his demeanour, so he marched him (some accounts say at the points of an agricultural fork) to the Police House at Bozeat, home of PC 23 John William Forth. PC Forth checked the identity card and when he asked the man where he came from he said he had come from Bedford to Yardley Hastings by bus and was heading to Kettering where he hoped to find work as a waiter. During the conversation the constable detected the man spoke with a foreign accent and his clothes looked both new and foreign in style. PC Forth telephoned his police divisional headquarters at Wellingborough who dispatched Inspector Sharman.

As they awaited the arrival of the inspector the stranger was kept under close watch. PC Forth's wife simply saw a scared and hungry man who kept nervously playing with the fringe of his scarf and would remember he was polite and expressed his sincere gratitude for the scrambled eggs she cooked for him.

Inspector Sharman arrived at 8pm and it was only then that the stranger was searched and a number of identity cards and a small pistol were discovered about his person. The man then admitted he had landed by parachute near a pumping station, his mission had been to collect and transmit weather information back to Germany. He was handcuffed and taken to the pumping station at Hollowell Plantation at Easton Maudit where he took his bearings and led Inspector Sharman and PC Forth to where he had hidden his parachute, harness and equipment. He was then removed to Wellingborough police station where he was taken into custody.[88]

Removed to Latchmere House, examination of his identity card revealed that, although there were no continental characteristics to the writing, it had been incorrectly filled in; instead of Phillips, A it should have had the full Christian name, Philips, Alfred. Under interrogation by Robin Stephens it appeared that the agent was willing to co-operate and revealed his real name as Karl Goose (although this may not have been his real name either). According to Guy Liddell MI5 had already been made aware of Goose from TATE. Goose was adopted by the double-cross programme under the codename of GANDER – who says MI5 didn't have a sense of humour? Liddell noted:

> *He has a one-way set of maps of the Liverpool area. His instructions were to hike about and report on morale (or as he puts it morals), roadblocks, weather conditions etc. He is going to work his set and we propose to run it as a very obvious double-cross in order to enhance the value of SUMMER and company.*[89]

Karl Goose should have been ideal for the role of agent in enemy territory, he had been a soldier in the *Abwehr*'s highly secretive Brandenburg commando unit, but it appears he had never wanted to be a spy. In his interrogation at Latchmere House he claimed it was only shortly after he joined the Brandenburgers a sergeant asked who spoke English and, eager to please, he put up his hand and before he knew it he was in espionage training.[90] This story was perhaps given some credibility by his obvious nerves and when the uniform and overalls he had parachuted in were discovered they were found to be spattered with his faeces.[91]

Attempts were made to send messages via Goose's set but as it could not receive messages and there seemed to be no intelligence from Germany that his messages were being received, GANDER was stood down as a double-cross agent transferring to Camp 020R (Huntercombe) and spent the rest of the war in captivity.

*   *   *

The Moray Firth viewed from Nairn, c.1939.

The Culbin Sands by Findhorn, Morayshire, Scotland where the sabotage team of Lund, Joost and Edvardsen landed on 25 October 1940.

The fourth and final *Hummer Nord* agents to land by dinghy in 1940 flew out from Stavanger on 24 October and landed south of the Moray Firth about 15 miles north-east of Inverness on 25 October 1940. Their arrival coincided with a Joint Intelligence Committee report that: assemblies of shipping and barges were still to be observed in Channel ports; it was believed Germany was still pushing on to complete arrangements in case the conditions became favourable for an invasion; or were continuing with what was an increasingly unlikely operation simply to prevent a fall in morale.[92]

There were a total of three agents, Legwald Lund, Otto 'Max' Joost and Gunnar Edvardsen. Lund was a Norwegian master mariner in his fifties who had threatened a German policeman during one of his drunken binges and deserted his ship. He claimed he had been met by German Secret Service officers who offered him the deal to undertake this mission as the only way he could escape punishment.[93]

Otto 'Max' Joost was a German who had fought for the Spanish government during the civil war and was given a similar option of going on the mission or being sent to a detention camp. The third man was Gunnar Edvardsen, a Norwegian journalist who had been conscripted as an interpreter for the German occupation forces in Norway, attached to the elite Gebirgs (Mountain) Division. He had received some training in espionage and had originally been a member of the Drüke, Vera and Wälti group.[94]

This latest unfortunate trio had been instructed that their mission was to bicycle across Scotland cutting telephone lines in an attempt to create alarm, and to perform acts of sabotage whenever they presented themselves. The three were told that their operation was in advance of the invasion that would be launched in about three weeks. They would then be expected to join with the invading forces to fight on for the conquest of Britain.[95]

As observed by Hinsley and Simkins in *British Intelligence in the Second World War*, 'Of all the spies sent in preparation for the projected invasion, these were the most ill-prepared.'[96] They were sent with no radio transmitter or receiver so had no way of communicating successes, failure, difficulties or observations with their base; only Lund had his passport, but not one of them had an identity card, ration book or any other paperwork to assist their cover and their survival during the mission. In fact according to Edvardsen, the only equipment they seemed to have been issued with to carry out their task were two bicycles, a revolver, a torch, insulated pliers and each man was given £100 in notes.[97] Suspicions were also aroused because many of the notes had consecutive serial numbers.[98]

After rowing for thirteen hours and discovering, as ever, that bicycles and rubber dinghies don't mix, they had ditched the bicycles over the side long before they landed at Culbin Sands by Findhorn, Morayshire, Scotland. Once ashore Edvardsen had 'knifed' their rubber dinghy but, according to Edvardsen, all three of them had intended to hand themselves in. They ditched or buried what equipment they had, except the money and Lund's passport, and all, feeling hungry, set off towards Nairn to get something to eat. As they were walking along the main road near the village the three were surprised from behind by Inspector Stewart of Moray and Nairn Constabulary and arrested. When challenged as to who they were, they used their prepared cover story of being refugees from Norway, so it is difficult to know if this truly was the intention of the three potential saboteurs.[99] Another 'cargo of meat'[100] is what Robin Stevens would describe in his report after their initial interrogation at Latchmere House as: *'sent over as part of the jitter war'*.[101] They were all interned for the duration.

* * *

Prime Minister Churchill had been asking since early October 1940 why some of the spies that had been caught in Britain had not been shot. Lord Swinton, Chairman of the Home Defence (Security) Executive, a position his lordship *'seemed to think made him head of MI5 and to some extent SIS'*,[102] continued to press for an example to be made and in 1941 he got his wish.

Even as the prospect of invasion faded, further away spies were still being sent to England. At 8.20am on 1 February 1941 smallholders Charles Baldock and Harry Coulson both from Puddock Drove, Warboys, Huntingdonshire were walking across farmland at Dove House Farm when they heard three pistol shots; they looked but could not spot anyone, so they kept walking. More shots were fired so they looked across the field in the direction the shots came from and about 150 yards away saw a man. Mr Baldock approached first, holding up his hand he told him not to shoot, as he would recount in his statement:

> *The man then put his hands up and we went across to him. The man was lying on his back and when we got to within 15 yards of him, he threw a revolver* [actually a Mauser pistol] *into a steel helmet which was lying close to him. When we got to him I could see a camouflaged parachute covering him. I asked him what he was up to and he said 'Solo flying.' I asked him where he came from and he said 'Hamburg, I am in no war.' He pointed to his leg and said 'Broken'. I stayed with him and sent Coulson for assistance. He told me he was a Frenchman sent from Hamburg and handed me a small cardboard box containing some rounds of ammunition.*[103]

Coulson found Harry Godfrey, a volunteer in the Ramsey platoon of the Home Guard, who rang the police then returned with Coulson and a horse

Captain William Newton, Officer Commanding (seated centre) and the members of the Ramsey Mereside Platoon, E Company, 1st Huntingdonshire Battalion, Home Guard.

and cart. They were soon joined by Captain William Henry Newton, Officer Commanding E Company, 1st Huntingdonshire Battalion, Home Guard who had been called by the local police to attend the scene; he was accompanied by Lieutenant John Curedale. Captain Newton took charge of the man's pistol and ammunition. They then helped him up as he could not walk unaided. He was seen to be wearing low boots and spats. The man was searched by the Home Guards and a wallet containing a blank ration book and two identity cards, one blank and the other completed, were found along with a wad of money to the value of £498 in £1 Bank of England notes. Beneath

Josef Jakobs photographed shortly after his capture.

him was a case buried in the ground but with one corner sticking up, a map of the local area – marked with the location of a local aerodrome and a triangle indicating the area where the man had landed – lay nearby and an amount of ripped-up cardboard (a code wheel the man had tried to destroy) was scattered around the area along with a small bottle of brandy, some sandwiches and a piece of German sausage. The case was also removed from the ground and the

135

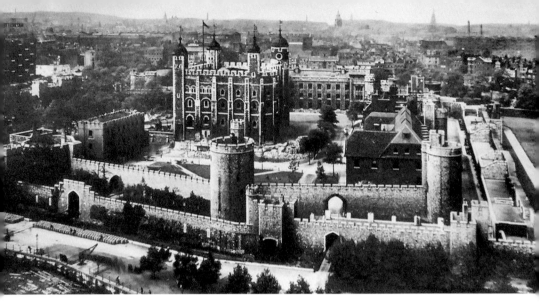

The Tower of London, the Miniature Rifle Range where Jakobs was shot stood on the right of this photo in the Outer Ward between the Martin Tower and the Constables Tower.

man taken to Ramsey police station. Once there he handed over the key and the case was opened to reveal a wireless set with headphones, dry batteries, insulated wire and some sheets of paper.[104]

The parachutist was delivered by Detective Sergeant Thomas O. Mills of the Huntingdonshire County Constabulary to Major T.A. Robertson and John Hayes Marriott, Cannon Row police station (part of the New Scotland Yard building) in the late afternoon on 1 February. Pronounced fit for questioning by the police doctor, he was interviewed by Robertson and Marriott and was then taken to Brixton Prison Hospital Infirmary for treatment on his broken ankle.

When interviewed by Robertson and in due course by Lieutenant Colonel Edward Hinchley-Cooke, he freely gave his name as Josef Jakobs, confirmed he was a German citizen and stated he was to send reports back regarding weather conditions. He also explained to how he came to be found in the field:

When I was ready to jump out of the plane they opened the trap-door in the floor of the plane. I put my foot through the aperture, but my parachute got jammed because the aperture was very small and owing to the pressure of the wind I broke my right ankle before I was able to get clear. I got clear in the end and came down by parachute. I landed in a soft freshly ploughed field where I lay all night …[105]

Jakobs' fracture required hospital treatment and he was removed to Dulwich Hospital on 3 February. Released to Latchmere House on 26 March he was returned to Brixton Prison Infirmary after a relapse a few days later and remained there until 15 April when he was returned to Ham Common.

On 23 July Jakobs was placed in the hands of the Military Police at Wandsworth Prison where he was charged under Section 2(1)(b) of the Treachery Act, 1940 on 24 July 1941. Hinchley-Cooke read over the charge to him in German and Jakobs replied '*I have nothing to fear.*'[106] Josef Jakobs was tried in camera before a General Court Martial held at the Duke of York's Headquarters, King's Road, Chelsea on Monday 4 -Tuesday 5 August 1941. Found guilty as charged, Jakobs was removed to the Tower of London. There he was held in a cell at Waterloo Barracks until he was executed in the Miniature Rifle Range, seated in a brown Windsor chair, by an eight-man firing squad from the Holding Battalion, Scots Guards at 7.12am on Thursday, 14 August 1941. Josef Jakobs was buried in an unmarked grave at St Mary's Roman Catholic Cemetery, Kensal Green.[107]

* * *

MI5 had a steep learning curve creating a double-cross network with the 'turned' agents that dropped by parachute or landed on the shores of Great Britain during the autumn of 1940. The main difficulties that confronted them were not only making sure the communications appeared authentic, but deciding what intelligence the double agent could communicate that would make them appear active and useful to their German masters.

On 16 September Guy Liddell took the initiative and set up a small committee to deal with the double-cross agents consisting of Malcolm Frost, Dick White, Jack Curry, Thomas Argyll Robertson and Felix Cowgill,[108] but still the sticking point remained of what genuine intelligence could they obtain for the agents to pass on to the enemy. The directors of the various intelligence departments were uncomfortable about taking responsibility for releasing any sensitive information and it soon became clear the scheme needed higher authority. Masterman recounted:

> *…in the autumn of 1940 MI5 and MI6 took steps to put the whole organisation on a proper footing and a memorandum was sent to the Directors of Intelligence explaining to them the importance of the double agent system, telling them also that it was becoming increasingly difficult, if not impossible, to maintain the agents unless sufficient information could be released to the enemy to retain the enemy's confidence and adding that it ought not to be impossible to strike a balance between the risks involved in releasing the minimum of true information required and the strategic losses which might result from closing the double agents down.*'[109]

The risks involved were carefully considered and it was agreed the double-cross agents were of great value. On 30 September 1940 a meeting was held at the instigation of the Director of Military Intelligence for the establishment of the W. Board.[110] Guy Liddell records the meeting in his diary entry for

1 October 1940, noting it had been attended by three Directors of Intelligence, George Steward of the Downing Street press office, a representative of MI9 and Cavendish Bentinck of the Foreign Office and of course Liddell himself as the Director of B Division. The aim of the meeting was to establish a board consisting of interested parties to centralise the dissemination of rumours and false information and to take stock of the channels through which such information could be distributed.[111]

The W. Board would make decisions on what information could or could not be passed by the double-cross agents. The board contained only senior directors and could not undertake the day to day supervision of the double agents, so a special sub-committee was created specifically for this purpose. Chaired and with a secretary provided by MI5, the original W. Committee consisted of representatives of the War Office, GHQ Home Forces, Home Defence Executive, Air Ministry Intelligence, Naval Intelligence Division, MI6 and Colonel Turner's Department. (Colonel John Turner's Department at the Air Ministry was given a deliberately vague title because it was responsible for K, Q and QL site dummy airfields, 'Starfish' bombing decoys and deception.) The double agent information element of the W. Committee evolved into the dedicated Twenty Committee, named so after the XX Roman numerals for twenty – two crosses, or a double-cross. The first meeting of the Twenty Committee was held on 2 January 1941. [112]

It was agreed that MI5 should shoulder responsibility for maintaining the agents and in June 1941 B1a was created, headed by Major Thomas Argyll Robertson. They could not have had a better man for the job. Major 'Tommy' Robertson, frequently referred to by his colleagues simply as 'TAR', from his initials, was a dapper, charismatic fellow in the mould of David Niven (in fact he had been at Sandhurst with Niven). With an infectious chuckle and the easy company of successful, well-mannered gentleman, crucially, he was also a shrewd and proficient MI5 officer who had experience in both military and political intelligence activities.

In fact the man was brilliant at his work. Lady Dundas summed him up well describing him as having: '*a certain sort of special brain that could see round corners*'.[113] 'TAR' would go on to be involved in the planning of such notable deceptions as Operation Mincemeat in 1943 and was the mastermind behind Operation Fortitude in 1944 which led the Germans to believe landings for the liberation of Europe were going to take place in the Pas de Calais instead of Normandy.

Double-cross worked and when more agents followed throughout the rest of the war it continued to work, J.C. Masterman would claim with some pride: '*for the greater part of the war we did much more than practise a large scale deception through double agents; by means of the double agent system we actively ran and controlled the German espionage system in this country.*'[114]

138

Chapter 8

The Undetected?

Look and you will find it – what is unsought will go undetected.

Sophocles

The problem with double agents is that if they have been turned once, they can potentially be turned again. One such individual was Arthur Graham Owens who back in the 1930s was an electrical engineer employed as a civilian contractor by the Royal Navy. He also worked in Germany, had contacts in the Kriegsmarine and had dabbled in some espionage for the SIS, providing them with information about the German shipyards where he had worked, until he was found to be reporting to the *Abwehr* without the knowledge of SIS. Owens was a Welsh nationalist and had little loyalty to Britain. He had been recruited by Nikolaus Ritter to work for the *Abwehr* in 1938 and was even issued with a radio transceiver in 1939 to enable direct communications between Owens and his handler.

Soon after the outbreak of war, fearing the consequences of being caught as a German agent, Owens was savvy enough to think he could make even more money and save himself from the gallows into the bargain by offering his services and what he knew of the *Abwehr* to Special Branch. MI5 were of the opinion that Owens could be of use as a double agent; he was initially imprisoned but was permitted to continue to use his transceiver under supervision. Owens appeared to be playing ball and was granted a release if he worked from a residence provided for him and sent messages that had been agreed with MI5.

Owens was given the codename SNOW. He provided his German handler with useful information for the Operation Lena agents, such as the correct code numbers for their forged identity cards, and acted as an emergency point of contact for the *Abwehr* if the agents needed help while in Britain. In the process he would know when to expect them and the place they would land and passed this information on to MI5. The problem was none of the agents Owens handed to MI5 were desperately well trained and some of them spoke only limited English. British intelligence officers could not believe the *Abwehr* were sending such inept agents and suspected they were more sacrificial offerings than a serious attempt to infiltrate agents into the country. Suspicions arose that Owens was simply a distraction operation and there was in fact a completely separate network of Nazi agents operating undetected in Britain.[1]

Ladislas Farago's book *The Game of Foxes* presents an engaging account of British and German intelligence operations during the Second World War. Although not annotated, it is claimed by the author to be based on microfilmed German bureaucratic paperwork containing *Abwehr* intelligence files captured by the Americans at the end of the war in 1945 and discovered in a dusty metal footlocker in a dark loft of the National Archives in Washington DC.[2]

Over recent years a huge amount of captured German papers from the Second World War have been digitised by the American National Archives as part of an ongoing process. The amount of material to sort has been vast, so the discovery he made back in the 1970s is possible and how they were packaged and stored certainly has a ring of truth about it. Farago's text clearly draws on his own research and interviews with those who may or may not have been telling the truth. It draws conclusions that may not always be as accurate as we can be today after so much more has been released for public access in archives around the world. That said, what he has to say is usually grounded in real incidents, characters and events. So, bearing that in mind, we do need to be cautious when he recounts a conversation between double agent SNOW and Nikolaus Ritter when the pair arranged to meet in Lisbon in February 1941.

The meeting is confirmed as having taken place in other documents[3] but the exchange Farago recounts regarding a lost LENA agent is entirely from Farago's research in which he claims Ritter had mentioned the loss of an agent who had remained unidentified and apparently undetected:

> *If ever an eccentric philanthropist decides to erect memorials to Hitler's follies, the odd man of the Lena team would qualify as the unknown soldier of Sea Lion. He was sent to Lancashire and came down in the Manchester Ship Canal near the Mersey estuary above Birkenhead. He drowned, helpless and alone, on the night of 7 September 1940. He was never missed. His loss was never felt.*[4]

It is not beyond the realms of possibility. The day of 7 September 1940 will always be known as 'Black Saturday' in Britain as it was the first time London was bombed and marked the beginning of almost eight months of nightly raids on the capital and many other industrial and ports around the country. It is possible that on that date or thereabouts a Luftwaffe aircraft, detected or not, could have delivered an enemy agent who unfortunately landed in the Manchester Ship Canal and, like many other aircrew who landed in deep water, was dragged down by his 'chute and drowned. If like, Karl Goose who would parachute down wearing his uniform and get changed into his civilian clothes after landing (it is worth noting that although he landed in Cambridgeshire he was carrying maps for the Liverpool area) on 3 October 1940, perhaps our man was found in Luftwaffe uniform and, if no espionage equipment was recovered with the body, it could have been assumed he was just another member of German aircrew.

There are also numerous stories of mysterious unidentified bodies in civilian clothes with items that could indicate that they were enemy agents being found around Britain during and over the years after the war. There is the chance that some of these could have been enemy agents outside those known to the British intelligence branches via double-cross. A distinct possibility is also that some of the wartime stories of these discoveries were deliberately circulated as part of the black propaganda campaign engineered by a variety of British intelligence organisations; the intention was that they would reach the ears of the enemy and deter those who were thinking of chancing their luck as an agent.

There is also the chance that bodies found in caves or woodland or washed up on the shores of our coastline, with foreign labels in their clothes and remnants of continental confectionery wrappers and similar ephemera in their pockets, may just have been some of the thousands who had fled from the Nazi terror to Britain. With features decayed beyond recognition and family and friends left behind in the occupied country and possibly in concentration camps, the one who had got away was laid in a common grave. Their identity and reason for being there would remain a mystery, especially in the minds of those privy to the discoveries. Such tales have certainly entered into urban legend in some parts of the UK. Over decades of research the author and his fellow historians have encountered many people who earnestly relate 'friend of a friend' stories of mysterious bodies during the war.

The Norfolk coast had some of the first bodies of dead German aircrew washed up on its shores during the Second World War. Over the winter of 1939 the incongruous sight of swastika-draped coffins borne on the shoulders of smartly turned out RAF men at full-honours funerals for German aircrew took place at Happisburgh[5] and Sheringham.[6] It was a legacy of the First World War that if aircrew landed on enemy soil the enemy would give them a decent burial befitting a 'knight of the air'. The air war fought over the county and the tides off its coast led to military rubber dinghies occasionally being washed up; admittedly some were lost during RAF air sea rescue training but on occasion they would be German.

Funeral of German aircrew with full military honours including coffins draped with swastika flags, Sheringham December 1939.

These could be explained as a boat from a crashed German aeroplane and the crew lost, but stories linger of clandestine activities off the coast, of enemy agents landing and leaving, particularly along the North Norfolk coast where the beaches provide ideal natural harbours for small craft and numerous Nazi sympathisers were known and suspected to live there.[7] It is no surprise Jack Higgins was inspired by his visit to North Norfolk to set his book *The Eagle Has Landed* (1975) there.

It does seem odd, even if the spies were being sent off as feints in the 'jitter' war, that agents were landed on the south coast where invasion was intended, but no agents are known to have landed anywhere on the other area of anticipated landing, along the East Anglian coast. During the interrogation of captured German agents Waldberg, Meier, Drüke, Schalberg and Wälti they all independently mentioned one of their instructors, *Oberleutnant* Werner Uhlm, who was originally at *Ast Wiesbaden* and later *Ast Hamburg*. He was lauded for having made a successful clandestine reconnaissance mission to England in 1940, landing by parachute in Norfolk and making his exit by boat off the coast of Cromer where he was picked up by a sea plane.[8] Uhlm's exploits were 'held up as a model for agents in training'.[9]

Liddell was quick to dispense with Uhlm's successful mission as 'obviously an untrue story' but offers no reason for his assumption. If the revelation had come from Vera Schalberg alone this could be understandable, but the story was told by spies from two groups, who landed at different times and a successful in-and-out mission would leave no trace, so Liddell may have been rather hasty in being quite so dismissive.

A curious incident was related in Tom Dewar's memoir *Norfolk Front Line* (1998). Dewar was a young subaltern in the 11th Battalion, The Royal Scots Fusiliers while they were engaged on coastal defence duties in North Norfolk during the invasion scares of 1940. Tom was acting second in command to C Company at Holkham (where the officers had their quarters in The Victoria Hotel) when a report was received of a badly damaged rubber dinghy having been washed ashore in the harbour at Wells-next-the-Sea. Fearing an enemy agent landing had been made, groups of his soldiers were sent out in patrols to search the coastline and countryside. The body of a man in civilian clothes was discovered at the beach end of the sea wall at a location he notes as 'near the point, at the base of the sea wall'. He had clearly been immersed in the sea and it was assumed from his injuries that he had attempted to scale the rocks near the wall but had fallen and dashed his head on the rocks below and had been battered against the rocks by the sea.

The battalion intelligence officer was sent for and on examination of the documents found in the dead man's pockets he concluded they were forgeries, as were the wad of bank notes in his wallet and a spectacle case found on

Grave marker for 'Two German Sailors' found drowned at Overstrand, Norfolk during the Second World War.

the body made by a well-known German company. A flick-knife of a type known to be carried by German agents lay nearby.[10] Dewar states reports were submitted to higher authorities, but the trail ends there, at least for the moment. No files relating to the incident have been identified in TNA and Dewar does not mention what happened to the body.

Just a few miles along the coast from Holkham and Cromer, in the cemetery across the road from Overstrand Church, a small memorial stone marks the grave of 'Two German Sailors' who were found washed up on the beach. Evidently, they were found with no identification tags to indicate who they were, and no record nor inquest papers appear to have survived explaining how they were identified, whether it be from the uniforms worn, clothing tags or items found about their person. Sadder still, no exact dates are recorded for the discovery of the bodies save for the fact that Dewar was stationed in the area during 1940 and the period can be narrowed to the months after June 1940 when the 11th RSF was formed. Dewar's mention that the battalion arrived on the Norfolk coast in the late summer fits well with the time frame of when the other agent landings were made.

With no dates and no identities for the two bodies in Overstrand, the *Volksbund Deutsche Kriegsgräberfürsorge* (German War Graves Commission) are unable to help and have, to date, shown little interest in trying to ascertain their identities by DNA. It leaves the tantalising possibility the body at Wells and the bodies carried on the tide flow and washed up near Overstand could have all been members of a previously undetected and only too typical three-man *Abwehr* espionage team.

Jack Higgins received a number of letters after the publication of *The Eagle Has Landed* from people who believed they personally witnessed incidents on the East Coast during the Second World War that could have inspired his book.

A typical example of such a story was mentioned in a letter from Derek E. Johnson, the author of *East Anglia at War* in a letter to Aviation Historian Bob Collis in March 1990 in which Johnson was trying to find out if there was any further information after being contacted by a 'Mr Hodges or Hodgseson', a former anti-aircraft gunner stationed near Woodbridge, who told him the story of when he and other members of his battery had been sent to guard a German bomber that had been brought down. Quoting the conversation, Johnson recounted:

> *It crashed in a lightly wooded area and me and my mates were dispatched to stand guard over the wreckage. There were several bodies scattered around and one of these looked as though he had tried to jump out of the falling aircraft, for he was embedded at least two to three inches in the earth. The*

strange thing about him being he was wearing civvy clothes and in his pockets he had British papers, a packet of English cigarettes – if I remember rightly they were Navy Cut – and English money. Whereas the other German crew members were taken away by British Service bobs, this bloke was carted off by plain-clothes characters.[11]

The German bomber crash could be traced; it was a Heinkel 111 from Stab1/ KG1 'Hindenburg' that had been shot down by a Blenheim night-fighter, which crashed at Wantisden, Suffolk on 5 September 1940. All the crew were killed (one of them was found over two years later still in the branches of the tree where he fell) but there is no mention in official reports found to date of a man in civilian clothes being found among the dead at the crash site. With only anecdotal evidence we are inclined to doubt such stories but they are told so earnestly, and rather like the tales described as 'urban legends' today they have a ring of authenticity about them and are also difficult to completely disprove, especially with the distance of time that has now passed.

*   *   *

Of the post-war discoveries the skeletal remains found in a shake hole near the well-known Yorkshire ravine Trow Ghyll, below Ingleborough mountain in the Pennines, West Yorkshire on 24 September 1947 is one of the best documented and investigated. The discovery, made by two young local pot-holers, Jim Leach and Harold Burgess, was brought to the attention of the police and an investigation ensued. Articles found with the body included a phial containing white crystals, a compass, a Yale key, a red and black Parker 'Duofold' fountain pen, a 15-jewelled wrist watch, a Velvet safety razor, two chromium-plated shaving tubes, a toothbrush, a propelling pencil, a pocket knife with two blades, a torch, a bottle of mineral water, a wallet emptied of all its contents and a small suitcase fitted with a short leather strap and broken carry handle.[12]

Both the body and the clothes were badly decomposed but a post mortem examination by Professor P.L. Sutherland of the Home Office North-Eastern Forensic Science Laboratory, revealed the remains were those of a man, 5ft 5¼ins tall with light brown to auburn hair, good teeth and aged between 22 and 30. His bones showed no evidence of deformity or fracture. He had been well dressed, wearing a grey suit with red and white stripes, a blue shirt and collar, necktie and a herringbone tweed overcoat with a brown shot silk scarf, a grey trilby hat and two pairs of shoes that had been repaired and fitted with rubber heels.[13]

Based on this description police enquires were able to rule out missing people from the area. At the inquest before Craven Coroner Mr Stephen

*Trow Ghyll below
Ingleborough mountain
in the Pennines, West
Yorkshire.*

E. Brown at Skipton Town Hall on 25 November, North-Eastern Forensic Science Laboratory Director Lewis Nickolls stated that the small phial of white crystals found with the body had contained sodium cyanide, although of a domestic type used to kill vermin; an ampoule containing the same substance was also found. Nickolls admitted the shape of the phial was not one he was familiar with.

Distinguished legal historian Brian Simpson, who was living two miles away in Clapham at the time the body was discovered, and having examined the case papers in more recent years, expresses the opinion the only known users of such an ampoule were German agents operating in enemy countries in order to commit suicide if they had been compromised and faced imminent capture. The body was in such a state of advanced decay it had not been possible to tell if the man had taken poison or not, no trace was found in his clothes or bones; in fact no cause of death could be determined. Judging by the state of decomposition, the dates on a few of the coins and dateable items found near the body, Nickolls had formed the impression that death had taken place in 1941. The jury returned an open verdict.[14]

*   *   *

There is, however, one agent that we know for sure went undetected. During one of the nights between 31 October and 2 November 1940 an enemy parachutist landed near Haversham, Buckinghamshire. Owens/SNOW had given no warning of his arrival. Guy Liddell noted the discovery in his diary on 5 November:

An enemy parachute landing was reported today. A complete parachute with harness, overalls and flying helmet was found neatly folded and placed in a hedge beside a bridle path on Hill Farm ... The parachute was wet but the clothing inside dry and it appears that it may have been dropped during the past two or three days. Inside the parachute was a paper wrapping for chocolate made in Belgium and a packet containing a white tablet, probably concentrated food [on examination it was found to be aspirin]. *The packet had recently been opened and contents consumed. The parachute had without doubt been used and the parachutist landed uninjured and is still at large.*[15]

The discovery of the parachute had been made at 12 noon on 3 November. On receipt of the report, and confirmation of the discovery of the parachute and harness, Buckinghamshire police contacted the local Home Guard battalion commander who immediately mobilised his men. They continued observation and searched through the night for the parachutist or any of his equipment. Special Branch was also informed along with Air Intelligence, Field Security, local military units, searchlight and RAF units. Neighbouring constabularies in Bedford and Northamptonshire were also put on alert and enquiries were made at shops, hotels, railway stations and other places that may have been used by the parachutist. At dawn on the morning after the discovery a thorough search of all woods and outbuildings was carried out with the aid of military units from Bletchley, Stony Stratford, Whaddon, Windlow, Lathbury, Hanslope and Cold Brayfield.[16]

The undetected spy, Jan Willem Ter Braak (real name Engelbertus Fukken).

Enquiries with the Observer Corps revealed enemy planes were plotted over Haversham district on the evenings of 30 October and 1 November. The

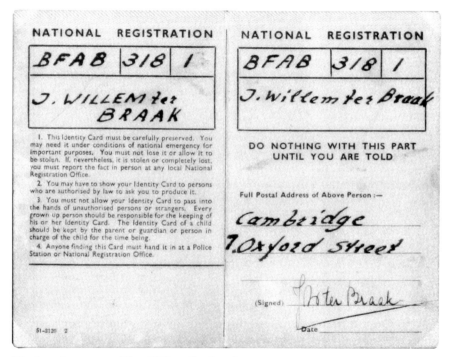

The forged passport of Jan Willem Ter Braak.

Radio Security Service was also on the case to try an intercept any messages being sent and on 5 November reported: '…*it seems likely that there is at least one wireless set being operated in the country*.'[17] The problem was detecting exactly where.

There was also consternation that the parachute had been found less than 20 miles from 'Station X', the top-secret Government Code and Cypher School (GC&CS) at Bletchley Park. Liddell would comment later that they had been expecting another agent around that time.[18] From previous experience the spies that had parachuted into Britain had either injured themselves or gave themselves away by some basic error. This agent, probably more by luck than judgement, just walked away into the darkness.

In his pocket the man carried a passport and identity card in the name of Jan Willem Ter Braak. He had arrived in Cambridge on 4 November 1940 and was operating under cover of being a Dutchman who had served in the Dutch forces, had escaped to Britain at the time of the Dunkirk evacuation and was now engaged with the Dutch Free Press that had its head office on Pall Mall.

Braak rented a back bedroom at 58 St Barnabas Road, Cambridge, the home of Mr and Mrs Sennitt. He was usually seen leaving the property about 10am and returned between 9.30 and 10pm each night. He was sensible enough to purchase new British clothes in Cambridge and Peterborough, so he blended in well. He seemed a nice enough gentleman and would often sit in the evening after his return from work with the Sennitts playing cards, darts or other games. He never seemed short of money and had even got Mr Sennitt to change American dollars into British pounds for him at the Lloyd's Bank on Mill Road.

On 31 January 1941 Braak told Mr Sennitt he was leaving for London. Some weeks later Mrs Sennitt saw Braak in Cambridge and asked him to call and collect the remainder of his clothes which he did a few days later.[19]

Braak was now staying at 11, Montague Road in another small back bedroom in the home of Miss Greenwood. He had never been any problem to her, he had retired to bed when she went up and she never heard anything of him during the night. On Saturday 29 March he had left the house with two cases and told her he was going to join the Dutch forces on the coast but would return. He headed for Cambridge Railway Station where he deposited his cases at the parcels office.

Around 11am on Tuesday, 1 April 1941 an electrician entered a public air raid shelter on Christ's Pieces, Cambridge to complete an installation. There he discovered the body of Ter Braak lying on his right side, his head in a pool of congealed blood, with a Browning automatic pistol lying nearby. Dr Donald

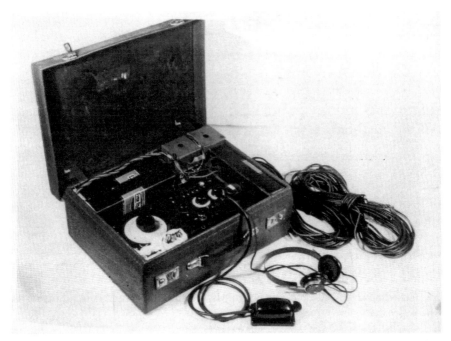

Ter Braak's radio that he deposited at the parcels office at Cambridge Station before committing suicide.

The body of Ter Braak as it was found in a public air raid shelter on Christ's Pieces, Cambridge 1 April 1941.

Cameron was called to examine the body and declared it was in an advanced state of rigor mortis; he had been dead for around twenty-four hours. Braak had shot himself in the head.[20]

Liddell recorded:

> *There is no doubt that he was the parachutist who was reported to have come down near Bletchley. We have obtained the wireless set which was in the cloakroom of Cambridge railway station. The joke of it is that in spite of our instructions to the police Ter Braak has been living within 50 yards of our RSLO in Cambridge. It seems the landlady did report his presence to the local police who merely said that they expected he would register before long. The man had been trying to get a ration book having run out of food and money, he presumably decided to shoot himself.*[21]

The Coroner, Mr W.R. Wallis agreed to hold the inquest in camera and it was impressed upon him that it was of paramount importance that no report of any kind should be published of the proceedings.

Despite thorough investigation by MI5 the only communication that could be found from or to Braak was the correspondence over the replacement of his ration book.[22] The batteries in his radio were found to be run down but it was not thought he communicated at night and tests revealed he would not have been able to obtain contact during the day because the frequency of his aerial was unsuitable.[23] There were also bus tickets found in his clothes that indicated that he had been to London, but nothing more.

The name on his Dutch passport, identity card and papers, the name he lived and was known by while in Britain was Jan Willem Ter Braak. Only in recent years after research by a family member has his real name been revealed as Engelbertus Fukken who had been born in The Hague in 1914 and had been recruited to the *Abwehr* by *Rittmeister* Kurt Mirow of *Ast Brussels*.[24] He was buried in secret and still lies in an unmarked grave in Great Shelford cemetery, about four miles south-east of Cambridge.

J.C. Masterman reflected: '*It is not altogether fanciful to speculate how much more happy and more useful his career might have been if he could have fallen into the hands of the Security Service and become a double agent.*'[25]

* * *

Then there was a certain Wilhelm Mörz aka Werner Mikkelsen; clearly he had been a person of interest to SIS for some time when they compiled their report on him in July 1939. It noted he had been a captain in the Hamburg Gendarmerie, but claiming he was an opponent of the Nazi regime and having narrowly escaped arrest by the Hamburg branch of the Gestapo, he had fled and arrived in Prague in 1935.

Mörz assumed the name of Werner Mikkkelsen and, along with another man known as Wilhelm Steiner, (real name Georg Schwarzloh or Schwarzlow, a member of the Social Democratic Party in Germany in the 1930s who had been detained by the Gestapo and had fled to Czechoslovakia immediately after his release) they were both taken under the wing of Dr Caspari. He was the former leader of *Schneidemuhl* (Social Democrat Party) who made the right introductions to Czech authorities as a result of which both men became members of the counter-espionage section of the Czechoslovak Ministry of National Defence.[26] Initially Mörz appeared to be a first class agent loyal

Wilhelm Mörz aka Werner Mikkelsen evaded the manhunt for him in 1940.

to his employers – indeed he was described as one of the best men they ever had – but the problem with Mörz all along was that he was a ruthless and 'dangerous double-crosser'.[27] SIS listed the instances of concern as:

A. *On many occasions Gestapo agents in Prague were pointed out to Mörz for arrest. These men were warned by Mörz and managed to flee the country.*

B. *Mörz enticed two German military officials to the Czechoslovak border, obtained information from them, which he sold to the Czechoslovak authorities. He denounced his informants to the Gestapo, which resulted in their being shot.*

C. *Through his connections with emigrant groups, Mörz obtained the addresses of German opponents to the Hitlerian regime and his denouncing them resulted in their arrest.*[28]

He was also believed to have been involved in money laundering, shady arms deals and revealing Czech military secrets to the Gestapo. Much of this was independently corroborated during the advisory committee interrogation of Schwarzloh (aka Steiner). He had fled Prague after Mörz had named him in an intrigue that had landed him in prison for a few days shortly before the Germans entered Czechoslovakia. Schwarzloh arrived in Britain in December 1938.[29]

Mörz himself was arrested when German forces entered Prague, but very soon afterwards he was taken by German army car to Holland where he maintained his claim that he was anti-Nazi. He was also known to be spending time in France and Switzerland where he was in direct contact with Dr Carl Spieker, with whom Dr Franz Fischer was also known to be in contact.[30] This was the same Franz Fischer who instigated the first meetings between British intelligence officers Best and Stevens and the supposed rebel German officers that culminated in their abduction at Venlo on 9 December 1939. Both Fischer and Mörz were known to be operating in The Hague at the same time.

Liddell recorded a view held by a number of those who had served in the Netherlands that Mörz was '*believed to have been responsible for the Venlo incident.*'[31] There was only circumstantial evidence Mörz was involved in the abduction of Best and Stevens[32] but SIS regarded him still being at large in Holland '*… as a tremendous danger to the Allied Intelligence Service there*'.[33]

The curious twist to this tale is that SIS were trying to enact their own Venlo-style sting on Mörz by attempting to entice him to France, but with no success and it was noted in the internally published minutes of a meeting dated 11 March 1940 that Allied Intelligence Services were then working on a plan to entice him to Britain. On hearing this Dick White was asked if Mörz did actually come would be possible to guarantee he would be locked up for the duration to which White responded: '*I rather rashly answered yes to this and feel strongly that this is a pledge which we shall have to honour at all costs.*'[34]

On 12 March Guy Liddell recorded in his diary: '*We are trying to get Morz over here and intern him … He will be a good bargaining counter for Best and Stevens.*'[35]

The following month he arrived in Britain, the problem was, apparently, that no security service appears to have been aware of his arrival or how he got here. Mörz remained undetected until the afternoon of 25 May 1940 when a former member of the Czech Intelligence Service, who had known and worked with him in Holland and who was living under MI5 protection in London, spotted Mörz purely by chance as he was getting into a taxi on Regent Street and warned his MI5 contacts of the sighting.

Even though MI5 did not have extensive files on Mörz, after consultation of what files they had and the agents at their immediate disposal, the potential danger he posed was clear and MI5 requested the Metropolitan Police Special Branch to commence search and enquiry at once. Armed with a description and the photograph MI5 had on file, officers began the man hunt at all London hotels in an endeavour to effect his arrest.[36]

The news of such a dangerous enemy agent being at large quickly rattled up the chain of command in the security services. MI5 Deputy Director Jasper Harker was only too aware of the threat Mörz posed and would state in a letter to the head of Special Branch, Albert Canning, at the height of the investigation:

We have reason to know here that the capture of Mörz would be a matter of the greatest significance at the present time. He is undoubtedly one of the cleverest secret agents the Germans have at the present time and after tremendously successful action in Belgium and Holland he has, no doubt, been drafted to this country to take charge of Fifth Column activities here. If Mörz could be captured it might mean that we should obtain thereby the means of breaking up a large part of the German network before it had a chance to operate.

The description circulated by Room 055 at the War Office to ports, airports and military commands on 26 May 1940 was also published as a special supplement to the *Police Gazette on* 28 May 1940:

Wilhelm MÖRZ, aka W. MORS, aka Wilhelm NOVAK aka Werner MICHELSON, most probably using the name Novak.

German – formerly had Czech passport – may now be travelling on any passport and under any name.
Age: 35 (looks younger) Height 5' 10'', hair sparse and fair, pale complexion, slim, inclined to slim build. Eyes probably blue, teeth very prominent projecting in the upper jaw. Speaks English quite well but cannot be mistaken for an Englishman. Said to be well dressed. This is a dangerous man, probably armed and prepared to defend himself. To be arrested on sight.[37]

Special Branch was mobilized onto the trail of Mörz and officers were sent out to enquire at all possible hotels. One of the early enquiries found the night receptionist clerk at the Cumberland Hotel recognised the wanted man as one who had stayed there in late March and who had sent a cable which he signed Novak. Other staff also recognised the man and recalled that during his stay there he went by the name of Wilhelm Novak. Another receptionist at Mount Royal Hotel, Marble Arch identified Mörz as a man he had seen six weeks previously in the company of 'Dawn' Karland, a dance hostess at the El Morocco Club on Albemarle Street.

Karland was soon traced and interviewed by Inspector Hunt, Special Branch. Despite giving the impression she was willing to help, she agreed she might have met him but said she saw so many men she could not remember him at Mount Royal. As plausible as she was, MI5 were not pleased when they learned a watch had not been maintained on her just in case she went to warn

Mörz.[38] Another club hostess, Mrs Glen Coutts at Murray's Club, also came forward and a picture soon emerged that Mörz liked West End restaurants and night club life and was recognised from his photograph as a man who gave his name as Collins to some and Morris to others.

The *Police Gazette* Special Notice was circulated nationally and enabled MI5 to track the movements of Mörz across Great Britain based on positive sightings and hotel registers. From 21–31 March he stayed at the Royal Hotel, Edinburgh, the County Hotel, Newcastle on 1 April and then on to The Queens Hotel, Leeds. In early May he had been to The Hague and back.

A case note on his file dated 29 May 1940 stated confidently: *Owing to the plans we have made it should be impossible for Mörz to leave this country by any way of the ordinary channels and escape discovery. A wide search was carried out throughout the whole London area and a hundred photographs were circulated at points where it is possible he may appear.*[39]

On 8 June 1940 another foreign agent exiled in London, who had known Mörz and had provided information on him to MI5, spotted him on Tottenham Court Road, even though his hair had been dyed chestnut brown. Mörz saw and recognised him too and immediately got on a bus. The agent got into a taxi to follow but to no avail; Mörz slipped away again.[40] Two Scotland Yard officers were employed continuously for nearly two months pursuing enquiries and keeping watch on the restaurants, cafes, night clubs and hotels of Knightsbridge, Kensington and the Tottenham Court Road.

Despite his description and photograph being supplied to many transport hubs Mörz simply departed from Croydon Airport for Basle under the name of Wilhelm Novak, a Czech engineer, one of his known aliases, on 15 June 1939. He even filled in his traffic card index honestly stating he had been staying at Lexham Garden Mansions Hotel in Kensington,[41] a hotel where it was soon discovered he had stayed in April, May and June 1940. By the time this was discovered he was long gone.

Mörz seems to have had an innate knack of just blending in but was distinctive enough for staff and hostesses to remember him well enough to successfully pick his face out of a selection of photographs. It appears he also dyed his hair from fair to chestnut, would occasionally sport a moustache, used a variety of identities and plausible personas and dressed like many other men of his day in suits, a long coat and trilby hat. The problem for those pursuing him was outlined by Dick White in one of the concluding minutes on his MI5 file:

… experience has shown over three months' search for him, Mörz's personal appearance conforms to a fairly common type. Working entirely from the

photo, I thought myself I had seen him in a waiter at the Chinese Restaurant at Piccadilly Circus. The likeness was almost exact. Nevertheless, on examination, the waiter did not turn out to be Mörz ... the police detained and questioned about a dozen people in the belief that they had caught him. Nevertheless, if he is here, he still eludes us ... He is in fact one of the cleverest agents the Gestapo has.[42]

Appeals for the capture of Mörz continued to appear in the *Police Gazette* and subsequent descriptions circulated to security control officers detailed his description as:

*... slim to medium build, upright carriage, round face, pale complexion, clean shaven or slight fair moustache, light brown hair (sparse), thick sensual lips, clean teeth (2 centre upper protruding slightly), walks with a sharp step and swings arms rapidly, generally quiet in manner, medical student type, speaks good English, is fond of drinking red wine with meals, likes company of women and night club life. The man who may use the name Joseph has posed as a Czechoslovakian and related harrowing stories of his treatment at the hands of the Germans. He is believed to be armed and would shoot on sigh*t.[43]

Finally, on 7 August 1941 Dick White wrote to the Deputy Commissioner Special Branch with a heavy heart to state MI5 had no objection to the description of Mörz being removed from the *Police Gazette* because '*There appears to be no longer any hope of tracing him in this country.*'[44]

Chapter 9

The Fifth Column

A nation can survive its fools, and even the ambitious. But it cannot survive treason from within. An enemy at the gates is less formidable, for he is known and carries his banner openly. But the traitor moves amongst those within the gate freely, his sly whispers rustling through all the alleys, heard in the very halls of government itself.

Marcus Tullius Cicero

The term the 'Fifth Column' originated during the Spanish Civil War (1936–39) when Nationalist General Emilio Mola spoke of his four columns of forces advancing on Madrid and a 'Fifth Column' of his militant supporters already within the walls who would rise up in support of the attack. The term remained in generally understood parlance and was applied to all manner of individuals (Fifth Columnists) or the supposed shadowy

" NITWITZ " THE NAZTY SPY

'" Rumbled I have been. To Hausfrau where I living am, a hated British neighbour Hausfrau saying is, ' Judgin' by 'is undergarments, Mrs. Cluppins, that lodger of yours is 'ardly ENGLISH, shall we say—'im wot's always snoopin' round, I mean ' "

From Blighty Magazine. February 1940.

organisation (The Fifth Column) that was believed to have been established, or was in danger of being established, in Britain by German nationals resident here, spies, British collaborators and Nazi sympathisers.

Just as in the First World War, there was also a body of literature by both British and international authors that spoke of the reality of the Fifth Column and warned of its methods. Among them was John Baker-White's *Dover-Nürnberg, Return* (1937), Ernest Hemingway with his anthology *The Fifth Column and the First Forty-Nine Stories* (first UK edition 1939) and *The Fifth Column* by John Langdon (1940)

J. Somerset Maugham took a great interest in the subject and pulled a few strings to meet with Guy Liddell to discuss what they were allowed to reveal under the restrictions of the time for a series of articles he was writing for the American press. Maugham featured the Fifth Column in his novel *The Hours Before Dawn* (1942). There were also a host of stories and articles, both factual and fictional, in newspapers and magazines and films like *Went the Day Well* (1942) that demonstrate how and why the menace of the disguised paratroops, the Fifth Column and enemy agents in Britain held the public's imagination and interest during those early war years.

The popular understanding of the methods of the Fifth Column in Britain consisted of spying on people, 'bugging' both public buildings and private houses with hidden microphones to listen in and record conversations, to commit acts of sabotage to damage the war effort and assist the enemy in any way they could in the event of an invasion. The mass hysteria that occurred in some places in Britain over suspected spies during the First World War was not repeated during the Second World War, but there was still a great deal of concern felt by the British public that the Fifth Column was indeed real. Many people harboured suspicions towards neighbours for a host of reasons – from xenophobia to ignorance and even through pure malice. There were many instances of suspicions being directed towards people simply because they were considered 'a bit odd' among their local community, or even because they had a German sounding name.

If the British population needed any proof of the existence of the Fifth Column they saw it in action on 9 April 1940 when Norwegian Fascist forces were mobilized under Vidkun Quisling in an attempt to seize a number of important communication centres, occupy military bases and spread false claims of successes to pave the way for the German invaders. The coup failed but the term 'Quisling' remained as a label for a traitor long afterwards. After German forces launched their advance into Holland on 10 May 1940 many British national and provincial newspapers carried the story of how German parachutists had disguised themselves in civilian clothes when they made

Heath Robinson's unique take on how to deal with disguised enemy parachutists, published in The Sketch, *July 1940.*

their landings to spearhead the attack. Leading the reportage was the *Daily Express*:

> *On the first day of the invasion parachutists dropped out of the sky like a vast flock of vultures. Most of them were disguised in Allied or Dutch uniforms,*

others came down in the uniform of Dutch policemen and began to direct the population in the streets and mislead the army. One 'policeman' told a group of isolated Dutch troops that their friends were round the corner. When the Dutch troops turned the corner, German troops barricaded across the road, slaughtered them … But, most fantastic of all, the steward of an English ship said that he and the crew had watched parachutists descend in women's clothing. They wore blouses and skirts and each carried a sub-machine gun.[1]

Lord Halifax also condemned the actions of the German forces in parliament, stating, '*Their parachutists had landed disguised not only in the uniforms of the Allied Forces but also as priests and women.*'[2]

Some newspapers even reminded readers '*that as long ago as last August a store of about 2000 uniforms of Dutch postmen, railway officials, gendarmes and soldiers was seen stacked in an office in a small German village in Westphalia. The reason for these collections is now revealed.*'[3] There were further comments about German civilians, undoubtedly Fifth Columnists, '*bearing special identification marks and charged with special missions were found where parachutists come down*'.[4] As the German offensive spread the French Prime Minister's office was swift to react and issued a statement reproduced in British newspapers:

In the course of the savage aggression which has been carried out against the Netherlands, Belgium and Luxembourg, the German Army has employed parachutists who, contrary to international law, have frequently worn Dutch or Belgian uniforms or civilian clothes. The French Government hereby publicly declare that any enemy combatant captured in France who is not wearing his national uniform will be shot.[5]

Almost to cue, *The Times* was able to report on the following day: '*A number of parachute troops were landed in North Eastern France. One, a fair-haired young man who wore dungarees over his clothes was arrested as he was attempting to tamper with communications near an important railway junction.*'[6]

The problem with all of these statements is that parachute troops played a minimal role in the assaults; in some areas they do not appear to have been deployed at all and the stories that ran abroad of disguised paratroopers that were accepted as fact have little or no proof to them actually having taken place, but the die was now cast. Ever since Hitler unleashed his Blitzkrieg things began to deteriorate rapidly in France. Concerns over a Fifth Column and similar parachute landings on British soil saw groups of men in villages and towns across Britain banding together in unregulated armed groups, keeping a watch and patrols for paratroopers and Fifth Columnist saboteurs in their local areas. Neither the police, military authorities nor the government were comfortable about such actions, but understood they would not have

The cover of The War Weekly *of 24 May 1940 reflects the fears of paratroop landing current at the time.*

Parachutes Over Britain *by John Langdon-Davies (1940), one of a number of manuals published by military experts on how to combat the paratroop menace.*

had much success in banning these groups; they would simply have been driven underground.

Fortunately members of the government and their military advisors recognised a ground swell among the British population, especially among those who had served in the First World War and were too old to serve in the armed forces in the current war, but who were keen to do something practical in the defence of their country. The idea was that there should be a civilian volunteer defence force (something very much along the lines that Churchill had recommended back in October 1939[7]) that led to the creation of the Local Defence Volunteers (LDV) which had its launch and first appeal for

German parachute soldier. Note sub-machine-gun, folding bicycle, portable radio.

One of numerous depictions published in books, manuals, magazine and newspapers of German paratroops and the various kit they were presumed to carry in 1940.

Home Guard and their mobile anti-parachutist and dive bomber team.

volunteers made in a radio address by the newly appointed Secretary of State for War Anthony Eden on 14 May 1940.

Over the next twenty-four hours after the broadcast some 250,000 men came forward and gave their names as potential volunteers. The first patrols of the new LDV platoons followed soon after and yet more concerns over Fifth Column activity were soon being reported. The British public was demanding something be done about the Fifth Column.

Under the Defence Regulation 18B all 'aliens' had to register with local authorities from the outset of the war. Defence Regulation 18, originally created to restrict the movement of aircraft, had an addition of Code B that slashed civil liberties in wartime. It enabled the arrest and detention of British citizens or German and Austrian naturalised British citizens, considered

Magazines and training manuals published illustrations warning of the dirty tricks you may face if you encountered a Fifth Columnist.

the most dangerous Nazis or members of pro–Nazi groups without trial. Those considered dangerous 'enemy aliens' would be detained under Royal Prerogative.

By 28 September 1939 the Aliens Department of the Home Office had established some 120 tribunals to consider the risk presented by the 73,353 German and Austrian 'enemy aliens' aged over 16 in the country. Those judged Category 'A' were considered the most dangerous, of whom there were 560, and they were interned within days of the outbreak of hostilities. Category 'B' covered 6,782 people who were not considered an immediate threat and were exempt from internment but subject to restrictions, specifically:

Captain Archibald Henry Maule Ramsey MP.

1. *They should report daily in person to a police station*
2. *They shall not make any use of a motor vehicle (other than a public conveyance) or any bicycle.*
3. *They shall not be out of doors between the hours of 8pm and 6am.*

They were also forbidden to have in their possession a camera, film camera, sketch book, wireless transmitter, telescope, binoculars, a bicycle, nautical charts or maps. They were also forbidden to keep carrier pigeons.

Category 'C' was applied to 64,200, most of them refugees who had fled Nazi Germany, were judged harmless, retained their liberty and initially were subject to no different laws or controls than any other UK resident.[8] In response to the mounting concerns over invasion scares, and in an attempt to destroy the Fifth Column male 'enemy aliens' (those of German or Austrian nationality), in Category B residents in coastal areas between Scotland and Hampshire were rounded up and interned on 11 May. This was extended yet further to all Category B aliens in Britain on 17 May.

* * *

Both in public and behind the scenes, issues with the BUF and other far right organisations had become acute. The aristocratic Scottish Unionist MP and rabid anti-Semite Archibald Maule Ramsay had formed the Right Club of like-minded aristocrats, upper class and well-placed individuals in 1939. With a view to keeping the membership of the club secret he gave the ledger containing the names of the members to one of its most junior members, Tyler Kent, a cypher clerk at the American embassy. The problem for Ramsay would be that Kent was already under suspicion of stealing top secret documents from the embassy. MI5 had received a tip-off that Kent's known associate and senior member of the Right Club, Anna Wolkoff, had been shown some of the documents and had supplied the information to her old comrade William Joyce, (one of the most infamous people to provide a voice, dubbed Lord Haw Haw by the British public) in Germany to use in his broadcasts on the NBBS.

US Embassy Cypher Clerk and spy, Tyler Kent.

In a move Ramsay could not have anticipated, US Ambassador Joe Kennedy, a man not known for his support for the British war effort, agreed to waive Kent's diplomatic immunity and he was dismissed from American government service on 20 May 1940. Kent's flat at the swish 47 Gloucester Place, Marylebone was raided by Special Branch, accompanied by MI5's Max Knight and a representative of the American embassy. During the course of their search it soon became painfully apparent that Kent had not only been abstracting originals of secret documents from the embassy, he had been copying them and, in some cases, lending them to Anna Wolkoff.

In one particular incident it was clear that these documents had been photographed. Tyler Kent was detained and Anna Wolkoff was arrested and interned under Section 18B of the Defence Regulations. However, among the papers discovered during the search was also the Right Club membership ledger. The concern was that if Kent had passed some of the sensitive documents to Ramsay, it was also possible he could have used his parliamentary privilege to speak about them in parliament and it would have been impossible for their publication to be prevented. MI5 wanted to leave nothing to chance and it really was no time for procrastination, but their requests to the Home Secretary regarding the extension of 18B regulations to tackle the Right Club, BUF and other far right organisations that were believed to be stockpiling weaponry, had gone unanswered.[9]

A meeting was arranged with Home Secretary Sir John Anderson at the Home Office on the evening of 21 May. The reason for inaction soon emerged, Anderson had formed the opinion that the BUF was in reality patriotic and he found it difficult to believe that members of the BUF would assist the enemy. Despite some of the underground activities of the BUF, Maule Ramsay and the Right Club, and their close association with Moseley and the BUF being explained to him 'quietly and forcibly'[10] by Max Knight (for Knight's own account of the 'Kent-Wolkoff Case' with his notes on the lessons to be learned for Intelligence Officers, see Appendix B), Anderson appeared unmoved. Even when Guy Liddell stressed the urgency of the matter Anderson still expressed his concerns over sanctioning the arrests without solid evidence and due process. Clearly, frustrated by the Home Secretary's stance, Liddell recorded in his diary:

I longed to say that if somebody did not get a move on there would be no democracy, no England and no Empire and that this was almost a matter of days … Either he is an extremely calm and cool-headed person or he has not the least idea of the present situation. The possibility of a serious invasion of this country would seem to be no more than a vague suggestion in Anderson's mind.[11]

'Enemy Alien' women boarding a train taking them to an internment camp. Defence Regulations 18B was extended to include them on 27 May 1940.

Anderson was however, at least in Liddell's opinion, *'considerably shaken by the end of the meeting'*[12] and asked for further evidence of a number of the points brought to his attention for the Cabinet meeting the following night. The meeting and the evidence clearly made an impression on Anderson and the Cabinet decided in favour of the detention of many members of pro-Nazi groups, predominantly members of the British Union of Fascists. A suitable amendment known as 18B (1A) was made to the regulations and the arrests ensued soon afterwards.

Internments under 18B were further extended on 27 May to include 'enemy alien' women who were also to be interned. A concession was made that permitted them to take their children with them. When Italy declared war on Britain on 10 June 1940 Churchill was in no mood for procrastination and it is said he simply barked 'Collar the lot!' and the 4,000 known members of the Italian Fascist Party resident in Britain were arrested and interned, along with Italians aged between 16 and 30 who had lived in the UK for less than twenty years, regardless of their political affiliations.

With the thousands involved in the internments of May and June 1940 most internees were initially held in designated prisons, often in old wings that were especially re-opened to cope with the numbers. They were then removed to various detention camps, in some cases tented camps surrounded by barbed wire fences, at various locations across Britain. Thousands of internees were removed to detention camps converted from old hotels; on the Isle of Man the men were at Peveril Camp, Peel and the women and children were held in a Rushen Camp at what was usually the summer resort of Port Erin in the south of the island. Many would spend months or even years behind barbed wire as tribunals sat and those who were judged 'of least concern' were gradually released.

Lists of British citizens or naturalised British citizens who were not interned, but considered to be likely to collaborate with German invasion forces, were drawn up by the chief constables of every city, borough and county constabulary across the country, would be agreed by their regional security committee and submitted to their regional commissioner for inclusion in the regional suspect list. The nature of the Fifth Column being a somewhat nebulous concept, security committees (in many ways a forerunner of regional crime squads) were established in each of the Civil Defence regions during 1940. The foundation meetings were addressed by Colonel Frank Brook HM Inspector of Constabulary who encouraged the senior officers who made up the committee to approach the matter in new ways, as recorded in the minutes of the first gathering of the security committee for the North East on 17 July 1940:

Colonel Brook opened the meeting stating he hoped this was the first of what he hoped would be a series of informal meetings held regularly to pool ideas so that they could be satisfied that they were on top of subversive activities, aliens and Fifth Columnists. He did not want them to concentrate on a mere elucidation of concrete cases, but to be constantly alive to possibilities of activities going under the surface. He instanced that in crime and other important police matters the need for combined action on a wider scale had been long recognised and similarly he wanted the officers present to regard the majority of the matters which came to their notice as being sufficiently important to bring to the notice of officers of other forces.[13]

The bulk of the thousands of reports of alleged Fifth Column activity or infiltration in Britain turned out to be the product of a widespread paranoia. This was fuelled by reports in national newspapers of infiltrations by operatives in disguises which had no doubt been inspired by the earlier reports of the landings of paratroopers dressed in civilian clothes and uniforms on the continent.

The story that seemed to catch the imagination of the British public was that German infiltrators were disguising themselves as nuns. As incredible as this may sound, during interviews with British veterans of the Battle of France, the author has heard the story repeated on a surprising number of occasions – German soldiers adopting that disguise and then being exposed by their hairy legs and jackboots while riding a bicycle. No doubt such tales reached home and gave rise and credibility to the stories of stubble-chinned, hairy-handed 'nuns' of the Fifth Column reported to have been spotted in Britain.

The story appears to have gained currency from around Sunday, 18 May 1940 when *Daily Herald* feature writer W.H. Ewer claimed he had first heard it in Buckinghamshire, *'from somebody who had it at second hand from the women who had discovered it'.* A woman had been travelling by train from London to Aylesbury and in the carriage with her were two nuns. One of the nuns had dropped a book and as she stooped to pick it up, *'From the folds of her habit, emerged a hairy, muscular, indubitably masculine hand.'* The woman kept her cool and did not intimate what she had seen until the nuns alighted from the carriage and she followed them; spotting a policeman she alerted the constable to the nuns who soon found out they were German spies and arrested them. The story concluded, *'She got her ten pounds reward.'*[14]

The story was reported and repeated as a real incident in a number of newspapers. It was embellished with descriptions of hairy arms with tattoos by others who claimed to have heard it from a friend or family member.[15] The chances are the whole thing was created as a deliberate rumour, but it got people looking out for enemies in disguise. Even intimating it would not only give the discoverer the satisfaction they had done their patriotic duty, but they had earned a cash reward worth having to boot, without any ministry actually having to make a genuine offer to pay a penny; it was all just a rumour.

In another rumour current at the same time, members of the British public were becoming convinced that German spies and collaborators must be communicating targets for German bombers, and the resulting bomb damage, back to Germany and we were being mocked using the information on the NBBS by Lord Haw-Haw. Stories always seemed to come from a friend of a friend, not the person who actually heard 'the German wireless say that Didcot [or insert any town or city of your choice] is going to be the first town bombed', or certain facts known only to local people such as the clock at so-and-so has stopped or a certain pub near an aircraft factory has run out of beer. These could all be easily disproved by anyone living in the areas mentioned by NBBS, but for those listening in other areas of the country it certainly sounded like NBBS was privy to detailed local knowledge.[16]

The Ministry of Information kept a record of Haw-Haw's broadcasts and, working with MI5, used regional security liaison officers to check up from that record as to whether or not the remarks were accurate or not. No evidence was found of NBBS having any prior knowledge of raids or privy knowledge of the damage inflicted.[17] However, the possibility that they could be transmitting coded messages hidden among their broadcasts for Fifth Columnists, was given expert analysis by MI5 and was considered a distinct possibility.[18]

Fifth Column scares were regularly brought to B Division, from 'suspicious' characters, such as the 'enemy alien' living on a house boat on the River Fowey in South Cornwall near the town of Fowey who, it was feared, might put a few floating mines on the river and do considerable damage,[19] to the joint B Division and Admiralty investigation of 'a lady of German origin' in Bacton, Norfolk who was believed to have tapped into an old telegraph cable to Germany and Holland from her bungalow on a nearby cliff.[20]

Then there was the 'German parachutist spy' in civilian clothes who had been arrested by Canadian troops because of his suspicious accent and brought MI5 officers speeding down to the Oxford area to interrogate him – he turned out to be a Welshman.[21] There was even an unfortunate apiarist in East Anglia who was reported to authorities for using his bees as couriers for messages. The police superintendent in charge of the enquiry reported earnestly *'that the practical difficulties of attaching and detaching the message would, in his opinion, render the scheme unworkable'.*[22]

* * *

After the Fall of France, despite the internment of Category B 'enemy aliens' and members of right wing groups, when air raids began to take place over Britain stories of supposed Fifth Columnists remained rife and MI5's B Branch recruited a number of new officers to assist with the huge workload of these reports. An insight into those times and the diversity of these reports is well illustrated by the record of Anthony Blunt's first day with B Division in June 1940:

1. *Dealt with letter from lady pointing out danger of sentries being poisoned by ice creams sold by aliens.*
2. *Report from a man who heard a Colonel making indiscreet statements.*
3. *Report about a mark (a lover's sign) on a telegraph pole.*
4. *Report about a Christadelphian Conscientious Objector giving training in engineering to prospective members of HM Forces.*

5. *Report on a hotel keeper in Scotland thought to have German blood in him.*
6. *Report from a woman who had received a map from an insurance agency showing reception, neutral and evacuation areas which she believed supplied valuable information to the enemy.*[23]

One of the regular reported concerns was that of supposed Fifth Columnists shining lights and flashing signals to enemy aircraft as they approached or were overhead to direct them to their targets; this became endemic across the country. In turn these incidents were reported to police and military authorities and used up thousands of man hours as each apparently credible or repeated allegation was investigated.

MI5 B Division regional officers were drawn into a number of the investigations into these lights. The Birmingham region attempted to plot the approximate locations of the lights reported to see if their source could be tracked down and attributed to causes such as flares or Very lights shot up by our own forces. There were other issues highlighted by a Merseyside Chief Constable:

The difficulty as far as the police are concerned does not arise at all from the fact that lights are used for signalling purposes. The difficulty arises from the fact that during an air raid the sky is lit up by many different types of lights. There is no doubt that the vast majority of these lights are caused by Anti-Aircraft guns.' [24]

He did however explain how they were addressing the problem:

Military and Naval authorities should send out bodies of watchers; the military acting on land and the Navy acting on patrol boats. As soon as a light is seen which is regarded as suspicious, the patrol warn the police. The police have arranged a flying squad of officers and immediately a report is received these officers dash off to the district where the light is alleged to have been seen.[25]

The result of such measures confirmed that the mystery signal lights were indeed from anti-aircraft guns. The problem in their area was that the Naval Intelligence Officer was frustrating local police forces with his assertion that Liverpool was full of Fifth Columnists and that the police were not doing their utmost to catch them.[26]

Although there were numerous successful prosecutions and some hefty fines imposed during the war years for blackout infringements, there was only one single case that was successfully prosecuted for 'signalling for a purpose prejudicial to the Defence of the Realm' that was brought to the notice of the government. The case was one of a woman brought before magistrates at Southampton who had been apprehended after she opened and shut the door of her house at night with the light on inside; but there was no evidence to suggest it was actually done with the intent of signalling to enemy aircraft. As a measure of immediate precaution, the woman responsible was ordered to be interned while further inquiries were made.[27]

Then there were the stories in a number of country areas of farmers painting their barns certain colours, red or black allegedly, to show they were pro-Nazi and avoid having bombs dropped on them or, more sinisterly, had created landing grounds for invasion forces and used the barns to signify their location from the air. The main incident of this nature was reported to MI5 by Captain Stephen Van Neck, the Chief Constable of Norfolk who had received reports from local people concerned about the East Anglian Real Estate Company which had bought up a great deal of land in Norfolk at Sporle, Buckenham, Beighton, Cantley, Halvergate, Paston, Guestwick and Southrepps since 1938. Officer Commanding RAF Watton reported his concerns common of each of the sites as:

> *Large area with hedges removed suitable land and take-off heavy aircraft all directions. Two barns painted red alongside … all have aspect of being specially prepared landing grounds [surfaces rolled hard] with easily recognisable features in barns.'*[28] The police investigated and reported *'hedges on a number of fields owned by this company have been removed and give the impression of preparations for a landing ground. All roofs of the farm buildings have recently been painted red.*[29]

The story was also brought to the attention of the Air Ministry, War Office and even the Prime Minister and generated a great deal of interest, especially because particular attention had been given to the obstruction and even mining of open areas that could potentially be used by the enemy as landing grounds for aircraft since May 1940 under the direction of Wing Commander Thomas G. Pike.[30] The Chief Constable of Norfolk was granted an order from the Home Office to apprehend the Dutch owners of the company, along with their wives. They were rapidly brought in and interviewed as their barns and properties were searched and the intelligence services began to investigate their backgrounds. It appears to have turned out to be another damp squib; the barn roofs had not been deliberately painted red, they were as supplied by the manufacturer, but none-the-less they were interned and the troops of Eastern Command wasted no time ploughing up the whole area and placing obstacles to prevent the landing of aircraft in the fields.[31]

Other tales told of how the 'collaborator' farmers arranged some of their mobile chicken coops in the form of a swastika and the remainder to form an arrow pointing in the direction of the nearest military installation or factory involved in production for the war effort. Guy Liddell recorded two cases on 17 June 1940:

> *The Air Force produced two very sinister photographs from the air. One had the appearance of an arrow, said to be pointing in the direction of an ordnance factory. It led from a church said to belong to the Unden Order. Then some 20 miles away was a bow in the middle of a plantation … Investigations have been carried out. The Unden Order turns out to be the Undenominational Church and when it was built the local borough council insisted there must be a car park. This car park made the head of the arrow … There was a wireless receiving set in the church, but it could not even pick up the national broadcasts. The bow was in the middle of a pheasant covert on Lord Iliffe's estate. It had been there since 1923 and showed up white on account of the chalky ground. At the moment it was planted with potatoes which have been put in in accordance with the Dig for Victory campaign. It would have been completely covered in green in about 10 days. The local air force unit took the law into its own hands, cut down the trees and laid them across the offending space.'[32]*

Another ground-to-air mystery were the mysterious piles of broken glass found deposited at intervals of 30 yards, for a distance of 1,000 yards, on the roadway near an aerodrome in Blackpool. Upon investigation a similar incident had been found to have occurred on the continent, the reflected light from the glass being placed on the ground to guide enemy aircraft.[33] Could it be that Fifth Column activists were deliberately playing up to scares to confound the authorities?

Even lovers' signs and the marks made by Boy Scouts and Girl Guide trackers on telegraph poles became viewed with suspicion during the Fifth Column scares, concerns that rattled up the line to General Ironside, Commander in Chief, Home Forces who wrote on 31 May 1940:

> *Fifth Column reports coming in from everywhere. A man with an armband on and a swastika pulled up near an important aerodrome in Southern Command. Important telegraph poles marked, suspicious men moving at night all over the country. We have the right of search and I have put piquets on all over the place to-night. Perhaps we shall catch some swine.[34]*

B Division Director Guy Liddell wrote candidly:

This office is being absolutely inundated with ridiculous enquiries from every possible quarter and the worst come from the highest circles. We have asked the Director-General to try and get some broadcast urging the public to report more accurately and to take steps to verify their facts as far as possible. I have also suggested that something should be done to ensure that stories are fully sifted here before being passed to the Prime Minister, Cabinet ministers and other officials. We are now harassed by a number of amateur detectives in high places.[35]

Some people had made up their mind that the Fifth Column didn't exist at all and even if it did it, posed no real threat. The view was even held by senior members of government as painfully illustrated by the conversation between Victor Rothschild, MI5's B Branch head of counter-sabotage and Lord Beaverbrook, Minister of Aircraft Production in August 1940. It was regarding a group of recently arrived German refugees who claimed to be Jewish. MI5 had received intelligence from a credible source that they were in fact German Fifth Columnists attempting to infiltrate British industry. Rothschild related the exchange to Guy Liddell who recorded it in his diary:

Beaverbrook:	*I am surprised that somebody with your name, your liberal views, your position and reputation, should go in for this witch-hunting. Those poor Jews have been hunted out of Germany and now they come here they are hunted back into concentration camps …*
Rothschild:	*The members of the Loewy firm that I came to see you about are not Jews. They are what is known as Aryan.*
Beaverbrook:	*They are Jews.*
Rothschild:	*They are not.*
Beaverbrook:	*They are Jews.*
Rothschild:	*They are not.*
Beaverbrook:	*They are Jews*
Rothschild:	*They are not.*
Beaverbrook:	*I am not going to start an argument …*
Rothschild:	*Do you think that MI5's investigations into Nazi agents in industry are of no value?*
Beaverbrook:	*No value at all. Even if thee Loewy people are agents, they can do no harm.*
Rothschild:	*Couldn't they sabotage plant?*
Beaverbrook:	*No. I watch them very carefully.*
Rothschild:	*Couldn't they convey information to the enemy about the geographical position of your extrusion presses and about*

173

> *the Ministry of Aircraft Production's aircraft capacity and production?*

Beaverbrook: *I don't care if they do know where the presses are. It is not easy to bomb a press even if your so-called agents were signalling to them. As regards our capacity, I hope the Germans do know …*[36]

And so, the to-and-fro rolled on, 'the Beaver' would not change his opinion, his parting words to Rothschild being: *'Good-night. You should not be in that organisation with the witch-hunters. It ought to be abolished. I do not think there is any danger from Nazi spies in this country. I do not think it matters if they are at large.'*[37]

* * *

Rothschild investigated numerous alleged acts of sabotage in factories, be it literally throwing spanners in the works, deliberate acts of damage or bad calibration and fires. There was even the strange case of the report of a bomb falling near a factory in Manchester. Work was stopped and the staff evacuated, but when the Bomb Disposal Squad investigated there was no bomb, just a hole deliberately dug to resemble a bomb crater.[38] The problem that most frequently confronted him, however, was discerning whether the act had indeed been committed by Fifth Columnists or if it was domestic industrial espionage, disgruntled employees committing acts of malice towards their employers, or former employees gaining revenge after being sacked.

Those who completely dismissed the existence of the Fifth Column were in a minority and most people had rubbed along satisfied the authorities had Fifth Columnists in check. The heightened scares of invasion in the summer and autumn of 1940 saw a 'jitter war' emerge with police and military authorities expending huge amounts of time and effort investigating spurious reports and false alarms of Fifth Column activities.

The Fifth Columnist scares, or what were quaintly referred to at the time as 'jitters' or 'flaps', of August and September 1940 usually concerned invasion scares and parachute landings by enemy agents or troops. But another chimera joined the canon in the form of 'mysterious' white powders after newspapers on 8 August ran accounts of patches of white powder found on the streets of a North Western town after an air raid. The substance was stated to be a sulphuric compound believed to have been found in other areas after propaganda leaflet parcels were heard to 'pop' and burst in the air.[39] Other papers consulted their experts who ventured it was possibly a bomb employed for aiding navigation over the sea; by breaking on the water it makes a big white patch, but they could not suggest a reason for one being dropped on land.[40]

In late August the scares ramped up like never before after reports appeared of packets of white powder being found near bomb craters after an air raid on a town in the South West on 25 August.[41] A few nights later patches of white powder were discovered on roads in a Midland town after enemy aircraft were heard overhead during the night,[42] followed by stories of 'white powder dropped by German aircraft on streets in a Welsh district' in early September.[43] Initially feared to be mustard gas in powder form, authorities were quick to assure the public that the powder was harmless and was not actually dropped by enemy aircraft.[44] However, because authorities were less forthcoming about exactly what it was and speculation rapidly set in about how it got there, it captured the imagination of the British public and alarms over Fifth Columnist activities involving white powder were soon occurring all over the country.

White powder scares had existed since before the war when patches of it were left on the ground after anti-gas exercises. It was actually a bleach

An Anti-Gas Decontamination Squad brushing their bleach power to neutralise a supposed use of gas spray or liquid during an exercise, Tenby 1939.

powder used for decontamination, but the misconception remained in the minds of some of those not involved with ARP work or training. The problem was, as seen before in the phenomena of the Fifth Column scares, that once one incident becomes the subject of gossip in one area it would not be long before someone else in the locality would be prompted by the story to see or think they see something else suspicious involving a white powder. So, it would spread as members of the public considered it their patriotic duty to keep their eyes peeled and report incidents of concern to the authorities.

Typical of the reports logged by the police was this example from the No 2 Region:

Man (50) 5' 8–9" dark suit, trilby hat and dark shoes, walking stick, smart appearance; and woman (25/35)5' 8–9" black coat, black hat, green frock, smart appearance seen depositing mysterious white powder from paper bag on grass verges and railings of the Leeds-York road at Copmanthorpe. Patches at intervals of 50 to 100 yards.[45]

Not all the white powders were man-made either, as Guy Liddell recorded:

There was a scare the other day about a curious substance looking like spider web which had descended on a policeman who had subsequently broken out in a rash. It was thought that this substance had been dropped by enemy aircraft. Enquiry showed that this was genuine spiders web, which forms on the ground at this time of the year under certain conditions. The dew settles on it and when it evaporates set up convection currents which raise the webs into the air. These webs take with them poison hairs from nettles which contain formic acid and it was these hairs which had caused the blistering to the skin that was thought to be due to mustard gas.'[46]

The first MI5 *Weekly Intelligence Summary*, published in October 1940, picked up on the white powder scares and wryly observed:

As Regional Officers are aware, there is a fairly complete organisation for the examination of objects suspected of being contaminated with noxious bacteria which might have been dropped from aeroplanes, or left about by saboteurs. Both the police and these scientists have been fairly heavily engaged in examining objects recently, these objects varying from white powders found to be chalk, packets of cigarettes, pink powders, pellets of starch, caterpillar faeces, dust off roads, rubber balloons filled with white powder which turned out to be barium sulphate, ampoules filled with ammonia, sand, clay, a fungus, cabbage leaves, tablets of hyoscine and common salt, to an unidentifiable object which may be an ornament off a woman's hat, or something to do with fishing.

It is clear that whether these objects are being released from enemy aircraft, deposited by German sympathisers or agents, or are simply fortuitous, they have a considerable nuisance value in occupying the time of the Police and of the Emergency Laboratory Service. It has therefore occurred to me that they might be being put about or taken to the police by 'Fifth Columnists' who wish to create alarm and occupy the Police and other experts when they might be doing more profitable jobs. It would therefore be advisable for those people who bring these objects forward to be questioned closely, and to have their background investigated to see that they really genuinely wish to assist the country.[47]

Enough was enough, scare reports had to be curtailed and the intelligence services set about quashing the belief in the minds of the general public that the Fifth Column existed. They did a very good job of it; the problem is it became accepted as the truth and was repeated in their official histories.

It is true to say there was no national organisation operating beneath the radar that co-ordinated a Fifth Column across Britain, although it had been highly likely that if the BUF had remained at large, and if there had been an invasion, they would have risen up as the Quisling Fascists had done in Norway. Even after the internments a dangerous Fifth Column did exist and how it was defined and understood by MI5 was explained by B Division Officer, Major the Hon. Kenneth Younger in a presentation for senior police and military security officers in September 1940:

The term 'Fifth Column' originated in the Spanish Civil War and had also been used to describe the minorities in Poland, Denmark, Norway, Holland and Belgium who assisted the German invasion. The term implies more than individual spies and traitors and means whole sections of the population who are willing to assist the enemy. All these countries were invaded without declaration of war, the main work of the Fifth Column was performed by the German Embassies, Consulates, Travel Bureaus and the German Colony generally, against whom no preventative action had been taken before hostilities broke out.

In Poland, Holland and Belgium considerable racial and political minorities existed which were openly unpatriotic. In Denmark and Norway, the Fifth Column consisted of a smaller number of highly placed people. There is no evidence that Communists assisted the invader in any of these countries. In Poland and Holland, the large scale military action was taken mainly by the German Colony and the Dutch NSB. Preparation made by those bodies had not been kept in any way secret before the invasion. Action taken included seizure of key-points and false orders issued by a few highly placed traitors disorganised the Norwegian defence.

Racial Minorities of Doubtful Loyalty

1. *Irish: This is the only section likely to take extensive action to assist the Germans.*
2. *Scottish and Welsh Nationalist Movements: Some evidence of German penetration, especially among the Welsh.*
3. *Germans: None still at large except some women of German nationality or extraction. Might give aid on a small scale to parachutists.*
4. *Other Refugees: 10,000 Czechs, 20,000 Dutch and Belgians. Some German agents must be expected, but the vast majority of these refugees may be considered anti-Nazi. British refugees 6,000 to 7,000 returned from the Low Countries many unable even to speak English.*
5. *Italians: Most of the members of the Italian Fascist Party have either left the country or have been arrested.*

Political Minorities of Doubtful Loyalty in Great Britain

1. *British Union: Membership in March 1940 about 8,000; 600 or 700 interned. Half the membership in London. Policy: authoritarian, anti-Semitic, anti-communist, anti-war. Not organised as a military Fifth Column but focus for people of Nazi sympathies. Subversive action so far discovered the work of individual extremists rather than the organisation. Some half dozen cases since the war show that members deliberately collect secret information. No evidence that they have means of transmitting it to the enemy but much of the information would be useless for any other purpose. Suggested method wireless transmission or crews to Lisbon.*
2. *Other Pro-Nazi Bodies e.g. Nordic League, Imperial Fascist League etc., small in numbers, now believed inactive.*
3. *Communist Party GB. Membership 20,000. Provided no breach of the peace is involved any attempt to stifle such agitation by police action would only arouse additional sympathy for the party.*

Conclusion

Subversive action by individuals more likely than mass action, except possibly by the IRA. Most likely methods: signalling to aircraft, bogus telephone calls, rumours, aid to parachutists, isolated acts of sabotage.[48]

Despite many of its leaders being interned, the activities of the Fifth Column in Britain were, for the most part, conducted by members of the British Union of Fascists. Right up to the outbreak of war the main conduit between the BUF and the Nazi Party in Germany was Rolf Hoffmann of the *Reichspressedienst* (Nazi Press Bureau). He was in regular correspondence with leading British Fascist Admiral Barry Domvile and time and again his name is mentioned in the case notes of interned and suspect list members of the BUF who would mention how they wrote to him to obtain copies of *News from Germany* and offered advice on how to circulate copies when it appeared some of the copies he was sending were being intercepted.

He supplied Nazi books and photographs of Hitler; one woman from Riseley, Berkshire gushed, *'I must thank you for the photograph of the Fuehrer which now has a place of honour on the mantel piece'.*[49] Hoffmann was also known to have had correspondence with extremist factions such as the Scottish Nationalist Party, notably a violent extremist cell known as the Scots Order that was based in Edinburgh and its leader Matthew Hamilton who expressed full sympathy with the Nazi cause in a letter to Hoffmann in May 1939. Hoffmann helped arrange British pro-Hitler supporters to attend the Nazi Party rally at Nuremberg and provided the first point of contact for many of those wishing to become naturalised Germans and attain their goal of becoming fully fledged members of the Nazi Party.[50]

Far from hiding himself with disguises and false passports, Hoffmann visited Britain to meet party faithful and to recruit a few more to the cause on a number of occasions and even gave interviews to the press. During his six-week 'good will' tour of Britain in 1938 he visited a number of the principal cities and towns between London and Edinburgh. During his visit to Sunderland and Wearside in March 1938, he gave an interview to the *Sunderland Echo* in which Hoffmann described himself as chief of the Nazi Germany government foreign press department. He spoke of his great admiration for the British road system and railways. During his travels in industrial areas he met a cross section of the public from businessmen to workers and spoke at a number of venues on Anglo-German topics in which he explained he liked to visit England as often as he could:

> *…to make contacts for the encouragement of better relationships between Germany and Britain … I have been particularly impressed by the ardent desire of everybody in this country to live in peace and friendship with all nations. The Englishman is fair, but it is unfortunate some people believe that German people are maintained under some sort of suppression. Nothing is further from the truth.*[51]

Hoffmann also revealed some of the doctrine he was expounding. When asked about his views on British youth contrasted with young folks in Germany he explained: *'German youth is by far more earnest in the attitude towards life and considerably less pleasure bent than the English. Hitler has given them a motto to be tough as steel, tenacious as leather and quick as greyhounds.'*

He observed the contrast between German and British women saying:

Few German girls use cosmetics. They believe that the open-air life is the greatest aid to beauty and refrain from putting artificial colour on their faces. I saw much exaggerated make-up on the faces of women in London but remarkably enough women in the smaller cities and towns of the country do not seem to have followed this fashion. It is to their credit – women are far better without it ... [adding] *The Nazi Government was especially interested in the improvement of the health condition through the 'Strength through Joy' movement.*[52]

Once war had broken out it became far more difficult to forge new covert links with Germany. Some of those who wished to enter into espionage activities for Nazi Germany suddenly realised they didn't have the contacts, nor had the know how to find them, and their attempts to find and make those contacts reached the ears of MI5 before they had a chance to do any harm. A case in point, was Dorothea Mary 'Dorie' Knowles (aka Knowles-Schulze). Born in Berlin in 1921 the daughter of a British father and a German mother, she was educated in Germany and had been living in Britain in 1934 working as a secretary. Her family life had been marred by the arguments between her father and mother. Dorothea would claim her mother, 'hates England like poison' and that she had instilled her own hatred of England in Dorothea, a view her father and sibling did not share and so she had become estranged from them.

In the autumn of 1939 Dorothea joined the Ealing Branch of the BUF where she made the acquaintance of Frank Millbank who she believed had contacts in German intelligence to whom she could pass on information she had relating to explosives being manufactured by the firm of chemical engineers where she worked.

Although Millbank himself was not above suspicion, he was also a member of The Link, but he communicated his concerns and produced letters he had been sent from Knowles with the police. Special Branch searched her room in December 1939. Among other things police found a collection of love letters to Kurt Schulze in which she wrote of her love of Germany and her desire to serve the Fatherland. '*I am ready to sacrifice all for my country – my life in espionage, it doesn't matter at all, only to know that I serve the great sacred German country.*' When questioned about these letters Knowles explained that she was keeping a record of her daily thoughts and doings so that she could let Schulze read it when the war was over.[53]

Guy Liddell commented: '*She is only seventeen but nonetheless a sophisticated and confirmed liar.*'[54]

Dorie Knowles was detained under 18B on 19 December 1939. During the early years of her detention Knowles made no bones about her devotion to National Socialist Germany. She had a visit from her relatives during January 1940 when she said she loathed England and the English people and belonged to Germany which she loved and wanted to serve. During her internment at Camp W on the Isle of Man, Knowles would claim she had a radical change of heart and no longer believed in Germany; her dream had been shattered and she wanted to do her bit for the British war effort. In 1943 the intelligence officer of Camp W sent in a report in which he described her as '*a most painful case of adolescence*'. She was released in 1944 and was soon reconnecting with fellow internee Gladys Fortune – it did not appear she had any real change of heart.[55]

* * *

BUF leader Sir Oswald Mosley had spoken a lot about patriotism and often chose to present his speeches in front of a Union Flag; the flag was also used in BUF insignia and thousands of people, albeit misguided, believing themselves to be patriotic had been drawn to the BUF. When hostilities broke out however, they were confronted with a stark choice of either taking the BUF stance of refusing to fight or doing their patriotic duty for King and Country. The National Service (Armed Forces) Act 1939 under which thousands of young men aged between 18 and 41 were 'called-up' for military service forced the decision. Thousands decided their loyalty was to Britain and a lot of the sting of the British Union of Fascists was lost as a result. For some, however, the cause of the BUF had to carry on.

One example of this can be found with the Bournemouth branch of the BUF whose leading members had left, most of them to join the Forces in 1939 and four women members '*carried on to the full all the activities of the branch*'.[56] One of them, the daughter of a titled lady, had already been fined £2 10s for using insulting words and behaviour in 1938 and fined another £5 for being caught daubing Fascist slogans on ARP signs in October 1939. She and others would also be removed by the police for their own safety after selling the BUF newspaper *Action* on the street during the Labour Party Conference at Bournemouth in May 1940. The daubing of Fascist slogans did, however, continue in the town but no one else was caught in the act of writing them. Was it surprising that no further slogans appeared after all four women who had taken over the leadership of the Bournemouth BUF branch had been interned?[57]

Internment of those who would and could have posed a threat at the height of the invasion scares of 1940 quashed any potential major national rising, but

"*She just says she does this cove* EVERY *year.*"

Cartoonist Rowland Emett's comment on the War Department restricted areas published in **Punch** *7 August 1940.*

after the internments there were those who continued to work towards BUF aims, some of whom would be interned when their activities or suspicions of their activities became known. Some attracted the attention of local police and the Security Services for their apparent attempts to indulge in espionage. A typical case was that of the wife of an interned BUF district leader in Suffolk. She had been a women's district leader and the pair had advertised their farm near Eye as a place where BUF members *'could stay in a National Socialist atmosphere'* as late as April 1940.

After the internment of her husband in June 1940 she went to live with her mother in Ipswich where they held frequent parties attended by a number of officers from HM Forces that continued to the early hours of the morning when the guests were observed to leave the worse for drink. There was considerable suspicion that during these parties, while the officers' lips were loosened through drink, the former BUF women's district leader was *'attempting to collect information which would be of value to the enemy'*.[58]

* * *

Just two miles off Hampshire on the south coast of England is the Isle of Wight, an island of just 22½ miles from east to west, 13 miles from north to south and home to around 100,000 people in 1939. It was a place where news travelled fast and it was difficult for much to remain a secret among locals. It was also one of the most sensitive of all the British Isles on account of its being the location of RAF Ventnor 'Chain Home' (AMES Type 1) station, one of the original twenty stations that formed part of an early type of RADAR that enabled the detection and early warning of enemy aircraft as they flew over the sea to Britain.

It was also slap bang in the middle of the Channel coast where it was strongly suspected the enemy would cross to make their invasion landings for the conquest of Great Britain. There was even a rumour during the summer of 1940, both in Germany and in Britain, that the Isle of Wight was already in the hands of the enemy. This was probably due to the erroneous assumption that could have been made that the Isle was one of the Channel Islands just off the coast of Normandy that had been occupied by German forces in June 1940.

So, with all of that in mind it is hardly surprising that some of those on the Isle of Wight, who wished to hedge their bets on the side of the enemy, came to the attention of the authorities. Some of the membership of the BUF were already known by 1939, such as Edward 'Pip' Davies who was the district leader for the Isle of Wight (later interned under 18B). He communicated with a particularly keen Niton woman who offered to hold meetings for the purpose of 'converting' her fellow villagers when the future of the BUF appeared threatened in the spring of 1940. When police investigated her house, it was found to contain '*a considerable amount of Fascist literature and propaganda*'. A restriction order was placed on the woman by the Home Secretary under DR 18A excluding her from being within an Aliens Protected Area and she went to stay in Surrey. She was permitted to return later in the war but was heard to express the same views she had expounded back in 1940.[59]

Another Isle of Wight BUF member brought to the attention of the authorities was a German-born woman who had married a British man who ran a private hotel in Ventnor. According to several reports from unconnected sources received by the police from 1939–40, she was expressing 'violently pro-German views'. In May 1940 she was requested to fill in form DR17 but would not disclose the whereabouts of her German brothers on the form; she was arrested and sentenced to three months imprisonment. She was later interned, the camp report on her noting she showed considerable affection and some admiration for Hitler and was a '*difficult and disagreeable woman*'.[60]

Another was a man who was described on this Suspect List entry as '*disgruntled and violently anti-British*,' he had been the subject of a number of concerned reports forwarded to the Chief Constable of the Isle of Wight over his pro-Nazi views and was even reported by his own wife who wrote to the Under Secretary of State warning that her '*husband hated England and wanted to get to Germany via Holland to take part in anti-British broadcasting*'.[61] He was also removed from the Isle of Wight by an order under 18a regulations and was not allowed to depart for Germany and join Lord Haw-Haw on NBBS. He went to live in Didcot instead.

Around 12.37am on 3 June 1940 East Cowes Air Raid Warden Arthur Board spotted a torch being shone out of a window. When he went to investigate he found local man Dennis Harper (24) leaning out of his window. On spotting the warden he shot back in and pulled down the sash window; his behaviour was suspicious to say the least. Board informed the police and Police Sergeant Winnard arrived at the house soon after. Harper was at that time on his verandah and on being challenged by the policeman he tried to climb in his bedroom window, the policeman managed to grab his trouser leg and had a word with him. Harper simply repeated it had been accidental. He was issued with a summons for displaying an electric light after dark.

Around 2.30am soldiers guarding the Kingston Electric Light Works, East Cowes spotted a man inside the barbed wire fence surrounding the works. As the figure approached Private John Driscoll, one of the three sentries on duty that night, challenged him to halt. The man ran away, Driscoll called out the guard and went in pursuit. The man was discovered in some bushes and was held at the fixed bayonet points of eight soldiers until the police arrived. When Police Sergeant Winnard arrived he soon saw it was Dennis Harper again. When asked what he was up to he claimed '*it was a mistake, quite an accident*'. Harper was taken to Cowes police station and Sergeant Winnard went to Harper's residence to search his room where he found a Nazi pennant bearing a swastika brought back from a visit to Germany in 1937 and a lot of correspondence written by Harper '*which showed the nature of his mind*'. Tried at Ryde Magistrates Court, Harper was found guilty of trespassing and shining a light and was sentenced to three months imprisonment with hard labour.[62]

The Isle of Wight was also the scene of one of the most bewildering espionage cases of the Second World War. Vincent and Dorothy O'Grady had moved from London to Sandown in the late 1930s to run a modest boarding house named Osborne Villa. Vincent had been in the London Fire Brigade and was recalled after war broke out leaving Mrs O'Grady alone on the island with Bob her black Labrador retriever as her only real company. With their guest house 'closed for the duration' Mrs O'Grady took to passing the days

Sandown on the Isle of Wight c1939.

185

taking Bob out on long walks. The problem was that she appeared to be taking a bit too much interest in the military emplacements and was starting to make a habit of walking long distances around fences and defences and finding entry into restricted military areas.

She was challenged by a sentry while in a defence area on the beach between Sandown and Shanklin and aroused suspicion by offering him a bribe to avoid getting in trouble with the police. The sentry had the presence of mind to report the incident and a summons was issued under Defence Regulations for her to appear before the magistrates at Ryde, but she failed to turn up. A warrant was issued for her arrest, but when police arrived at her guest house they found it shut up.

After about three weeks, during which there was a sudden flurry of malicious cutting of telephone wires, O'Grady was traced to a boarding house at Alum Bay where she was living under the name of Arland (an alias she had used back in younger days when she worked as a prostitute in London). Removed to Yarmouth police station, her property was searched and a number of highly detailed maps of the Isle of Wight were discovered.[63] Drawn

The cliff walk from Sandown to Shanklin on the Isle of Wight. Note the RDF towers and antennas of RAF Ventnor over the hillside in the background.

and sketched in her own hand, they showed all the various military defences, gun emplacements and troop dispositions.[64] They would have contained vital information for the enemy planning an invasion of the island.

When archives were checked Mrs O'Grady's past soon caught up with her and her criminal record was found to stretch back to her youth when she was sent to Borstal for forgery and had numerous convictions against her for prostitution. Hinchley-Cooke had interrogated O'Grady at Holloway Prison but still drew a blank when it came to her naming her enemy contacts; some began to wonder if she had made contact at all. Guy Liddell noted in his diary: *'She still refuses to say whether she was acting for anybody in particular. She evidently dislikes this country. I am a little inclined to think that she may be the type of person who has to be in the limelight.'*[65]

O'Grady faced a number of charges, the most serious of which were breaches of the Treachery Act. Her trial was held in camera at the Hampshire Assizes at Winchester. The jury found her guilty and Dorothy O'Grady had the dubious honour of being the first woman to be the sentenced to death under the Treachery Act. On hearing of O'Grady receiving the death sentence Liddell sagely commented: *'Personally, I doubt she is guilty of anything more than collecting information. She probably pictured herself as a master spy and cannot bring herself to say that there was really nothing behind it at all.'*[66]

O'Grady was fortunate to have the conviction quashed by the Court of Appeal on 10 February 1941 and a sentence of fourteen years' penal servitude was handed down for her offences under the Official Secrets Act instead.[67]

* * *

Events over recent years have tragically revealed that fundamentalist terrorist cells and even individuals can undertake vicious and deadly attacks in their own right and groups of Nazi sympathisers with equally dark intent most certainly existed back in 1940. One of the most ambitious plans for an armed rising by Fifth Columnists was revealed by Tim Tate in *Hitler's British Traitors*. It was devised by composer, conductor and expert on the Welsh bardic tradition Dr Leigh Vaughan-Henry, a man who was also a rabid pro-Nazi and anti-Semite. Henry and his confederates had raised eighteen 'cells' of twenty-five terrorists across London in preparation for an armed coup to pave the way for the German invasion forces landing in Britain.

What Henry did not realise was that he had already been infiltrated by two MI5 moles and as he began to ramp up his plans he openly shared them with those he thought he could trust. His ideas were very similar to those of Quisling in Norway and on 10 May 1940 Henry's house was raided and the whole sordid story was told in the report of Inspector Arthur Cain of Special Branch who executed the warrant:

> *In London Vaughan-Henry has organised district 'cells' under 'sergeants' who use code terms and keep in touch with him by telephone. He claims that when all the Government defence authorities in England have been disorganised, his group would come on the streets and assume control.*
>
> *Amongst the documents was a code, which [Henry] stated he had devised for communicating with his wife in Germany. There are also draft plans for a subversive organisation to establish an authoritarian system of Government.*
>
> *The methods to be adopted include illegal printing, a transport section to convey the members in their various activities, an extensive arrangement of accommodation addresses and various aliases for leading members of the organisation. Among Dr Henry's chief associates in these political activities have been Captain Ramsay MP, Jock Houston, Samuel F. Darwin Fox and Norman Hay.'[68]*

There was also evidence of serious negotiations for the purchase of weaponry and munitions to arm the group.[69] Vaughan-Henry would spend the rest of the war interned on the Isle of Man; others would hang for far less under the Treachery Act. Tate suggests a possible reason for his escape from the gallows or even a trial was that Henry's plot included such senior figures from Britain's political and military establishments they could not risk a trial, even in camera, for fear of some or all the names leaking out and becoming known to the public. It could also be argued MI5 would not have wanted to risk the loss of such valuable undercover agents through exposure. The chances are we will never know the truth because the files that name those involved or the exchanges of opinion between MI5 and Director of Public Prosecutions (DPP) don't appear to exist anymore.[70]

MI5's hunt for Fifth Column cells and lone terrorists was on. The men and women who tracked them down – some of them becoming the moles inside the cells – were a diverse patchwork of operatives. Some were members of independent private organisations with no official backing, like John Baker-White's 'Section D'.[71] some were concerned citizens and others were members of the groups who feared what they were part of and its repercussions, reporting their concerns to the authorities. Some had been 'turned' by MI5, others were MI5 agents all along. All of these operatives are usually referred to in the case files simply by title, such as those run by Max Knight who bore designations such as M/F and M/M, while those who were not MI5 agents would be referred to by a title and a letter such as Miss A or Mr B, not only to protect their identities, but to enable them to be used again. Most remain unidentified or their identity the subject of erroneous speculation. One such agent was known only by his operational name of 'Jack King' until files relating to his cases were released and opened for public access at The National Archives in 2014.

It had been speculated that 'King' was in reality the aristocrat John Bingham, 7th Baron Clanmorris,[72] who had worked for MI5 for decades and even provided the inspiration for John le Carré's character, the spymaster George Smiley.[73] The files revealed a very different story. 'King' was in reality Eric Arthur Roberts a 34–year–old clerk at the Euston Road Branch of the Westminster Bank. On the surface he would have appeared to be a very ordinary family man living with his wife and children at Tattenham Corner, Epsom. When the request to release Roberts from his employment arrived at their head office they were clearly bemused how this clerk could be of such importance to the war effort and the assistant controller haughtily replied:

> *… if the Bank were satisfied that the release of Mr Roberts was of real national advantage they would release him at once … However, what we would like to know here is – what are the particular and especial qualifications of Mr Roberts which we have not been able to perceive – for some particular work of national importance which would take him away from his normal military call up …*[74]

How MI5 replied is sadly not recorded, but Roberts was released from his employment. It is almost certain Westminster Bank were never aware, to

Eric Arthur Roberts. A man with 'a particular set of skills'.

Eric Roberts' forged Gestapo identity card in the name of Jack King

paraphrase Liam Neeson's character in the notorious line from the film *Taken*, he had a '*particular set of skills acquired over a very long time*'. This unassuming bank clerk could speak Spanish, French, some Portuguese, Italian and German and would list on his security service confidential personal record his recreations and membership of such sporting clubs as Ju-Jitsu and the Anglo Japanese Judo Club. Significantly, Roberts had also been involved with espionage for years, previously having been Max Knight's first successful infiltrator in the BUF back in 1934.[75]

When the request was made for Roberts to become a fully-fledged member of MI5, the application to Guy Liddell, was written by Francis Aiken-Sneath head of B7, the section with responsibility for monitoring the BUF and other right wing organisations, confidently stated: '*Roberts is thoroughly familiar with everything connected with the various pro-Nazi organisations in this country and Maxwell Knight has the highest opinion of his character and abilities...*'[76]

It would not be long before Roberts had the chance to put all this to the test on his first mission as an MI5 agent. In late July MI5 received a tip off from a former member of the BUF who had got involved with a small group of other former members who were discussing ways and means of continuing the organisation and assisting the Nazi cause by 'direct action'. Specifically, these were throwing bombs in the black-out, sabotage in factories and aerodromes and the passing of information of military importance to Nazi intelligence.

Knight was confident Roberts was the ideal man to travel to Leeds in his first outing under the audacious cover of being a senior BUF operative acting as an agent for the Gestapo. The plan was for the informant to tell the Leeds group that he was an acquaintance of Roberts and would introduce him to them. Roberts would go and meet the group to see if he could ascertain how advanced they were with their plans and to assess their ability to carry them out.

Roberts travelled up on 24 August 1940, planning to stay a few days up in Leeds in a modest hotel. His informant met him and first introduced Roberts to Reginald Windsor, one of the known members of the BUF terrorist cell, in his newsagent's shop on Otley Road. Windsor was a former BUF district leader for North Leeds who had managed to stay under the radar and escaped internment. After preliminary greetings Windsor soon relaxed with Roberts and invited him to come to his private address that evening. In the privacy of his home and with people who he believed to be fellow BUF members Windsor relaxed and over conversation it soon became apparent he was violently anti-Semitic.

The following day, Saturday 25 August, they met again and after meeting a few of the group's contacts Windsor spoke openly about sabotage and arson,

Otley Road, Headingley where Reginald Windsor had his newsagents and the underground BUF terrorist cell held its meetings in 1940.

The Leeds BUF terrorists planned to throw bombs from the top of trams as they passed through streets like New Briggate in Leeds city centre.

particularly his idea to throw bombs from the top of a tram car while it was in motion through the city centre of Leeds. He then bragged of an arson attack on a shop run by a Jewish family on Kirkstall Road, with another former BUF member Michael Gannon, during an air raid alert in early August. Windsor claimed it had been on the spur of the moment and he had started the fire by pushing ignited cotton wadding from a lighter through the letter box of the shop. The fire brigade was soon in attendance and damage was limited, but having started they wanted to continue with bigger and better planned arson attacks and he spoke of being *'very anxious to contact someone in authority who could give him instructions to how best he could get to work.'*[77]

On day three, Sunday 26 August, Windsor organised a secret meeting of former BUF members in the back room of his shop and Roberts was introduced to more of the Fascists. These included Sidney Charnley, the brother of a Hull BUF district leader who had been interned, who appeared suspicious of Roberts, took every opportunity to question him and attempted to denounce him as a police agent. One of Eric Roberts' gifts was he was not easily riled, he remained calm and collected throughout and, being a man blessed with an easy charm and a smile worth winning, he was successful in not only refuting the allegation to the satisfaction of the others present by drawing on his many years as a member of the BUF, but also turned the tables on Charnley so that he came under suspicion. Charnley then addressed the group and spoke more calmly with Roberts.

Charnley was mainly interested in keeping the BUF alive for what he would simply refer to as 'The Day' when German forces would invade Britain. He also spoke of the existence of a shadow organisation which would come into being when the occasion arose. The leader of this shadow organisation, he claimed, was the senior BUF officer Major General J.F.C. Fuller and named an important link with Fuller as 'Colonel Fane, a Fascist leader living near Lincoln'.[78]

Charnley expanded his thoughts: *'If the object was to bring off a revolt and challenge the Churchill Government by force, then he felt that every Blackshirt in the North would obey any order issued by Fuller whether it came from a shadow organisation or not.'*[79]

On 27 August Roberts was introduced by the informer to Miss Angela Crewe, a 19-year-old shop assistant at the Leeds branch of Marshall & Snelgrove's on Bond Street, who claimed that she had contacts among serving officers and could obtain information regarding the location of aerodromes and vital factories in the Leeds district. The subsequent MI5 Divisional intelligence summary contained an account of the meeting:

Though he posed as a German agent he endeavoured to persuade Miss Crew to think twice before going in for espionage. He warned her of the seriousness of what she was proposing to do and asked her if she realised that she was selling her own country. She nevertheless held to her resolve. Her answer to his question as to why she wished to sell her own country was illuminating. It was 'because I am a National Socialist and a follower of Oswald Mosley'. She insisted on collecting information and passing it to R. [Roberts] who agreed to transmit it to the Germans.[80]

Guy Liddell was delighted with the outcome of Roberts' mission:

There have been some melodramatic developments in the case of the BUF at Leeds. There is now a definite conspiracy to obtain military information through a young girl who is friendly with an officer and to pass this information to the Germans. There is also a scheme to obtain arms and explosives.[81]

Shortly after Roberts' return Home Office warrants were imposed on Windsor, Charnley and Miss Crewe but these yielded surprisingly little. It later emerged from a soldier reporting on Windsor's activities, independently of the Roberts investigation, that the old BUF network still had very useful contacts when Windsor told him that he was aware that his letters were being opened through a friend in the Post Office. This explained why Windsor and Charnley did not send Roberts the reports on their plans and activities that they had promised him.[82]

Despite the concern Roberts may now be under suspicion after the discovery of the HOWs, the decision was made he should pay a return visit to the Leeds group. The date set was 5 November and soon after he arrived Roberts found that the group still welcomed him; he was subjected to awkward questions, but as ever Roberts pulled it round again and he soon discovered the group had planned and attempted arson attacks on firms and warehouses in Leeds. Then it came to the crunch: members of the group decided they would set fire to Morley's warehouse on 11 November and Roberts would go with them to keep watch. Roberts ensured the RSLO and the police were informed and in place to deal with any attempt to start the fire. The Leeds terrorists actually used a different door to that staked out by the police but fortunately, yet again, the fire failed to take hold.

As a result of Roberts' findings, it was clear that if the Leeds BUF terrorists were left at large they would eventually cause a serious fire, or worse. Application was made to the Home Secretary for Orders under 18B to be applied to the some of the members of the group involved in the arson attempts, including Windsor and Gannon, and they were duly tracked, arrested and interned. Despite being an *agent provocateur* Charnley had not taken an active part in the acts of sabotage attempts and it was decided '*he might be of more use to the authorities if left at large*'.[83]

With regard to Major General Fuller, the MI5 report on the Leeds cell commented hopefully:

> *Fuller has for some time been the subject of close investigation by this office, but he is extremely cautious and astute. We are not yet in a position to say anything regarding the nature of his activities, but we shall probably have obtained valuable information from quite another source within the next week or so.*[84]

Fuller had now been named in two serious coup attempts, but still he was not arrested as other senior officials of the BUF had been in May 1940. Even Mosley expressed 'a little puzzlement'[85] that 'Boney' had not ended up with him in Brixton. It has been suggested he was protected because of his knowledge and known close associations with other senior officers, including General Edmund Ironside (Commander-in-Chief Home Forces until July 1940) who, it was feared, he could have taken down with him, or at least caused acute embarrassment that would have been crippling to morale at a time when Britain faced invasion.[86]

Despite her attempts at betrayal of her country the efforts of Miss Crewe were so amateurish it was considered, '*She had not and was not likely to do any serious harm by her communications, it would be better to leave her at large in order not to cause any further suspicions in Charnley's mind.*' [about Roberts].[87]

The report on the case published in the Intelligence Summary concluded: '*The case of Miss Crewe in particular shows how an otherwise perfectly normal and decent person can be completely subverted by Nazi doctrines. It is unlikely that the majority of B.U.F members were fanatics of this type, but the movement undoubtedly contained a fair number.*'[88]

Curiously, when brought before the advisory committee during his incarceration in May 1941 Windsor was to claim he suspected Angela Crewe of being a Nazi agent.[89] Her photograph was removed with authority from Windsor's MI5 file as late as September 1961.[90]

Roberts carried on his false flag operations for the duration of the war, notably operating as Jack King, the Gestapo's 'stay behind' representative in Britain working from a block of flats on the Edgware Road. Roberts' flat was rigged with microphones and numerous men and women Fascists were recorded providing him with the locations of factories, arms dumps and military camps and secrets they believed would be of benefit to the Nazi war effort. Some also discussed acts of sabotage.

MI5 even reproduced a few Nazi War Merit Crosses that would appear to have arrived from Germany as a reward to those who remained so loyal to the Reich and provided particularly valuable information. The operation curtailed the actions of many others of similar intent to the Leeds BUF cell and dangerous individuals, every one of them a potential Fifth Columnist, before they acted on their plans. It undoubtedly saved many lives in the process years after the invasion threats of 1940.

Chapter 10

The British Black List

I've got a little list — I've got a little list
Of society offenders who might well be underground
And who never would be missed — who never would be missed!

W.S. Gilbert

The infamous German *Sonderfahndungsliste G.B.* (Special Search List Great Britain), otherwise known as the 'Black List' of British people they would wish to track down and arrest on the grounds they were considered likely to be subversive to the Nazi regime, has become the topic of numerous books and articles over the years. Less known was the German 'White List' of those who they considered would be likely to collaborate in the event of an invasion, but almost unheard of is the British 'Black List', or to give it its correct title, the *List of Suspected persons who might be disposed to assist the enemy in the case of invasion, prepared in accordance with Home Office circular of 24 August 1940.*

Fears of a 'Fifth Column' existing in Britain had rumbled around the press and public rumour since the late 1930s. Before the war a list of some 800 names of German suspects had been compiled by MI5, but the majority of those named on the list avoided arrest by leaving Britain before the outbreak of war in September 1939.[1]

When British forces in France had been knocked into a fighting retreat in the wake of the Blitzkrieg fears of a 'Fifth Column' in Britain rose dramatically. Despite the news media attempting to lift hopes many people were under no illusions. France was falling, Britain was going to be Hitler's next target and the 'Fifth Column' in Britain was limbering up to go into action any day to pave the way for the German invaders.

General Sir Guy Williams GOC Eastern Command had become particularly worried about 'Fifth Column' activity in his area during May 1940. He had been passed a map by Lincolnshire Constabulary which seemed to indicate some plan for a parachutist landing in the area of the Wash and contacted MI5 expressing his belief it was of paramount importance that all members of the 'Fifth Column' should be interned immediately. He made it clear he was prepared to go to the Prime Minister to get the matter addressed if necessary.[2]

The problem was by the nature of the 'Fifth Column' being a secret and shadowy network of spies, collaborators and saboteurs; nobody was sure who its members were. However, as soon as it was given serious consideration it rapidly became apparent there were plenty of likely candidates and the military personnel of Eastern Command started to take matters into their own hands. In one instance they arrested a man (who turned out to have served as an officer with a fine record during the First World War) and kept him and his wife under detention for seven days without any justification except that he had a German sounding name. Guy Liddell noted:

Prime Minister Winston Churchill took a personal interest in the development of Suspect Lists in 1940.

> *Some of the units appear to have prepared a kind of Black List of their own. When the balloon goes up they intend to round up or shoot all these individuals. The position is so serious that something of a very drastic kind will have to be done.*[3]

MI5 officer John Maude was sent to investigate and discovered:

> *... particularly the 55th Division in the Eastern counties have badgered the local people into giving them a list of people with whose bona fides they are not altogether satisfied. If and when the balloon goes up, the military intend to take the law into their own hands and arrest these people. We have got hold of these lists which do not seem to have much in the way of a common-sense basis. One man's only crime appears to be that he is a dentist. Another is a member of the PPU.*[4]

Prime Minister Winston Churchill had also had the lists brought to his attention and was enquiring why the people had not been arrested already. As Maude progressed his enquiries, he encountered the Eastern Command security officer who seemed anxious to cover the whole area with another network of intelligence officers. Maude commented:

Personally, I can see no use for the Command Security Officers except in so far as they may act as a kind of brake on the soldiers, through keeping them assured that things are being done and that of the many rumours which are circulating, the majority are ill founded.

Maude also had a visit from one of the intelligence officers who, when asked what his functions were, said that he was concerned with civil intelligence in the area. He seemed somewhat vague about his duties and in fact when challenged said that he had orders from the senior security officer not to let Maude know what he was doing. Maude was left with the opinion it was hopeless to try to withdraw the lists because he was pretty sure the units concerned would just keep a copy and act upon it, so he suggested that MI5 should work with the chief constable to compile lists of people 'concerning whose reliability there is some sort of doubt' and arrange for them to be arrested by the civil power in the event of invasion. They could then show the military the lists and hopefully put their minds at rest.

There would still need to be issues ironed out, such as how the order to initiate these arrests would be given and under what circumstances and, if a landing is made in one place in the country was it an order to be given nationally or by region affected? It would also need to be established if the police would need additional powers if the scheme was to be adopted.[5]

Just over a month later the Home Office circular of 24 August 1940 authorised all regions to undertake the compilation of their own suspect list. The process was to be carried out by all chief constables and would be submitted to their relevant regional commissioner. Some regions certainly embraced the idea with gusto, the Region 11 Headquarters in Edinburgh was sent returns from chief constables in their area that amounted to a list of some 1,700 names, but after discussions between the regional commissioner and the chief constables approximately sixty names were entered on the Suspect List for Scotland.[6] After the first submissions, sifts and reconsideration, each of the twelve regions of Great Britain ended up with between 46 (Region 3 HQ Nottingham) and 104 (Region 2 HQ Leeds) names on their lists.

Regional meetings of police security officers had been established under Colonel Brook, HM Inspector of Constabulary, in July 1940. These gatherings would usually include the regional inspector, a police staff officer and chief constables and detective superintendents from the various constabularies in the region (in 1940 there were still city, borough and county police in every county). There would also be representatives of officer rank from military units based in the locality (usually the intelligence officer) and similar from both fixed and mobile military defences, a field security officer, field security police, the regional security liaison officer (MI5), RN and RAF security officers and the security control officer for ports.

By the time the suspect lists were established, the regional security meetings had also found their feet, the suspect list was added to the agenda and the forum would discuss additions and deletions and update the group about any persons named on the suspect list who had moved in or out of their area.[7] It was also suggested chief constables should circulate photographs of enemy aliens who they consider might return to Britain as parachutists.[8]

Most of those who ended up on the regional suspect lists tended to fall into two categories: those who had not been interned but had one parent who was German, or were German born and had become naturalised British having married a British man. This may sound unfair but reading the accompanying statements it often appears the person(s) concerned had been outspoken in their support for the Nazis. Others had been active members of the BUF and similar pro-Nazi groups (in some cases they were both). There are a few examples of individuals from other political groups such as the Communist Party of Great Britain, but they are in very low numbers.

Every suspect on the list would be submitted by the chief constable of the area where they resided with a brief case report, although some of these ran over several pages for particularly active Fascists. There were, of course, the obvious suspects, such as those who had been members of the BUF that were described as 'being of the thug type' who had absolutely no regrets for being active and committed members of the BUF, then there were those considered 'a dangerous liar' who tried to mask their associations when interrogated, but continued to spout their pro-Nazi and anti-Semitic beliefs even while they were in detention or even those who saw it as an opportunity 'endeavouring to get rich quick, who would not shirk anything for money'. Phrases such as 'a dangerous person to be at large should an invasion of this country take place' and known to express 'subversive and anti-British views' were frequent comments on the chief constables' case reports.

In its most simple form a recommendation would be like the following example for a BUF activist from Llanelly, Wales. The chief constable of Carmarthenshire Constabulary noted on her file:

In view of the following facts:

1. *Prior to the outbreak of war she was very strong in her pro-German views and has given no indication that these views have since been changed.*
2. *She has attended a Nazi Party conference at which a record of those in attendance was undoubtedly kept with the result that any enemy agents*

would naturally proceed to her home with a view to seeking assistance or information

3. *That she can speak German.*

I am of the opinion that in the event of an invasion or similar emergency she should be interned.[9]

The reports could have come from anyone, from a shopkeeper concerned at the things being said by customers, or things said to and seen by neighbours. The question has to be was it a report from paranoid busybodies? Was it xenophobic or motivated to settle old scores or simply to be malicious? It was up to police, Special Branch, CID and field security police to investigate, but it was down to chief constables to submit the name and the summary of the case and the security committee to be satisfied for them to be included, with the regional commissioner having a carrying vote if required. In every case it seems that names were added to err on the side of caution and would remain on the list until the case had been investigated.

All walks of life could be found on the list, young and old, from retired British Army officers, civil servants and businessmen to teachers, publicans, shopkeepers, domestic servants, roundsmen, factory workers and farm labourers. There was a German-born mother living in Crowthorne, Berkshire who held pro-Nazi views which she shared with her daughter who turned Hitler into her poster-boy and decorated her bedroom wall with magazine pictures of large postcards of *der Führer*. In June 1940 local police had received complaints after the mother had been heard to say that the British people would soon 'be crawling on their haunches' to Hitler and when British losses during the Battle of France were published both mother and daughter clapped their hands and laughed.'[10]

When BUF activists had been arrested their premises and homes had been searched and uniforms and propaganda material were often found, but some certainly took things to a different level such as the district leader of the Maidenhead branch of the Imperial Fascist League whose house revealed when it was searched by police in May 1940: '*two rugs with swastikas woven thereon, two swastika car mascots, two revolvers, two knuckle dusters, 28 copies of Moseley's* 'Tomorrow We Live' *and numerous Fascist, Nazi and anti-Jewish books, pamphlets etc.*'

In another flat on Muswell Hill there was found: '*a complete fascist uniform, a photograph of Winston Churchill with a jack-knife inserted in the throat, a quantity of fascist literature and correspondence,...a rotary duplicator and a bundle of sticky back labels, some of which advertised the New British Broadcasting*

Corporation.[11] Rest assured, they were all added to the Suspect List when they were released from internment.

There were whole families that came under suspicion like the parents and their grown up children in Rownhams, Southampton described in a field security police report in July 1940 as '*all ardent members of the Fascist Party*'. A neighbour informed the police '*a good number of persons visit the house every Sunday evening by car and on foot*'. It did not take much investigation to reveal the house was being used for meetings of the local branch of the BUF. The chief constable of Southampton was satisfied they would be likely to assist the enemy if they had the opportunity and the name of the father of the family was put on the list.

It was even known for a wife to report her husband – such as the wife of a man on the Isle of Wight who was described in his suspect list report as '*a disgruntled and anti-British individual*'. On 6 March 1940 his wife wrote to the Under Secretary of State, saying that her husband hated England and wanted to get to Germany to take part in anti-British broadcasting with Lord Haw-Haw.

Defeatist talk, pro-Nazi talk, Nazi sympathies reported to authorities, anti-British talk, anti-Semitic talk, BUF, Link, Nordic League or Right Club membership; preaching the Hitler doctrine, and associated behaviour such as daubing anti-British messages on walls and signs; distributing pro-Nazi literature; promoting the New British Broadcasting Service; those who were considered likely of collaboration, that had local knowledge of waterways or military installations could all land you on the list if it was witnessed and reported and believed credible by the police. Like the West Wycombe blacksmith who was heard by two witnesses on 16 May 1940, to say '*Germany is a better country than England. England is not worth fighting for; I would not hesitate to help Germans if I had a chance.*'

Another man who had fled to Britain from Denmark in July 1940 and was working in Monmouthshire when he was 'reported for making anti-British remarks'. Two witnesses stated he said: '*If a fleet of planes came over and bombed your dirty little country and they left a little bit of it to me I would see that there was nothing left of your dirty little country.*'

Or even the German-born woman living in Ipswich, Suffolk who was claimed by a neighbour in May 1940 to have said if German parachute troops landed anywhere near her house she would go and welcome them. The chief constable recorded she was of '*hostile origin and in view of her general attitude she is considered a likely person to assist the enemy in the event of an emergency*'.[12] They were all investigated and entered onto their region's suspect list.

Names were removed if the allegations proved false, transfers to different regions were also recorded. Some of those who were interned, but considered still to be a risk, were monitored, a number of them connected with their old cohort of BUF members after their release, and were returned to the list, as were those who in the opinion of their local chief constable *'still had their sympathies lie with Germany and were likely to assist the enemy in the event of invasion'*.[13]

Suspect lists had been initially compiled after the internment of enemy aliens and some members of the British Union of Fascists who had been considered the most dangerous were included. There were, however, still plenty who remained on the outside and were joined in the latter months of 1940 by many of those being released from internment after having faced and satisfied the tribunal that they were no longer a threat – even if MI5 had commented that they felt the release of the individual was not advisable.

It is not thought that anyone on the list was aware that they were on it, but if they did move, their relocation would be noted when they re-registered their identity card the relevant regional committee would be alerted accordingly. Sometimes this process would take as long as two weeks, which was an unsatisfactory situation, especially in one case experienced by the chief constable of Norfolk who had the first intimation of the release of a North Norfolk Fascist with the announcement of the individual's wedding in the local press, followed almost immediately by the arrival of the man himself at the police station to ask for the return of his BUF black shirt and belt. The chief constable considered him *'the most dangerous man in Norfolk'*. He was most certainly put on the Suspect List.[14]

To activate the arrest of those named on a regional Suspect List in the event of an invasion an order applying Regulation 18B (1b) would be sent to the regional commissioner by the Relay Dispatch-Carrying Scheme. Chief constables would then be notified by the Regional Police Staff Officer (RPSO) by use of a code word, (in the North East Region it was 'Meccano' in other regions they would have had their own code words to minimise the chances of the order being given in error) and the arrests would be made. Police would then transport the arrested persons to the collecting centres (often a large military camp with a secure stockade) or prison in their region.

Security officers were asked when advising the RSLO of any suspects whom it had not been possible to arrest, to give particulars of any action taken to trace the missing persons. Arrangements were also made to circulate the description (and photographs where available) of missing suspects through the RPSO and police forces.

Suspect Lists were maintained and updated across the Civil Defence regions until late 1944 when the fear of invasion finally passed after the success of the campaigns for the liberation of North-Western Europe.

Chapter 11

In the Event of Invasion ...

We shall fight on the beaches, we shall fight on the landing grounds, we shall fight in the fields and in the streets, we shall fight in the hills; we shall never surrender.

Winston Churchill

On 27 May, as the first troops were evacuated from the beaches of Dunkirk, General Edmund Ironside, Chief of the Imperial General Staff, was appointed Commander-in-Chief, Home Forces with the heavy responsibility

Issued by the Ministry of Information on behalf of the War Office and the Ministry of Home Security

STAY WHERE YOU ARE

IF this island is invaded by sea or air everyone who is not under orders must stay where he or she is. This is not simply advice : it is an order from the Government, and you must obey it just as soldiers obey their orders. Your order is "Stay Put", **but remember that this does not apply until invasion comes.**

Why must I stay put ?

Because in France, Holland and Belgium, the Germans were helped by the people who took flight before them. Great crowds of refugees blocked all roads. The soldiers who could have defended them could not get at the enemy. The enemy used the refugees as a human shield. These refugees were got out on to the roads by rumour and false orders. Do not be caught out in this way. Do not take any notice of any story telling what the enemy has done or where he is. Do not take orders except from the Military, the Police, the Home Guard (L.D.V.) and the A.R.P. authorities or wardens.

What will happen to me if I don't stay put ?

If you do not stay put you will stand a very good chance of being killed. The enemy may machine-gun you from the air in order to increase panic, or you may run into enemy forces which have landed behind you. An official German message was captured in Belgium which ran :

"Watch for civilian refugees on the roads. Harass them as much as possible."

Our soldiers will be hurrying to drive back the invader and will not be able to stop and help you. On the contrary, they will

Stay Put *and* **Stay Where You Are** *were very much the tone of the early invasion leaflets that also warned of deadly consequences if you did not.*

Fifteen million copies of If the Invader Comes *were printed to be distributed to every household in June 1940.*

Issued by the Ministry of Information in co-operation with the War Office and the Ministry of Home Security.

If the
INVADER
comes

WHAT TO DO — AND HOW TO DO IT

THE Germans threaten to invade Great Britain. If they do so they will be driven out by our Navy, our Army and our Air Force. Yet the ordinary men and women of the civilian population will also have their part to play. Hitler's invasions of Poland, Holland and Belgium were greatly helped by the fact that the civilian population was taken by surprise. They did not know what to do when the moment came. *You must not be taken by surprise.* This leaflet tells you what general line you should take. More detailed instructions will be given you when the danger comes nearer. Meanwhile, read these instructions carefully and be prepared to carry them out.

I

When Holland and Belgium were invaded, the civilian population fled from their homes. They crowded on the roads, in cars, in carts, on bicycles and on foot, and so helped the enemy by preventing their own armies from advancing against the invaders. You must not allow that to happen here. Your first rule, therefore, is :—

(1) IF THE GERMANS COME, BY PARACHUTE, AEROPLANE OR SHIP, YOU MUST REMAIN WHERE YOU ARE. THE ORDER IS " STAY PUT ".

If the Commander in Chief decides that the place where you live must be evacuated, he will tell you when and how to leave. Until you

receive such orders you must remain where you are. If you run away, you will be exposed to far greater danger because you will be machine-gunned from the air as were civilians in Holland and Belgium, and you will also block the roads by which our own armies will advance to turn the Germans out.

II

There is another method which the Germans adopt in their invasion. They make use of the civilian population in order to create confusion and panic. They spread false rumours and issue false instructions. In order to prevent this, you should obey the second rule, which is as follows :—

(2) DO NOT BELIEVE RUMOURS AND DO NOT SPREAD THEM. WHEN YOU RECEIVE AN ORDER, MAKE QUITE SURE THAT IT IS A TRUE ORDER AND NOT A FAKED ORDER. MOST OF YOU KNOW YOUR POLICEMEN AND YOUR A.R.P. WARDENS BY SIGHT, YOU CAN TRUST THEM. IF YOU KEEP YOUR HEADS, YOU CAN ALSO TELL WHETHER A MILITARY OFFICER IS REALLY BRITISH OR ONLY PRETENDING TO BE SO. IF IN DOUBT ASK THE POLICE-MAN OR THE A.R.P. WARDEN. USE YOUR COMMON SENSE.

of the defence of Britain. Roadblocks, sentries and defences had been in place around the coast and in areas considered vulnerable to sabotage by enemy agents since 1939. As the situation declined in France, Ironside ordered measures for the defence of the coast against invasion forces and these were acted on with vigour. Troops set about installing both military designed and improvised roadblocks, digging weapons pits, sandbagging and reinforcing defensive emplacements at vulnerable points across the area, including on the main roads. Orders stipulated a special watch was to be maintained for enemy parachutists.

Ironside and his team of advisers rapidly got to work and Britain was soon feeling like it was on an anti-invasion footing. On 31 May orders were given for all signposts to be taken down, milestones uprooted and all names of streets, railway stations and villages to be obliterated in an attempt to confuse any invading enemies. On 13 June 1940 it was announced the ringing of church bells was banned and henceforth they would only be rung by the military or the police to give warning of invasion to the civilian population. Three days

A Bren carrier passing through one of the many roadblocks on the North Norfolk coast, 1940. Note there are also anti-tanks blocks on either side of the road.

The Norfolk Broads Flotilla patrolling the waterways for enemy seaplane landings, 1940.

later fifteen million copies of the leaflet *If the Invader Comes* were ready for distribution to every household. The leaflet offered practical suggestions for members of the public to help foil invasion forces, such as not to believe or spread rumours, be observant and report 'anything suspicious' to your nearest police station with details of time and place; be aware the enemy might send paratroopers disguised in police and ARP uniforms and if unsure of the uniformed person giving orders, to check with officials you do know before acting on them. It also pointed out:

> *Remember that if parachutists come down near your home, they will not be feeling brave. They will not know where they are, they will have no food, they will not know where their companions are. They will want you to give them food, means of transport and maps … Do not give the German anything. Do not tell him anything. Hide your food and your bicycles. Hide your maps. See that the enemy gets no petrol. If you have a car or motorcycle, put it out of action when not in use. It is not enough to remove the ignition key; you must make it useless to anyone except yourself.*

Once road signs were removed people were instructed not to give directions: 'I'll tell nobody where anywhere is', **Punch** *24 July 1940.*

The leaflet emphasised 'You must not be taken by surprise' but said nothing of resisting the invader. The message which had been said before in official literature and would be repeated again was – 'stay put' unless told to do so by military authorities or members of the LDV. It also warned that attempts to move might just block the roads needed by the military coming to deal with the enemy and, if that was not enough warning, the leaflet also pointed out: *'If you run away, you will be exposed to far greater danger because you will be machine gunned from the air ...'*

As the danger of invasion intensified, thousands of children who had been evacuated to coastal areas in 1939 were evacuated again to safe areas further inland, as were those who had already returned to their families during the 'Phoney War'. Some coastal areas also

General Sir Edmund Ironside was appointed Commander-in-Chief, Home Forces on 27 May 1940.

displayed posters urging civilians not engaged on essential war work to leave and the invasion coast became a restricted area where a person would have to have a permit to reside or visit.

Railway companies issued emergency orders marked 'Secret' which dictated the evacuation of locomotive and rolling stock away from invasion areas and ordered its destruction if it could not be moved. Food officers were appointed with appropriate supplies in the event of invasion and local authorities worked with farmers to plan the slaughter of livestock if they could not be removed, so they would not be of use to the enemy.

Ironside despatched an array of officers on reconnaissance missions to assess the British coastline for beaches and depths of water that would be suitable for invasion attempts, and to consider defences inland. His first priority was to construct a defensive 'crust' along the south, south–east and east coastlines. It was a massive undertaking consisting of hundreds of miles of scaffolding designed to tear the bottoms out of landing barges. Behind the scaffolding tens of thousands of mines were laid and thousands more were on order. Behind the mine fields were evenly spaced lines of 13-ton anti-tank blocks designed to impede enemy tanks and steep anti-tank ditches.

'If the Invader Comes'—How He Will Be Repulsed

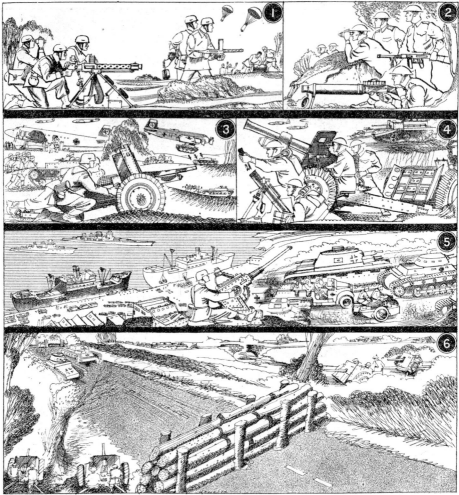

Britain's defence against invasion falls into three main parts :

(A) Timely warning by our air forces of impending enemy action ; preparation at points likely to be threatened first or mainly ; air and sea action against the invaders on the sea and in the air.

(B) Defence of our coastline by fixed and mobile artillery and by aircraft ; naval operations against transports and enemy escorts by our naval forces based on ports, to prevent or limit enemy landings ; shore defence by our land forces, mobile bodies of whom would be rushed to threatened points to reinforce the troops normally massed there ; defence against aerial landings : L.D.V. patrols by night (perhaps later by day), backed up by patrolling units of the regular forces.

(C) Action against any troops landed by the Nazis. Roads would be blocked and defended ; threatened areas would be evacuated of most civilians and brought under military control. Zonal rather than linear defences are probable, and any forces securing a foothold would be isolated and dealt with piecemeal after they had penetrated a little way into the country.
Specially drawn for THE WAR ILLUSTRATED *by Haworth*

OFFENCE

Stage 1.
Parachute troops would be dropped followed by parachute containers with machine-gun, sub-machine-guns, dynamite and ammunition, etc. These troops would be intended to take and hold a given piece of country until reinforcements arrived.

Stage 3.
Large troop-carrying 'planes full of heavily armed shock troops would then arrive. Some of the 'planes would carry light field artillery and heavier types of machine-guns. The Nazis are supposed to have dropped small tanks from the air in Holland. If this is so they would probably be introduced at this stage.

Stage 5.
Assuming that the Germans were able to hold off our defenders, and if they were able to take possession of a harbour or landing ground, they would bring in troop-ships and supply ships. To do this, of course, would mean facing our Navy, including submarine and torpedo boats, not to mention our heavy bombers. If successful they would then try to land medium and super-heavy tanks and various types of artillery. One of the first would be anti-aircraft guns to keep our bombers away whilst they rushed mechanized transport along the roads.

DEFENCE

Stage 2.
Local Defence Volunteers, having spotted the Germans, would give the alarm, and regular troops, armed with service rifles, tommy-guns and Lewis guns, could be rushed to the spot in fast trucks.

Stage 4.
Bren gun carriers mounting anti-tank rifles and Bren guns should be quickly concentrated. These, together with the very mobile gun-howitzer and trench mortar crews, would be able to give adequate support.

Stage 6.
By this time the intentions of the invaders would be clear, all roads would be blocked, and anti-tank devices brought into operation. Heavy mobile artillery rushed into position farther back could pound away at masses of vehicles and tanks thus held up. The Germans would undoubtedly use dive-bombers in an attempt to dislodge strong defence posts. During the evacuation from Dunkirk our fighter 'planes were able to deal very effectively with these dive-bombers. All this time more and more troops, guns and tanks could be brought up and concentrated where needed, and the same process could be repeated wherever and however often the Nazis attempted to invade.

The War Illustrated *shows the weaponry, defences and forces of Britain 'If the Invader Comes' 12 July 1940.*

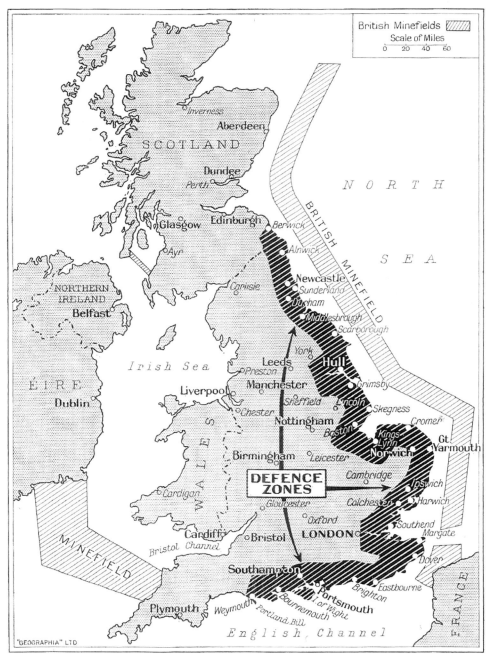

The anti-invasion defences of Britain 1940.

Emergency gun batteries were to provide the most formidable component of the coastal defences. Construction of what were predominantly twin batteries began in June 1940 armed with 6-inch naval guns. Smaller batteries were fitted with 4-inch guns with 12-pounder Q.F. (quick-firing) guns to

One of Britain's coastal defence batteries, July 1940.

cover harbour entrances. However, weaponry issued to the batteries was often far from up to date, many of the guns and their mountings were noted by those operating them to date back to the early twentieth century.

Behind the beach area were huge coils of barbed wire defences stretching across the dunes, interspersed with concrete pillboxes and gun emplacements at strategic positions. At the height of construction during the summer of 1940 some 18,000 pillboxes were built in key positions for the defence of Britain.[1] In answer to scares that enemy troops could be landed by aircraft onto roads, large metal hoops that arched over open roads were installed in many open areas considered vulnerable to such landings. Large lakes, lochs and wide, still waterways such as the Norfolk Broads were also considered vulnerable to troop landings by sea planes and were mined; unmined waterways were patrolled by armed motorboats.

Inland defensive lines or 'Stop lines' were also constructed. The longest, known as the 'GHQ Line', would bisect most of England to seal London and the Midlands from the coast, which was divided into defence sectors. Concentric rings of anti-tank defences and pillboxes were built in and around London which comprised: The London Inner Keep, London Stop Line Inner (Line C), London Stop Line Central (Line B) and London Stop Line Outer

DANGER of INVASION

Last year all who could be spared from this town were asked to leave, not only for their own safety, but so as to ease the work of the Armed Forces in repelling an invasion.

The danger of invasion has increased and the Government requests all who can be spared, and have somewhere to go, to leave without delay.

This applies particularly to :—
SCHOOL CHILDREN
MOTHERS WITH YOUNG CHILDREN
AGED AND INFIRM PERSONS
PERSONS LIVING ON PENSIONS
PERSONS WITHOUT OCCUPATION
OR IN RETIREMENT

If you are one of these, you should arrange to go to some other part of the country. You should not go to the coastal area of East Anglia, Kent or Sussex.

School children can be registered to join school parties in the reception areas, and billets will be found for them.

If you are in need of help you can have your railway fare paid and a billeting allowance paid to any relative or friend with whom you stay.

If you are going, go quickly.

Take your
NATIONAL REGISTRATION IDENTITY CARD
RATION BOOK
GAS MASK

ALSO any bank pension payment order book, insurance cards, unemployment book, military registration documents, passport, insurance policies, securities and any ready money.

If your house will be left unoccupied, turn off gas, electricity and water supplies and make provision for animals and birds. Lock your house securely. Blinds should be left up, and if there is a telephone line, ask the telephone exchange to disconnect it.

Apply at the Local Council Offices for further information.

Private Car and Motor Cycle owners who have not licensed their vehicles and have no petrol coupons may be allowed to use their cars unlicensed for one journey only and may apply to the Police for petrol coupons to enable them to secure sufficient petrol to journey to their destination.

ESSENTIAL WORKERS MUST STAY

particularly the following classes :—
Members of the Home Guard
Observer Corps
Coastguards, Coast Watchers and Lifeboat Crews
Police and Special Constabulary
Fire Brigade and Auxiliary Fire Service
A.R.P. and Casualty Services
Members of Local Authorities and their officials and employees
Workers on the land
Persons engaged on war work, and other essential services
Persons employed by contractors on defence work
Employees of water, sewerage, gas & electricity undertakings
Persons engaged in the supply and distribution of food
Workers on export trades
Doctors, Nurses and Chemists
Ministers of Religion
Government Employees
Employees of banks
Employees of transport undertakings,
    namely railways, docks, canals, ferries,
    and road transport (both passenger and goods).

When invasion is upon us it may be necessary to evacuate the remaining population of this and certain other towns. Evacuation would then be compulsory at short notice, in crowded trains, with scanty luggage, to destinations chosen by the Government. If you are not among the essential workers mentioned above, it is better to go now while the going is good.

Evacuation of all but essential war workers was called for in many coastal and defence areas along the south and east coast of Britain during the invasion scares in 1940.

(Line A) that was built in the countryside north of London from Watford. It followed the course of the River Colne through Potters Bar, Cuffley and Nazeing and then south through Epping Forest, Loughton and Chigwell using natural ditches and rivers in addition to anti-tank ditches and new fixed defences.

In eastern and southern counties, the stop lines were constructed using the same methods, including defending towns and villages with the intention that they would become buffers for holding up the advance of enemy forces if they managed to penetrate the coastal crust. Over 100 stop lines were constructed across the country by the summer of 1940. A central corps size reserve would be created to act as a rapid reaction force in the event of a major enemy penetration. Local mobile columns would also be created to deal with localised attacks and parachute landings. Bridge crossings over the rivers along forward stop lines formed a 'demolition belt' of key structures that would be blown up to frustrate the advance of enemy invaders.[2]

A London North Eastern Railway poster produced in July 1940 for the coastal evacuation period.

IMPORTANT NOTICE

The civilian evacuation of certain East Coast towns on Home Office instructions makes it necessary to suspend a number of ordinary passenger and goods train services in the Eastern Counties while the evacuation is proceeding. After the evacuation, services to and from the areas concerned will be adjusted to suit the new conditions.

During the period of evacuation, tickets can only be issued and traffic accepted to and from stations in the Eastern Counties where services are available and on the understanding that the Railway Companies cannot be responsible for any delay, damage or loss which may arise through the curtailment or interruption of the services.

Once Ironside's plans were revealed criticism was swift. At a meeting of Vice-Chiefs of Staff Air Marshal Richard Peirse pointed out many of the key operational airfields concerned with the defence of Britain would be overrun by enemy forces before they reached the GHQ Line. Meanwhile 3rd Division Commander General Bernard Montgomery – never an agreeable man but a master tactician – reflected the opinion of many of the divisional commanders and would recall finding himself *'in complete disagreement with the general approach to the defence of Britain and refused to apply it'*.[3] 'Monty' expressed his concerns to Churchill during a visit the PM paid to 3rd Division. On a visit to Southern Command Churchill and Sir (Lieutenant General Sir Alan Brooke) held a long conversation during which the pair had the chance to discuss counter-invasion strategy.

Churchill wrote: *'We were four hours together in the motor-car on this July afternoon and we seemed to be in agreement on the methods of Home Defence.'*[4]

One of thousands of pillboxes still standing across Britain in mute testimony to the invasion threat of 1940.

A local Home Guard Platoon on parade at Hackbridge, Surrey. Similar scenes would be repeated all over Britain. The Home Guard stood ready to join in defence their country.

<table>
<tr><td>

ENEMY TROOP MOVEMENTS AND/OR LANDINGS.   REPORTING PROCEDURE.

REMEMBER — Troop movements are essentially of a moving character and information must be fresh to be of use.

ACTION BY POLICE AND WARDENS

RING POLICE H.Q.—ASH 2883/7 or from Police Box (If it is possible without loss of time to report to a nearby H.G. Post, etc. it should be done, but the message should afterwards be given to Police H.Q. as quickly as possible).

IN REPORTING GIVE -

(a) Rank and Name, time and place of origin of report.
(b) Strength and type of enemy seen. (Infantry, paratroops, armoured, etc.)
(c) Exact location & direction of movement.
(d) Time of event.
(e) Whether engaged by our troops.
(f) Any outstanding feature, (disguise, etc.)
(g) Particulars of informant, if event not witnessed personally.
(h) Details of any military unit, etc., informed

P.T.O.

</td><td>

REMEMBER

(1) Speed is vital.
(2) **FACTS** not rumours are wanted.
(3) Report only what is seen.

WHO saw it
WHAT he saw
WHEN it was seen
WHERE it happened

If carrying a message of enemy troop movements endeavour to:

(1) Reach Police Stations or Wardens Posts by detours.
(2) Keep out of line of fire.
(3) Carry verbal messages accurately.
(4) Implement message carried if other enemy troops seen on way.

ACT QUICKLY - SUBMIT ACCURATELY SPEAK CLEARLY

</td></tr>
</table>

A locally produced card to remind Special Constables of what to do in the event of spotting enemy troops.

The conversation crystallised the new approach Churchill wanted in his mind and he had found just the man to implement it. Ironside counted senior BUF officer Major General Fuller as a trusted advisor. The rumblings of a coup involving Fuller had not escaped Churchill's notice either and his fate was sealed. On 19 July 1940 Ironside was called to the War Office and was informed he was to be replaced by Lieutenant General General Sir Alan Brooke as Commander-in-Chief Home Forces.

Brooke called an immediate halt to many of Ironside's defences and implemented a greater emphasis on offensive action to repel any attempted invasion. Under his new scheme Brooke introduced an intricate system of anti-tank 'islands' and three categories of defended localities known as 'nodal points' were rapidly developed across the country:

Category A: Locations not more than 15 miles from the coast, provided good anti-tank defence localities and commanded the nexus of roads.

Category B: Defended towns and villages on routes of re-enforcing formations.

Category C: Defended villages of military and or tactical significance such as road junctions and bridging points.

The idea of the stop lines was to hold the enemy at bay rather than deliver a decisive blow against him, buying enough time to establish the direction of the attack. The units charged with this task were primarily Home Defence battalions, but due to insufficient troop numbers to hold a second or reserve line in strength, Home Guard units in nodal point towns would be deployed into this role along with any available troops, such as fighting personnel from Field Ambulances, Royal Engineer Field Companies and Royal Army Service Corps. With the Home Guard under operational control, these soldiers would be organised into garrisons for towns where the local officer commanding troops of each town would have his defence scheme planned.

In villages and other localities the defences would be also manned by the available local military forces and Home Guard. Divisional military commanders were in no doubt of the dedication of the Home Guard, particularly in the

4th/7th Dragoon Guards with their new standard 'Beaverette' armoured cars at Halstead, Essex July 1940. The urgent need for mobile troops led to the production of these light armoured cars instigated by Lord Beaverbrook, hence the nickname.

forward areas on and near the coast; more than one official report stated confidently, *'They would, if required, fight to the last round and the last man.'*[5]

The defence of the nodal points was intended to allow time to bring up the reserves of troops to counter-attack as the navy deployed at sea to engage the enemy landing vessels and support craft. As defences became more organised it was decided that each nodal point town or village should have its 'keep' made tank proof by means of roadblocks and concrete blocks between houses and that an outpost ring of defences would be constructed on the outskirts. The

Lieutenant General Sir Alan Brooke.

expression 'fortress' came to be used to designate the main inland towns that were selected for fortification along these lines.[6]

Many town centres had their own large pillboxes or defensive structures built into more urban settings and disguised as part of the extant buildings or painted to appear more like the other building surrounding it. Some had their town centre pillbox disguised as a plinth for a statue and even had a figure placed on top of it, others were painted to look like shop fronts, taxi offices, news stands, parked cars, lorries or petrol stations. Disguise was not limited to the town centre defence structures, pillboxes on the coast could also be found painted as bathing huts, as fairground attractions or were even built unobtrusively into historic castles, buildings and ruins. By October 1,697 miles of wire, 440 miles of anti-tank obstacles and 73 miles of anti-tank minefields and anti-tank ditches had been built, excavated and set up across the Eastern Command Area alone.[7]

* * *

While the War Office was concerned with the construction of Britain's defences, ministries with specific portfolios and intelligence services made far less known plans for 'in the event of invasion'. Immediate protection of the Royal family at Buckingham Palace and St James's Palace was provided by the 'King's Guard' drawn from the holding battalions of the Brigade of Guards who also provided guards for the inner defences of Westminster and regularly undertook dusk to dawn patrols in Hyde Park.

216

Their Majesties King George VI and Queen Elizabeth, 3 September 1939.

The first winter of the war from 1939–40 the Royal Family continued to spend the festive season and New Year at Sandringham, but in wartime security had to be increased and a specially selected company of men from the 5th Battalion, The Royal Norfolk Regiment were sent over as 'King's Bodyguard' based at York Cottage. Anti-aircraft guns were installed and security was maintained by specially assigned Metropolitan Police detectives. Armed police officers from Norfolk Constabulary were on the beat around

Norman Gate and Round Tower, Windsor Castle c1939. The king and queen resided here far more often than at Buckingham Palace during 1940.

Sandringham House, the Royal Family's retreat in Norfolk pictured during a public open day before the outbreak of war in 1939.

Norfolk Chief Constable Stephen Van Neck seated centre left with police superintendent on right and the sergeant, constables, plain clothes officer and special constables of Dersingham Police Station that carried out many special duties in and around the Sandringham Royal Estate during the Second World War.

Officers and men of the 5th Battalion, The Royal Norfolk Regiment who provided the 'King's Bodyguard' for the Royal family for Christmas and New Year at Sandringham 1939-1940, photographed in front of York Cottage.

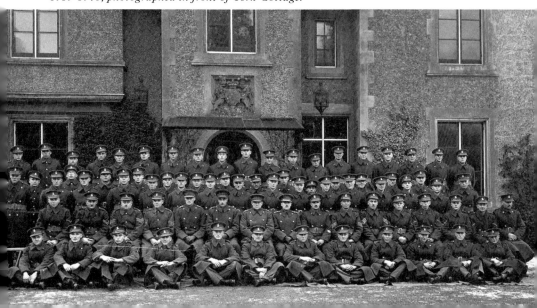

Ruth Urquhart-Dykes, former 'Brooklands Belle' and FANY Driver for HM King George VI inspects the royal pennant on the royal car.

the perimeter and on duty at perimeter entrances to the estate.[8] The small coterie of specially trained drivers for the king and the queen on their official visits was also joined by former racing driver Ruth Urquhart-Dykes, one of the 'Brooklands Belles' who had set a new 'twelve hour' speed record with her husband at Brooklands driving their Alvis in 1929.

On their return to Windsor early in 1940 the royals could rest easy protected by their loyal troops, anti-aircraft guns, a total of ten Bren carriers and two armoured cars specifically for the young princesses.[9] However, as the situation in France declined in May 1940 plans were made for the evacuation of the Royal Family away from the London area in the event of invasion. The man chosen for this secret and sensitive operation was Major James 'Jimmy' Coats MC of the Coldstream Guards. He began by selecting a special company of hand-picked officers and men from the Holding Company, Coldstream Guards, every one of them interviewed personally by Coats, who would travel with the convoy as an armed royal protection squad for what was soon dubbed 'The Coats Mission'.[10]

A small detachment under the command of Lieutenant W.A. 'Tim' Morris, consisting of Lance Sergeant John Thurston and eight other ranks (all of them trained machine gunners) from the 12th Lancers, equipped with four Guy armoured cars and a Lanchester, that became known simply as 'The Morris Detachment', were detailed with the specific duty of the evacuation of the king and queen.[11] An additional troop from the 2nd Northamptonshire Yeomanry equipped with four Guy armoured cars, under Lieutenant Mike Tomkin, based at Windsor Castle, were responsible for the evacuation of Princesses Elizabeth and Margaret in what would become known as Operation Rocking Horse. The armoured cars originally used for the transportation of the royals were far from ideal and were soon replaced by 'Special Ironside Saloons' with specially built bodies by Thrupp and Maberley and armour manufactured by Spear and Jackson of Sheffield.[12]

If mobilised, the Coldstream Guards on the royal protection detail would travel in the royal convoy in Leyland buses driven by men of the Royal Army Service Corps. In turn the convoy would be escorted by motorcycle outriders provided by members of the Military Provost Company of the 1st London Division under the command of the legendary land and water speed record breaker Captain Sir Malcolm Campbell. Their duty was to scout the way ahead for security or traffic issues.[13]

Two principal refuges were earmarked for the royal family: Madresfield Court, near Malvern, Worcestershire, owned by Earl Beauchamp and codenamed 'Harbour' and Newby Hall codenamed 'Security' near Ripon, Yorkshire owned by Major E. Compton. There were also Pitchford Hall owned by Sir Charles Grant and Burwarton House, the property of Viscount Boyne, both in Shropshire, that were kept as reserves. Referred to in the secret correspondence regarding them as 'Accommodation reserved for Special Purposes', the primary houses were fitted with defensive works, machine-gun emplacements, barbed wire entanglements and reinforced shelters in

Territorial Provost Company Commander, Captain Sir Malcolm Campbell on his Triumph motorcycle 1939.

anticipation of the arrival of the 'special guests'. [14] If Britain did appear as if it would fall it was planned for the royal family to evacuate to Canada via Liverpool or Holyhead.

Famously, Queen Elizabeth commented that she could '*finally look the East End in the face*' after Buckingham Palace was bombed, but few realised the Royal Family resided there infrequently during the war, preferring to stay out

Madresfield Court, near Malvern, Worcestershire. Codenamed 'Harbour', it was to be the primary refuge for the British Royal family if Britain was invaded.

of London in Windsor Castle. It was also to the safety of that ancient royal bastion that the Crown Jewels were removed in 1939 for the duration of the war. A story related by Royal Librarian Owen Morshead told of how only copies of the crown jewels were sent over to Canada after it was feared the risk was too great of the ship transporting them being sunk by a U-boat. The king personally dismantled the real jewels along with Morshead and Mr Mann from Garrard's, the Royal jewellers. Queen Elizabeth was also aware of what had been done and the four kept the secret. Once the priceless gems had been prised out of their settings Morshead wrapped the precious stones in cotton wool and placed them inside a glass jar which was then placed in a Bath Oliver biscuit tin and sealed with surgical tape. The tin was then hidden down a 12ft shaft that had been dug beneath an 'obscure little room' situated between the York and Lancaster Gate and the Sovereign's Entrance at Windsor Castle.[15]

* * *

The British Government was not going to take any chances by leaving Britain's gold reserves in the country either and organised for the first £30 million in Bank of England bullion to be sent to Canada in two light cruisers, HMS *Southampton* and HMS *Glasgow*, each carrying fifteen million, that sailed from Portsmouth to Quebec, Canada in May 1939. More would follow but Churchill was not going to risk losing the rest when invasion loomed and under the codename of Operation Fish (as in Gold Fish) the Bank of England gold bullion was packed into wooden crates and taken by a number of heavily guarded trains in absolute secrecy up to the Clyde where it was loaded onto waiting battleships and former passenger liners bound for Halifax, Nova Scotia, Canada.

The bulk of the gold, running to tens of millions, was removed between June and August 1940. The final ship arrived in April 1941 and once all was accounted for the bullion amounted to £470,250,000.[16]. That equates to almost £24,000,000,000 (24 billion) in today's money (2020). The secure vaults of Canada under the Sun Life Assurance Company Building in Montreal and the Bank of Canada in Ottawa held more gold than anywhere else in the world outside Fort Knox. It remains to this day the largest country-to-country transfer of wealth of all time.

The art treasures in the National Gallery were also evacuated from London in 1939 and were initially dispersed to a number of locations including the University of Wales's Pritchard Jones Hall in Bangor, The National Library of Wales at Aberystwyth, Caenarvon Castle, Penrhyn Castle, 'Old Quarries', Lord Lee's country house in Avening, Gloucestershire and a slate mine in Manod, near Blaenau Ffestiniog, Wales. This latter facility proved ideal

In the event of the 'Black Move' being necessary Parliament would relocate to the Shakespeare Memorial Theatre, Stratford-upon-Avon.

A wartime view of The Bank of England (left) and the Royal Exchange, London.

and over the course of the war the galleries beneath the Welsh mountains were enlarged and became the home to the majority of the artworks.[17] The V&A's bombproof stores under the museum were ideal for its smaller items such as miniatures and jewellery; its larger items were evacuated in secret to Montecute House in Somerset. The British Museum followed suit and evacuated treasures to a number of locations across Britain including the Aberystwyth Quarry in Wales and deep underground in London where the Elgin Marbles spent the war in a disused tunnel at Aldwych tube station.

The security of the senior members of government was also planned. Day-to-day two small armoured cars were placed at the disposal of Churchill and the Cabinet.[18] In the event of London suffering extensive damage or facing imminent invasion, the 'black move' was planned whereby our government would evacuate to the West Midlands with Prime Minister Churchill relocating to Spetchley Park near Worcester, War Cabinet Ministers to Hindlip Hall near Worcester, the Cabinet secretariat to Bevere House at Bevere Green and Malvern College. Parliament would sit in Stratford-upon-Avon at the Shakespeare Memorial Theatre, the Lords in the conference hall and the Commons in the auditorium.

*   *   *

But what would happen to the civilian population of Britain? In 1939 an order within the Ministers of the Crown (Emergency Appointments) Act transferred the statutory powers of the Home Secretary, Secretary of State for Scotland and the Lord Privy Seal, to the Minister of Home Security and the Ministry of Home Security was created as a result. The ministry is best known for overseeing the Civil Defence Services of Britain. It was an enormous undertaking that had the oversight of central and regional air raid precaution schemes, Civil Defence organisation, supplies and the provision of gas masks and air raid shelters for millions of people. Indeed, the first minister to head the Ministry of Home Security was Sir John Anderson, whose name will always be associated with the domestic 'Anderson Shelter' that many people installed in their gardens.

In April 1939 the Ministry of Home Security set up twelve Civil Defence regions across Britain, each with an appointed regional commissioner to co-ordinate officials of government departments and local authorities in Civil Defence work. In May 1940 their powers were extended under Defence Regulations to direct local authorities in Civil Defence matters and were empowered to issue orders in, or control entry to, defence areas. Every region also had a 'war room' to collect information concerning air raids, report numbers of casualties and request assistance from other regions, if required, to the central Home Security War Room in London.

Each regional commissioner would have headed quite a team of personnel too. They would have a deputy and each region's 'war room' would be staffed by duty officers, administration staff and telephonists twenty-four hours a day. There would also be specialist officers appointed for specific tasks or to address issues such as refugees, supplies, rehousing of those made homeless due to air raids and the organisation of the clearance and salvage of bomb-

EASTERN CIVIL DEFENCE REGION
OFFICE OF THE REGIONAL COMMISSIONER

Telephone No. : CAMBRIDGE 54237

Telegrams : EMREGCOM, CAMBRIDGE

ST. REGIS,

MONTAGUE ROAD,

CAMBRIDGE.

Our Ref...

Your Ref..

All official communications should be addressed impersonally to the Principal Officer.

Letterhead of the Commissioner for the Eastern Region, 1940.

226

damaged buildings. Regional Information Officers reported to the Ministry of Information and co-ordinated the distribution of government information circulars and public information leaflets. There were also advisers from the Ministry of Works, an inspector from the Ministry of Health, Regional Technical Intelligence Officers and a Regional Security Liaison Officer from MI5.

The problem was that although many regional commissioners were public figures there were elements of their work that had significant security implications and could not be discussed openly. It is likely MPs got wind of some of these additional duties and a question was addressed in the House of Commons to the Home Secretary to explain the precise functions of each of the Civil Defence Commissioners appointed in the London area. Parliamentary Secretary William Mabane replied on behalf of the Home Secretary:

> *There are three Regional Commissioners for Civil Defence in the London Region, the Right Hon. and gallant Member for Hornsey (Captain Wallace), Sir Ernest Gowers, and Admiral Sir Edward Evans. They may in certain circumstances assume the powers of Government; but in the meantime they are engaged in co-ordinating measures of Civil Defence in the London Region and are responsible for certain aspects of Civil Defence delegated to them by the Ministers of Home Security and Health. Admiral Evans is giving special attention to shelters.*'[19]

The assumption of the power of government by regional commissioners 'in certain circumstances' that was broad brushed in the answer given in the House of Commons alluded to an aspect of the duties of regional commissioners the Ministry of Home Security did not want to become public knowledge. The ministry was responsible for the preparation of secret plans of action with regard to the civil population in the event of Britain being invaded, and if communication between government and regions broke down, the primary purpose of regional commissioners was to assume full civil powers in their region. The official letter sent to all regional commissioners on the extension of their powers in 1940 stated:

> *The representatives of the departments who are associated with you have powers delegated to them by their Ministers and normally any authority required for measures taken have been given by them on behalf of their Ministers. If, however, communication with the Government becomes very difficult or impossible, it may be necessary for you to act on behalf of the Government and emergency measures outside the powers of the Departmental representatives may have to be taken without consultation with Ministers.*

In such circumstances you will, on behalf of the Government, take such steps as in your judgement are necessary for the public safety and you will be entitled to expect all persons to give you facilities or assistance in pursuance of their duty to co-operate in the defence of the realm. Such action, duly recorded, will be supported by the Government and Government will ask Parliament to give you whatever indemnification may subsequently be found necessary.[20]

Regional security liaison officers – in effect the field officers of MI5 – had key roles to play in the event of an invasion and drew up action plans with their regional commissioner which would have been presented to the security committee meeting. The first regional action plans in the event of invasion were drawn up in 1940 and were reviewed throughout the war. Many were destroyed with each revision. A rare surviving example exists for No.1 Region in the North East dating from early 1941:

In the event of invasion being directed against this region we must be prepared for a state of confusion, no proper communications, harassed officials and conflicting reports, accompanied by prolonged bombing attacks and flights of enemy parachute troops. Apart from the usual civil security work, etc.

A. *Regional Headquarters will be in constant touch with Military Headquarters and the RSLO will have dual responsibility towards the regional commissioner and Northern command. He has arranged to send after 'stand to' a daily report to 9th Corps headquarters under the following headings:*

(1) Arrests of individual civilian suspects
(2) Sabotage
(3) Activities and capture of enemy agents
(4) Subversive organisations
(5) Rumours
(6) Civilian morale
(7) Riots and panic
(8) Evacuation and subsequent refugee vetting problems

The RSLO would be grateful if police officers would bear this table in mind and keep him informed of any developments under the above headings.

B. *Suspect Lists round up.*

C. *The rich and influential 'peace at all costs with Hitler' man must be disposed of before he has time to do damage.*

D. Large scale sabotage

E. Single enemy 'civilian' agents and saboteurs will penetrate and drop on to back areas controlled by the civil authorities. As long as it is possible to communicate with the RSLO these suspects of course will be held by civil police and dealt with according to present arrangements. If communication with the RSLO is no longer possible it is obviously desirable that the military authorities should be informed and contact should be made with a Field Security Officer and, failing him, the nearest military Headquarters.

F. The spreading of rumour and panic, whether intentional or irresponsible, will be widespread and must be quashed and the offenders punished before either rumour or panic have been given time to gain hold.

G. Evacuation and subsequent vetting problems

The RSLO is particularly interested in any indication that there is a PLOT and in all INDIVIDUALS organising such plot, whether it be espionage, sabotage, rumour spreading or panic making. The activities of the Communist Party and kindred bodies are also of course of great interest. The RSLO would therefore be grateful for reports on all such individuals who are combining in any plot. If any movement passes out of police control and has to be met with military force, it means of course that civil security has probably failed to prevent the growth of the same plot. In such circumstances the RSLO is only interested in the ringleaders, although his office will be making arrangements to prevent any similar uprising in other parts of the region or country. As long as regional Headquarters control any substantial unoccupied part of the region, the RSLO will remain at Regional Headquarters, keeping in close touch with the Acting Inspector of Constabulary, the RPSO and MLO. The assistant RSLO may go to Corps headquarters but it is hoped that a third officer will be sent up to assist in the efficient maintenance of a 24-hour service.[21]

*　　*　　*

Britain was the only country to recruit, organise, train and equip a top-secret resistance network that stood ready to give their all in the event of an invasion. Officially, they were simply known by the innocuous title of Auxiliary Units. In 1940 Colonel Colin McVean Gubbins, a decorated and experienced officer with a particular interest in irregular warfare, was given the task of creating the Auxiliary Units under the aegis of Home Forces. A letter to him from the offices of the War Cabinet outlined their desired objectives for the Auxiliary Units:

A) *They are intended to provide, within the framework of the Home Guard organization, small bodies of men especially selected and trained, whose role it will be to act offensively on the flanks and in the rear of any enemy troops who may obtain a foothold in this country. Their action will be particularly directed against tanks and lorries…ammunition dumps, small enemy posts and stragglers. Their activities will also include sniping.*

B) *The other function of the Auxiliary Units is to provide a system of intelligence whereby Regular Forces in the field can be kept informed of what is happening behind enemy lines.*

The letter went on to point out that each unit would comprise no more than a dozen men, they were to be provided with weaponry and equipped with wireless and field telephone apparatus. Each unit was to be accommodated in specially designed camouflaged and concealed (usually underground) operational bases (OBs) where food, water, weapons and ammunition would be stored. Once training got underway the Auxiliaries were also taught how to disrupt enemy railways by blowing up tracks, destruction of petrol and ammunition dumps and how to immobilize enemy aircraft on occupied airfields.

In practice the Objective 'A' Auxiliary Units were to become known as Operational Patrols and usually comprised between four to eight men in each unit. Patrols would only operate in an area within 15 miles of their base and they would have no knowledge of the other units in nearby villages. In the event of a successful invasion and enemy occupation they were not to communicate in any way with army command; they had to be isolated and autonomous until a successful counter-attack was made, or they were wiped out. All Auxiliaries were warned that their operational life expectancy, if there was an invasion, would about fifteen days – if they were lucky.

Objective 'B' units became known as Special Duties Section and Signals. These units contained both men and women who were trained to identify vehicles, high-ranking officers and military units, and were to gather intelligence and leave reports in dead letter drops. The reports would be collected by runners and taken to one of over 200 secret radio transmitters operated by trained civilian signals staff.

Gubbins began his recruitment drive with a team of twelve hand-picked intelligence officers. When the units had taken shape their expansion, recruitment, administration and training was placed in the hands of officers dedicated to each county. Over the years of its existence these men would be remembered by those who served in patrols under them for both their professionalism and charisma. Among them was surfing pioneer Major

Colonel Colin Gubbins (centre) with Hugh Dalton, Minister of Economic Warfare (right), talking to a Czech officer during a visit to Czech troops in Warwickshire, 1940.

Nigel 'Oxo' Oxenden, Peter Fleming, the brother of James Bond creator Ian Fleming, and a certain Captain Anthony Quayle, the man who would go on to international stardom in such films as *Ice Cold in Alex*, *The Guns of Navarone* and somewhat ironically, he would also play German intelligence service Chief Admiral Canaris in *The Eagle Has Landed*.

Every man who was to serve in the Auxiliary Units had to be very carefully selected. The officers and NCO instructors were mostly drawn from the Regular Army while the members themselves were drawn from the Home Guard and a huge variety of backgrounds, from civvy street to farm labourers, gamekeepers, factory workers and fishermen, to clerics, doctors, dentists, local council officials, aged and from their teens into their seventies. They would need to be resourceful, have the ability, if required, to blend into the countryside around them and have the willingness to undergo specialist training in guerrilla warfare. They would need to quickly become proficient and to follow such orders that they fight, if necessary, to the last round and to the death. Their one common bond was they, above all, had to be able to keep this work a secret. They would find out over time it was a secret that was hard to keep, especially when they faced awkward questions from their wives and were frequently ostracised by their local communities for not appearing to be doing as much as they could for the war effort.

Recruitment of auxiliaries was very cloak and dagger. The potential recruit would often be called upon by name at their place of work by a well-dressed gentleman claiming to be on 'government business'. Only after being taken to an unmarked car or secluded location would the true purpose of the visit be revealed. After a brief explanation of how it was feared that Britain may well be invaded and that an organization was being set up to 'deal with Germans when they get here', the potential recruit would be told he had been highly recommended and would be asked if he would be prepared to join. If he agreed, the potential auxiliary would be told to report to the Post Office, Highworth, Wiltshire where he would present proof of identity to its innocuous looking postmistress Mabel Stranks. She would then disappear through a door and upon her return announce, *'Somebody's coming to fetch you.'* An unmarked transport would then arrive and take our man to nearby Coleshill House,

Home Guard demonstrating a night raiding party at a public display. Such events would be watched by Intelligence Officers for potential recruits for Auxiliary Units.

the top-secret training headquarters of Auxiliary Units. Here, during the war years about 4,000 Auxiliaries were trained in advanced guerrilla warfare including unarmed combat, assassination, sabotage and demolition.

Each county would also have an administrative centre and a radio communications and control station. There would also be local training areas and firing ranges for regular shooting practice and special courses in weapons handling and explosives. Patrols would be instructed in fieldcraft and how to set and deal with trip wires and how to carry out night exercises by army instructors appointed to the auxiliary units. Instructors would be met at agreed, secluded locations by members of the local unit, if he needed to go to their OB he would probably be blindfolded and led there to maintain secrecy.

In the event of invasion the patrols knew their duties only too well due to their training. Most patrols were issued with one hunting rifle complete with scope and they would only know exactly what was expected of them when they opened a sealed envelope that had been entrusted to them. Under their solemn oath they would not open it unless they had received warning invasion had actually taken place.

Sergeant Geoff Deveraux of the Broadheath Auxiliary Unit in Worcestershire recalled one of his comrades opened his envelope and was taken aback to discover: *'one of things he had to do immediately was to eliminate the Chief*

Home Guard Manual of Camouflage by English surrealist artist and camouflage pioneer Roland Penrose.

Wartime Gale & Polden Training Manual for fighting patrols.

Constable'[22] the reason being the local police chief had vetted the auxiliaries before they were recruited; he remained aware of their identities and too many other secrets and he had to be eliminated before he had chance to collaborate or was tortured to tell what he knew. Numerous members of Auxiliary units have gone on record over the years to confirm they too were issued with sealed instructions for the elimination of individuals considered dangerous collaborators, names that undoubtedly came from the Suspect List held by the Regional Commissioner and Chief Constable for their area.

A Northumberland farmer who only consented to give an interview if he was simply known as 'Mr. F.' revealed to *Newcastle Chronicle* reporter Eric Forster in his *The*

DISARMING (PISTOL)

No. 30(a). Disarm, from in Front (Alternative Method)

Fig. 127

Fig. 131

Fig. 132   Fig. 133

How to disarm a parachutist from W/E. Fairbairn's Fall in Fighting.

Secret War series in 1981 that he was the leader of a two-man cell with orders to kill off potential collaborators. He explained: '*There were at least two such cells operating within striking distance of Newcastle ... Each was largely unaware of the other's existence.*'

Each man was '*given the names of two people to be "removed" when the Germans landed in the North-East. They could perform that task by whatever means presented themselves.*' Mr F. refused to name those on the list presented to him; one of them was still alive at the time and he was moved to comment: '*I know him. The horrifying thing is that he has never since shown any potential to become a traitor and had never said anything in public which would give an inkling why he was on a death list.*'[23]

Once they had completed their grim task the men of the Auxiliary Units would then go to ground, allow the main body of the enemy forces to pass and would then rise up and begin 'picking off stragglers and, if possible, messing up bodies'. They had been trained in 'the messing up process' which would involve such things as hanging the dead bodies upside down and mutilation such as castration achieved by the use of cheese wire. That

Home Guard Training chart for tackling an enemy with concealed weapons.

said, Mr F. explained, '*it was my opinion that the only way to survive in those conditions was to make a clean kill and then get out of it.*'[24]

Looking back on events in 1940 the men of the Auxiliary Units would shudder at what they had trained and forswore to do and the reprisals they or their families may have faced as a result but there was not one of them who expressed any doubt; if the invasion had taken place they had been given their instructions and they were quite prepared to carry them out.

German map of the new front and targets against England 1940.

Chapter 12

The Invasion That Never Was

People in England are filled with curiosity and keep asking 'Why doesn't he come?' Be calm. He's coming. He's coming!

Adolf Hitler

There have been claims that there were no plans for the invasion of Great Britain before the Fall of France, but German commanders were only too aware of the whims of Hitler. They were under no illusion and *der Führer* was not alone among the senior military commanders of Nazi Germany in harbouring desires to redress the old scores left lingering after the First World War – to conquer Europe, occupy the countries and bring them to heel under The Third Reich.

German plans for the invasion of Great Britain can be found long before the outbreak of war in 1939. The Luftwaffe had conducted a clandestine aerial reconnaissance of Great Britain since 1936 and feasibility studies for the bombing of Britain had been undertaken since the Munich crisis in September 1938. Even the visits of the *Graf Zeppelin II* (LZ 130) along the East Coast during May and August 1939, despite assurances from Germany that its visits were perfectly innocent, were later to be confirmed as being used to reconnoitre Britain's coastal defences, notably the tall radio towers that had been erected along the North Sea coast from Portsmouth to Scapa Flow. The sites were photographed and the experts on board conducted a series of radiometric tests which suggested the radio towers were involved with some form of radar. Indeed they were part of the then top-secret Chain Home Radio Direction Finding (RDF) known as AMES Type 1 (Air Ministry Experimental Station) which provided long-range detection of aircraft.

The Luftwaffe also pushed their luck, sending formations of their aircraft to within seven miles of the Norfolk coast before turning away during their 'air exercises' in 1939.[1] Fearing bombing or even an enemy commando raid to snatch scientists or technical information from the Air Ministry's top-secret radar research station at Bawdsey Manor on the Suffolk coast, the scientific establishment moved to University College, Dundee in September 1939.

It would appear Hitler's focus up to May 1940 had been on the conquest of his neighbouring countries and France, but he was intent on the conquest

Bawdsey Manor, the Air Ministry's top-secret radar research station on the Suffolk coast, 1939.

of Britain too. In a secret meeting with the chief commanders of his armed forces on 23 May 1939 Hitler proclaimed, '*Our aim will always be to bring Britain to her knees…Britain is the main driving force against Germany.*'[2]

Among the earliest known invasion feasibility studies was the 94-page *Studie Blau*, published three months before Britain's declaration of war in September 1939. It claimed that a strategic campaign in the air by the Luftwaffe could achieve significant damage to the RAF and Great Britain.[3]

Shortly after the outbreak of war, in November 1939, Grand Admiral Erich Raeder selected *Konteradmiral* Otto Schniewind, his Chief of Staff of the *Seekriegsleitung* (SKL), to organise a technical study for the invasion of Britain. Schniewind, in turn, selected a small, hand-picked team led by *Korvettenkapitän* Hans-Jürgen

Grand Admiral Erich Raeder.

238

Gegen Briten und Franzosen

Marsch nach der Melodie: Siegreich woll'n wir Frankreich schlagen
Worte und Musik von Herms Niel

Als Soldaten Adolf Hitlers
ziehen wir zum Kampfe aus
gegen Briten und Franzosen,
niemand bleibt zu Haus, zu Haus,
gegen Briten und Franzosen
niemand bleibt zu Haus, zu Haus.

Deutsche Frau'n und Kameraden,
streitet alle tapfer mit,
nieder mit den Plutokraten,
Franzmann und dem Brit', dem Brit',
nieder mit den Plutokraten,
Franzmann und dem Brit'.

Ladet eure schärfsten Waffen,
drückt auch nicht ein Auge zu.
Siegreich woll'n den Feind wir schlagen
und die Welt hat Ruh', hat Ruh'.
Siegreich woll'n den Feind wir schlagen
und die Welt hat Ruh', hat Ruh'.

Haben wir den Feind vernichtet,
pflanzt nach gutem deutschem Brauch
auf das Grab des Kameraden
einen grünen Lorbeerstrauch,
auf das Grab des Kameraden
einen grünen Lorbeerstrauch.

Refrain: Lebe wohl, mein Kind, denn im Westen pfeift der Wind, der Wind.
Leb wohl, Mütterlein, heut muß geschieden sein.

German song card of German forces against France and Britain.

HORN'S Bildkarte

„...Denn wir fahren gegen Engeland!"

Heute wollen wir ein Liedlein singen,
trinken wollen wir den kühlen Wein,
und die Gläser sollen dazu klingen,
denn es muß, es muß geschieden sein.

Kommt die Kunde, daß ich bin gefallen,
daß ich schlafe in der Meeresflut,

Unfre Flagge und die wehet auf dem Mafte.
Sie verkündet unfres Reiches Macht,
denn wir wollen es nicht länger leiden,
daß der Englifchmann darüber lacht.

weine nicht um mich, mein Schaß, und denke:
Für das Vaterland, da floß fein Blut.

Kehrreim: Gib mir deine Hand, deine weiße Hand, leb wohl, mein Schaß,
leb wohl, mein Schaß, leb wohl, lebe wohl; denn wir fahren, denn wir fahren,
denn wir fahren gegen Engeland, Engeland!   H. LÖNS

Aus der Sammlung „Der kleine Rosengarten", Verlag von Eugen Diederichs, Jena

One of a series of German propaganda postcards promoting German forces against Britain 1940.

Reinicke who took two weeks to draft out a brief of twelve pages outlining a scheme of invasion entitled *Studie Röt* (Study Red). This suggested a narrow beachhead assault of around 60 miles along the south coast of England but took pains to warn of the numerous factors against its success, such as the strength of the British coastal artillery, mobile troops and the threat posed by British submarines. Indeed, they only envisaged any chance of success if both the Royal Air Force and the Royal Navy had been defeated.[4]

A copy of *Studie Röt* was sent to *Oberkommando des Heeres* (OKH), the high command of the German Army under General Walter von Brauchitsch who ordered a German Army general staff study of their own. He turned to Colonel Heinrich von Stülpnagel his head of Army Operations who selected Major Hellmuth Steiff, a young officer who had come to prominence for his organisational skills, to co-ordinate the project. What resulted was *Studie Nordwest* that proposed an assault launched from Low Country ports. It would be the responsibility if the *Kriegsmarine* to neutralize the Royal Navy and clear mines as the invasion flotilla, complete with its own specially designed landing craft, crossed the North Sea. It would also fall to the *Kriegsmarine* to provide the covering fire for the main landings as they were made along the east coast of England from the Wash to the Thames estuary, with a beachhead created in the Great Yarmouth-Lowestoft area.[5]

Far more positive and driven in its outlook, surprise would be the key. A diversionary attack north of the Humber would draw troops up from Norfolk and Suffolk as a division of paratroops fell inland behind them. Three or four infantry assault divisions would make their landings at carefully selected beaches along the East Anglian coast, followed by two panzer divisions and motorised troops. As they moved inland from the coast, a third wave would then hit the beaches and move rapidly inland with the objective of cutting off London.

The OKH plan was ambitious, it would require landing craft to carry over 100,000 men. The problem they had was the sheer lack of resources, the sizes of ports such as Great Yarmouth and Lowestoft were not suitable for the vast amount of supplies required and, no matter how many troops were quoted, they still needed to cross the Channel. Germany simply did not have the number of landing craft required and they would still need to knock out the RAF and the Royal Navy.[6]

As soon as the Allied forces in France began to fall into retreat the *Kriegsmarine* revisited *Studie Röt*, placing the matter in the hands of *Konteradmiral* Kurt Fricke who drew up the new *Studie England* report of 27 May 1940. The old threat of RAF and Royal Navy were still recognised, as were the issues over landing craft, the necessity to neutralize anti-parachutist defences in

German forces marching through St Peter Port, Guernsey 1940. The Channel Islands were the nearest the Germans came to occupying Britain.

drop zones and natural hazards of weather conditions and tides. However, although it was more of a check list of 'things to do', it had a drive about it that appealed to many who read it and some solutions were offered. It was suggested the Royal Navy ships could have been kept at bay by lining the flanks of the invasion forces with mines; optimum conditions for an invasion crossing could be predicted from tide charts and weather reports. Significantly *Studie England* suggested shifting the area of the planned landings from East Anglia to the south coast of Britain, a far closer option of around 21 miles across the Strait of Dover, once German forces had consolidated their victory in France.[7]

Generalfeldmarschall *Erhard Milch.*

Generalfeldmarschall Erhard Milch, the Inspector General of the Luftwaffe was one of those who pondered the invasion question and, being only too aware that the RAF needed to be crushed before an invasion was launched, came up with the daring suggestion that this could be achieved by paratroops who would seize airfields in southern England providing safe landing grounds for fleets of Ju52 troop transporter aircraft for more men, ammunition and weapons. Ten infantry divisions could then be shipped across the Channel to push on and conquer Britain.

Göring resented Milch, his deputy, for his original thinking and ran the idea past Hitler knowing full well he would turn it down because he was still holding out hope that Britain would agree peace terms after the Fall of France. If the plan had been carried out at that time the Luftwaffe did not have sufficient troop transporter aircraft to get the requisite number of paratroops over the airfields to carry out the operation.

On 20 June 1940 Major Gerhard Engel noted: *Von Brauchitsch briefed the Führer on the urgent need either to make peace with Britain or prepare to carry out an invasion as soon as possible. The Führer is sceptical and considered Britain so weak that, after bombing, land operations will be unnecessary. The army will move in and take up occupation duties.*[8]

Hitler clung on to his belief Britain would come to terms and a peace agreement would be achieved and, for the time being at least, his mind was focussed on France. Some of his military staff urged caution, others were keen to capitalise on the victory and did not wish to not lose the impetus to press on.

On 26 June 1940, buoyed up by the final surrender of France, General Franz Halder, OKH Chief of Staff noted in his diary *'It is not impossible that we shall be compelled to land in England.'*[9] Despite all the carefully worded cautions in all *Studie* produced to date, there were still those who suggested to Hitler that an invasion could be possible, some of them no doubt wishing to placate the *Führer* with positive ideas rather than the more risky path of giving emphasis to the impracticalities.

Hitler had grown impatient with Britain, he wanted peace agreed, on his terms of course, and was not afraid to use force to achieve it. He ordered Generals von Brauchitsch and Halder to a conference on 13 July. The meeting lasted just two hours, and all three seemed to steam through the plans, save the *Führer*'s usual obsession with the danger presented by coastal artillery; but for the most part they shared one vision in what was required in the preparations for invasion. General Halder recorded: '*Recommendations are as a basis for practical preparations. Order for practical preparations, which are to start immediately, given.*'[10]

Hitler issued *Führer* Directive No.16 *On preparations for a landing against England on 16 July 1940*, in which he brayed:

> *Since England, despite its hopeless military situation, still gives no sign of any readiness to come to terms, I have decided to prepare for an invasion of that country and, if necessary, to carry it through. The aim of the operation will be to eliminate England as a base for carrying on the war against Germany and should it be requisite, completely to occupy it.*

The code name for the assault would be *Unternehmen Seelöwe* – Operation Sealion.

* * *

Even before the First World War, German military planning, at least on paper, was renowned for its thoroughness. The likes of Sir Ian Hamilton would bemoan his lack of brief for the Gallipoli campaign, believing that had he been a German general he would have been provided with meticulously detailed plans that would have been compiled months or even years before just in case a need for them arose.[11] As we have seen in the previous chapters intelligence gathering for Nazi coercion and military purposes was carried out by an array of Germans, both resident and visiting Great Britain, throughout the 1930s, especially those under the guise of students, reporters, businessmen, engineers, servants, sportsmen, tourists and even Hitler Youth 'spyclists'.

By 1940 the box files of the German intelligence services were bulging with a wealth of British material. There were photographs from holiday snapshots to reconnaissance photographs, travel guides, holiday brochures, gazetteers, ordnance survey maps and business prospectuses, many of which followed the new vogue for including aerial photographs of the city, port or county town they wished people to visit or the impressive factory they wished to encourage people to trade with. All of this would now be drawn upon to compile a military guide for German forces on a very unwelcome visit to Great Britain.

It has often been suggested these guides were prepared in haste when the decision was made to invade Britain. The production was undoubtedly rapid, but preparation of the guides was the fruit of years of research. *Abteilung für Kriegskarten und Vermessungswssen (IV.Mil.-Geo.)*, the German Army High Command Department IV Military Cartography and Surveying, known as Mil-Geo IV, for short, had begun as a small unit in the 9th Division of the German general staff operating from a central office, often simply referred to as 'Zentrale' in Berlin, in 1935. It consisted of a total of eight staff including their 'chief,' Colonel Schmöckel, draftsmen-photographers, a librarian, filing clerks and typists. Regional offices were also set up across Germany to undertake surveys and research to ensure the records held at Zentrale were as up to date as possible, ready for when the next edition of the maps was printed. Zentrale had also received, collated and indexed material from German intelligence services that had been obtained by their 'researchers' abroad for years before the outbreak of the war.[12]

As military operations began to be prepared during the summer of 1939 the staff at Zentrale were joined by geographers from four of their regional offices and an additional typist. While Hitler's campaigns rolled out across Europe Mil-Geo IV established outposts in countries as they were occupied and recruited military geographers of all ranks (it was their knowledge that mattered) and brought in university professors with specialist knowledge to prepare a number of country studies. With necessary additional clerks to deal with the growing workload, Zentrale had expanded to around twenty-five staff in four divisions by 1940:

1. *Referat Inland* (Germany)
2. *Referat Ausland Öst* (German occupied territory East: Lithuania and Poland)
3. *Referat Ausland West* (German occupied territories West: Netherlands, France and Belgium)
4. *Referat Ausland Süd* (German occupied territories South: Czechoslovakia.)[13]

Militärgeographische Einzelangaben über England

Objektbilder

zu den militärgeographischen Objektkarten 1:250000 und 1:10000
der Mappe

9

Ost-Anglia

Abgeschlossen am 30. September 1941

Generalstab des Heeres
Abteilung für Kriegskarten und Vermessungswesen (IV. Mil.-Geo.)
Berlin 1941

Cover of the German military geographical guide to East Anglia 1941.

So, when the call came for the military guides for Britain in late June 1940, *Mil-Geo IV Zentrale* were well-honed in such projects. They had already collated and indexed a considerable amount of material and in some cases it was already prepared, consequently they were more than capable of producing *Militärgeographische Angaben über England,* (the term England was often used in German parlance to refer to the whole of Great Britain) in quick time as a reliable compendium of maps and guides for invasion forces aimed at the conquest of Great Britain.

The set, first published in August 1940, consisted of three thick A5 and A4 card folders containing booklets packed with hundreds of half-tone photographs showing bridges, factories and landmarks by region. There were city plans, road maps of over 160 British towns, gazetteers and a series of 1:1,000,000 scale maps including an isorhythmic map of population densities, and maps of the telephone system and radio installations, the electricity grid, waterways and transport systems. *Militärgeographische Angaben über England* provided German military commanders planning Operation Sealion with accurate geographical information including an *Objektverzeichnis* [object dictionary] that identified and described strategic targets, provided images

246

The Riverside Works of Boulton & Paul, Norwich copied from a pre-war factory catalogue to create one of the illustrations for **Militärgeopraphische** Angaben über England *guide.*

to assist the German forces to recognise landmarks in the area where they were landing and would provide valuable information for after the area was consolidated and occupied.

Folder A covered England and Wales by region, including street plans of cities and towns. Folder B surveyed London in photographs and maps and Folder C provided booklets of photographs and maps of the English coast aimed at providing the German senior officers with information about the beaches and terrain where they would be landing.[14] There was even a booklet of English place names with how they should be pronounced.[15]

Most of the maps did not have to be redrawn, lithographs of British ordnance survey maps with a few details and keys around the border in German and the street plans of the towns and cities were taken from standard gazetteers originally produced in the UK. What they did innovate, however, were the illustrated guides showing landmarks, the *Operationskarte* that was created to show types of terrain, its 'trafficability' and in some cases even suggested billeting capacity. Military and Naval Geo also worked together to develop the maps and guides to the coastal areas of the south

247

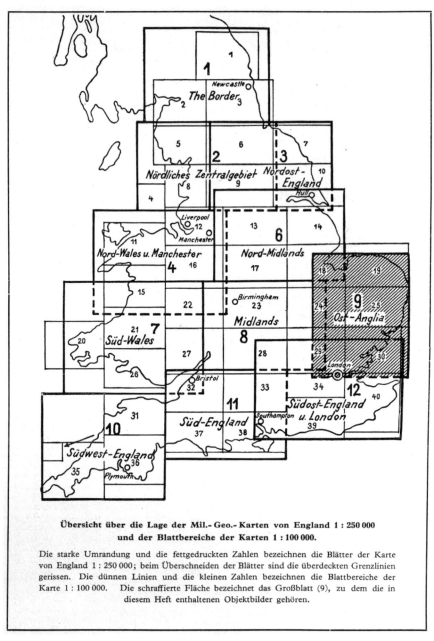

Übersicht über die Lage der Mil.- Geo.- Karten von England 1 : 250 000
und der Blattbereiche der Karten 1 : 100 000.

Die starke Umrandung und die fettgedruckten Zahlen bezeichnen die Blätter der Karte
von England 1 : 250 000; beim Überschneiden der Blätter sind die überdeckten Grenzlinien
gerissen. Die dünnen Linien und die kleinen Zahlen bezeichnen die Blattbereiche der
Karte 1 : 100 000.   Die schraffierte Fläche bezeichnet das Großblatt (9), zu dem die in
diesem Heft enthaltenen Objektbilder gehören.

Guide to the map sheets in the Militärgeographische Angaben über England.

where the invasion forces proposed to make their landings .[16] It is, however,
interesting to note that although there was rivalry between the various
German forces 'Geo' units they would co-operate when required, but in
the case of *Militärgeographische Angaben über England* there is little or no

indication of input from the Luftwaffe and their target maps for strategic air operations remained a separate entity.

*　　*　　*

The finalised orders for Operation Sealion were issued by General von Brauchitsch, Commander-in-Chief of the Army HQ OKH General Staff/Operations Branch on 30 August 1940:

Instruction for the Preparation of Operation Sealion
Proposed Method of Execution
a) *The Luftwaffe will eliminate the British air force and the armament production which supports it and it will achieve air superiority. The Navy will provide mine-free corridors and supported by the Luftwaffe, will bar the flanks of the crossing sector.*

b) *The Army's landing forces will win local bridgeheads with the specially equipped forward echelons of the first-wave divisions. Immediately afterwards, they will widen these bridgeheads into a connected landing zone, the possession of which will cover the disembarkation of the following troops and ensure early uniform control on the English shore. As soon as sufficient forces are available, an offensive will be launched towards the first operational objective, i.e. Thames estuary-heights south of London-Portsmouth. As the British will make counter-attacks against the German troops who have landed first, and as they will resist with every means further German gains in terrain, bitter fighting is to be expected. Command and organization of troops must be equal to the decisive significance of these initial actions.*

c) *After gaining the first operational objective, the further task of the Army will be as follows: to defeat the enemy forces still holding out in southern England, to occupy London, to mop up the enemy in southern England, and to win the general line Maldon (north-east of London) –Severn estuary.*
     Orders concerning further tasks will be issued at the proper time.

d) *The current enemy situation, as before, will be periodically forwarded to army groups and armies.*

<u>*Command and organization of forces*</u>
At first, Army Group A (with 16th and 9th Armies) will be entrusted with the execution of the tasks allocated to the Army. Whether elements of Army Group B will also be employed as operations proceed depends on the development of the situation.

Tasks of army groups and armies

a) *Army Group A's task. Beginning on orders from OKH, the Army Group will force a landing on the English coast between Folkestone and Worthing; and it will, first take possession of a beachhead, where the landing of further forces, aided by artillery fire in the direction of the sea, can be ensured and where it will be possible to create the preliminary conditions for continuing the attack. Early utilization of dock installations on the enemy coast is desirable for the rapid disembarkation of following forces.*

  After the arrival of sufficient forces on English soil, the Army Group will attack and secure possession of the line Thames estuary-heights south of London-Portsmouth. As soon as the situation permits, mobile formations will be pushed forward to the area west of London in order to isolate it from the south and west and to capture crossings over the Thames for an advance in the direction of Watford–Swindon.

b) *Initial tasks of armies. 16th Army will embark in the invasion ports situated between Rotterdam (incl.) and Calais (incl.). Landing on a broad front on the Folkestone-Hastings (incl.) section of coast, the Army will occupy an area at least as far as the line: heights halfway between Canterbury and Folkestone–Ashford–heights 20km north of Hastings. Speedy capture of the dock installations at Dover is important. The Ramsgate–Deal section of coast, which, for naval reasons, can only be approached when the coastal defence is eliminated, must be taken from the landward side as soon as possible.*

  Arrangements will be made to use paratroops for the speedy capture of the high ground north of Dover: this operation will take place at the same time as the landing. 9th Army, landing simultaneously with 16th Army between Bexhill and Worthing, will occupy a beachhead at least up to the line: heights 20km north of Bexhill to heights 10k. north of Worthing. It must be realized that only the first echelons of three first-wave divisions can be shipped across the Channel for the Army direct from Le Havre; the fourth division and the later echelons and waves, starting from Boulogne, must cross under the screen cover of 16th Army better-protected crossing-sectors, and must be disembarked east or west of Eastbourne as the situation dictates. The use of paratroop units for the capture of Brighton will be arranged.

  Boundary line between 16th and 9th Armies: Boulogne (9) – Hastings (9) – Reigate (16).

  Separate orders will be issued regarding the time of landing on the English coast. The intention is to land at daybreak. Dependence on weather and tides, however, may necessitate a landing in broad daylight.

> *In this case, extensive use of smoke is ordered (with the aid of aircraft, vessels, and artillery).*
>
> *(c) Army Group B's task. Army Group B will not participate in the initial phase of the operation. If the naval situation develops favourably, the Army Group, starting from Cherbourg, may be employed later to force an air and sea landing in Lyme Bay, and to occupy, first, Weymouth and the high ground 20km. north of Weymouth – 15 km north of Lyme Regis. From here, an advance would, on instructions from OKH, be made in the direction of Bristol. Captain for Later, elements of Army Group B may receive the task of occupying the counties of Devonshire and Cornwall.*
>
> *Army Group B will, in conjunction with the naval authorities, decide on embarkation ports and determine their capacity. Its landing troops will be assembled in readiness, so that, on orders from OKH, they can be brought up for embarkation within five days. The following instructions for assembly and organization of forces, which primarily concern Army Group A, are also valid, where applicable, for Army Group B.*

A further, secret adjunct to the invasion plan was the abduction of the British Royal Family so they could be used as a bargaining counter to obtain a cease fire among British forces, curtail resistance and perhaps even hasten a surrender. A similar attempt had only narrowly missed Queen Wilhelmina of the Netherlands on 10 May 1940. *SS-Hauptsturmführer* Otto Begus, the man who had led the Wilhelmina Kommando snatch squad was given the mission to kidnap King George VI, Queen Elizabeth and Princesses Elizabeth and Margaret and even Queen Mary. Begus was supplied with recent photographs of each of the royals and plans of Buckingham Palace and its grounds. The plan was to utilize the grounds of Buckingham Palace as a drop zone for 400 parachute troops to take on the defending

General Walter von Brauchitsch, Commander in Chief of the German Army, the man who would have been in command of the occupation forces of Britain, 1940.

251

forces, followed close behind by a further 100 parachute troops including Begus's team with the specific mission to rush the royal apartments and secure the members of the royal family present there. Begus was even given instructions for him and his men to observe:

On entering the presence of Their Majesties, we were to salute in a manner of the German Armed Forces [not a Nazi salute]. *Whoever captured a member of the royal family was to address them in English as follows: 'The German High Command presents its respectful compliments. My duty, on the instructions of the Führer is to inform you that you are under the protection of the German Armed Forces.'*[17]

* * *

Hitler had made it clear if invasion was successful it would have been the German Army that would take up occupation duties and a number of proclamations were prepared in anticipation. One of the first series were to be from the immediate military commander, General von Brauchitsch:

Proclamation to the People of England

1. *English territory occupied by German troops will be placed under military government.*
2. *Military commanders will issue decrees necessary for the protection of the troops and the maintenance of general law and order.*
3. *Troops will respect property and persons if the population behaves according to instructions.*
4. *English authorities may continue to function if they maintain a correct attitude.*
5. *All thoughtless actions, sabotage of any kind and any passive or active opposition to the German armed forces will incur the most severe retaliatory measures.*
6. *I warn all civilians that if they undertake active service operations against the German forces, they will be condemned to death inexorably.*
7. *The decrees of the German military authorities must be observed; any disobedience will be severely punished.*

The proclamation would have been published on the front cover of all newspapers. Its tone and content is very much in line with all other proclamations posted up immediately after the entry of German occupation forces to conquered countries, and there is no reason to suppose Great Britain

Gauleiter *Ernst Bohle, the man tipped to be* Reichsprotektor *of Britain in the event of a successful invasion.*

SS-Standartenführer *Dr Franz Alfred Six who would have been Chief of the SD in Britain, photographed after capture and facing trial for war crimes in 1948.*

would have enjoyed any favour or more lenient treatment than any other country subjugated under the Nazi heel.

Even those who had demonstrated their support for Nazism through membership of BUF and the various pro-Nazi forums would be little more than tools to the ends of the Nazi occupation forces. There would have been no seat at the right hand of Hitler for Moseley, Fuller or any of their cronies, even if they thought they had handed the Nazis the country on a plate after an armed coup at the seat of power. The *Gauleiters* for Britain would have been the military commanders that had taken the regions assigned to them before the invasion.

The more political appointment of *Reichsprotektor* would follow to establish Nazi government in Britain. The man tipped for the job was *Gauleiter* Ernst Bohle the leader of the *Auslandsorganisation*. Born in Bradford, Yorkshire to German parents, he had moved with his family to South Africa in 1906 and returned to Germany in 1914. Bohle was fluent in German and English and had acquitted himself well in Britain before the war. He was on the staff of Hitler's deputy, *Reichsminister* Rudolf Hess and had even been tipped in the foreign press as a successor to Ribbentrop.[18]

* * *

One of the most sinister forces would also have arrived with the occupation forces, the *Sicherheitsdienst* (SD), the Nazi Security Police. The man selected by Reinhard Heydrich as the Chief of the SD in Britain was an odious individual, *SS-Standartenführer* Dr Franz Alfred Six, the head of *Amt VII* the 'idealogical research' department at the *Reichssicherheitshauptamt* (RSHA) Reich Security Main Office. His appointment document explains his duties and authority:

> *Reichsmarschall Göring decided on 1.8.40 that the Reichsführer SS's Security Police will commence their activities simultaneously with the military invasion in order to seize and combat effectively the numerous important organisations and societies in England which are hostile to Germany. Your task is to combat, with all requisite means, all anti-German organisations, institutions, opposition and opposition groups which can be seized in England: to prevent the removal of all available material and to centralise and safeguard it for future exploitation.*[19]

To gain some idea of how Six would have operated and what actions he would have undertaken one only needs to see the likes of Adolf Eichmann in Prague. Indeed, the pair were acquainted and there is every reason to believe Six would have followed his methods of moving into occupied countries with streamlined arrangements for the extermination of Jews. Britain's Jews, men, women and children, like other Jews in Western Europe were destined for the gas chambers of Auschwitz, Treblinka and Birkenau. Homosexuals, the mentally ill, people with physical disabilities, TB Patients, many Freemasons and gypsies would have all faced similar fates. All the horrors seen in Nazi-occupied countries in Europe could have been inflicted on Britain.[20]

To assist them in their task was a book, *Informationsheft GB*, which had, like the *Militärgeographische Angaben über England*, also been collated in June 1940 but in the case of this volume it was the work of a small *Sicherheitsdient* (SD) team headed by *SS-Oberführer* Walter Schellenberg, Chief of *Amt VI* and his deputy and comrade in the Venlo Incident, SS-*Hauptsturmführer* Walter Christian.

It was a very different volume indeed. *Informationsheft GB* was a classified document of little or no use to the front line soldier, instead it was in effect a field guide for the Gestapo, a potted history of every British organisation or faith that could potentially pose a threat or cause offence to the Nazi regime, be they Jews, Catholics, Methodists, Freemasons, refugees, Boy Scouts, Trade Unionists, Communists or Marxists. Royalty was declared 'obsolete' and a host of other organisations were described so they could be identified and dismantled by the Nazi Security Police. Dr. Six already had his team from *Amt VII* with their remits allocated:

Jews (to be immediately arrested) to be rounded up by 'Jewish expert' *SS-Hauptsturmführer* Rudolf Richter.

Freemasons (to be immediately arrested) were to be dealt with by *SS-Hauptsturmführer* Dr Rudolf Levin.

Churches and all ministers to be investigated by Protestant church expert *SS-Hauptsturmführer* Kurt Stiller.

Liberal organisations, political parties etc to be examined by *SS-Hauptsturmführer* Horst Kunzer and *SS-Hauptsturmführer* Helmut Jonas.

Communists and Marxists to be dealt with by *SS-Hauptsturmführer* Dr Horst Mahnke.

At the rear of the handbook was *Die Sonderfahndungsliste GB*, [The Black Book] the special wanted list which contained the names of 2,820 individuals, organisations and establishments in Great Britain that would be of 'special interest' to the Nazi occupation forces. The spellings and the inclusion of the names of some who had already passed away or emigrated bore mute testimony

Seagoing barges arriving in a French port to join the invasion fleet 1940.

Gebirgsjäger *practising a beach landing from a converted barge, France 1940.*

Gebirgsjäger *(note the edelweiss badge on his cap) 'climbing fish' putting on life vests ready for another practice landing, France 1940.*

PAK gun teams on the turntable of a manually pivoted wooden platform that simulated the movement of an invasion barge at sea for gunnery practice, France 1940.

to the haste with which the arrest list was drawn together. Nonetheless there were plenty more on the list to keep the *Einsatzgruppen* (death squads) – Dr Six planned to be established in London, Bristol, Birmingham, Liverpool, Manchester and Edinburgh – more than busy.

Across the Channel barges from France and its occupied neighbours were being brought to ports where the German invasion fleet was being assembled. There they would be converted to have fall-front ramps to enable rapid loading and unloading of troops and vehicles; other vessels were also reinforced and converted for the purpose of invasion landings. German troops spent the summer and autumn of 1940 training for invasion at a variety of locations along the Channel coast of France. Troops gathered on beaches for pep talks, manoeuvres and to watch and practise 3.7cm PAK light field gun drills amongst the dunes and practise firing, as they would have to from a vessel at sea, from the turntable of manually pivoted wooden platforms. Auxiliary minesweepers sped out of ports laden with troops wearing their life vests, crammed onto decks with inflated rubber boats to practise launching and loading the *flossack flotille* with troops and weaponry and rehearsing seaborne landings.

The assault troops were a mixed group of infantry, artillery, tanks and *Gebirgsjäger* (mountain troops) who proudly wore on their caps the edelweiss badge which belied their specialist training. These troops were scheduled to

An auxiliary minesweeper crammed with troops and rubber boats for a practice invasion landing, Boulogne, France 1940.

German troops clambering from landing craft to rubber dinghy during an invasion exercise, France 1940.

Lowering a PAK light artillery piece into a landing craft during an invasion exercise, France 1940.

Having decamped from their transport ships, German troops of the rubber boat 'flossack flotille' row for the shore, during an invasion exercise at **Blankenberge** *near Zeebrugge, Belgium 1940.*

land from the assault craft and scale the high cliffs of southern Britain as part of the landings, hence they were soon nicknamed 'climbing fish'. RAF aerial reconnaissance photographs clearly showed the build-up of invasion barges and British forces built their defences and stood ready to repel the invader.

* * *

During the 'invasion summer' and into the autumn of 1940 in Britain there were a number of localised invasion scares brought on by 'jitters' and mistaken sightings of invasion craft on the horizon, but there was only one night the 'Cromwell' code word was given.

The day of 7 September 1940 will go down in history as the first day of the blitz on London and late that same afternoon British chiefs of staff met to consider a report on the intensification of the likelihood of German forces making the invasion assault on Great Britain. The main features of the report stated:

1. *The westerly and southerly movement of barges and small ships to ports between Ostend and Le Havre suggested a very early date for invasion, since such craft would not be moved unnecessarily early to ports so much exposed to bombing attacks.*

2. *The striking strength of the German Air Force, disposed between Amsterdam and Brest, had been increased by the transfer of 160 long-range bomber aircraft from Norway; and short-range dive-bomber units had been re-deployed to forward aerodromes in the Pas de Calais area, presumably in preparation for employment against this country.*

3. *Four Germans captured on landing from a rowing boat on the south-east coast had confessed to being spies, and had said that they were to be ready at any time during the next fortnight to report the movement of British reserve formations in the area Oxford – Ipswich – London – Reading.*

4. *Moon and tide conditions during the period 8th/10th September were most favourable for a seaborne invasion on the south-east coast.*[21]

The chiefs of staff were satisfied the factors for invasion appeared to have reached a point of critical mass; the possibility of invasion was now imminent. What happened next has been the subject of speculation over the understanding of what the Cromwell code word was actually intended to mean. Some accounts state it was issued as a warning for troops to be placed on alert, while others receiving the warning believed it was given because invasion landings had actually taken place. The account published in *Hansard* in November 1946 states:

Most military officials who received the message immediately put their troops onto a war footing, auxiliary units made ready to go operational and a number of Home Guard commanders called out their men by ringing church bells which, in turn, raised alarm that landings were being made by enemy parachutists. In such circumstances senses and fears are heightened and the effect of cloud and shadow on the sea and innocent fishing boats generated a number of false alarms of German E-boats being 'spotted' approaching the coast.[23]

German troops and rubber boats laden with equipment coming ashore during an invasion exercise, France 1940.

In Eastern and Southern Commands roads were instantly locked down, defences manned and primed, explosives were rigged ready to destroy bridges, roads were mined. Telephone operators refused to accept non-official calls and in some areas the church bells were rung. Before the immediate action orders could be rescinded or clarified a number of people suffered injuries, a few bridges were demolished by Royal Engineers and, near Mablethorpe, Lincolnshire Major Henry Cleaveland Phillips and his driver Private Arthur Scovell of 2nd Battalion, The Hampshire Regiment, serving in the 1st (Guards) Brigade, suffered fatal injuries when their car was blown up after running over mines that had been laid on the road they were driving along as a result of the 'invasion imminent' warning.

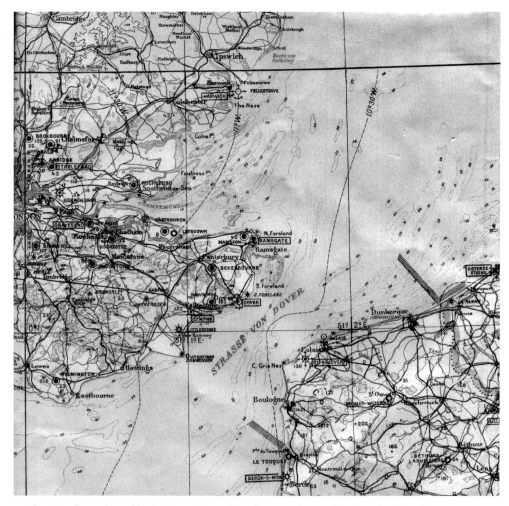

Section from the rubberised map issued to German forces showing the French coast, Dover Strait and South coast of Britain for Operation Sealion.

Luftwaffe **Flakkorps** *gunners freshly arrived at an embarkation port posing for the camera with their France-England invasion map, France 1940.*

Over the days and weeks after the 'Cromwell' codeword invasion scare a story began to circulate of how a German invasion attempt had actually been made on that night. Some stories claimed there had been some sort of accident as the Germans set off, or that they had been 'cut up' while at sea by the Royal Navy and bombed and machine gunned by the RAF.[24] The story rapidly spread as a rumour 'from the best authority' which claimed the Channel was 'white with bodies'[25] of German dead, some of the beaches on the south and east coast were claimed in some accounts to be littered with the bodies of thousands of dead Germans. In one tale the beach at Southend had been so inundated the corpses were being cleared away with the help of corporation refuse carts.[26]

Nothing was being said from official British sources and British national and provincial newspapers drew on reports published in American newspapers of a failed invasion attempt. Typical of these was the letter claimed to have been received by French residents in New York, published in the New York newspaper *The Sun*:

> *The invading German fleet is said to have started from St Malo, Brittany, with the expectation of landing on the west coast of England. Reports received it is said that the result was 'nothing short of suicide.'*[27]

263

RAF reconnaissance photograph showing the massed invasion barges at Boulogne, France 1940.

The account of the invasion scare published in Hansard in 1946 attributes the belief to being: *'based partly on the fact that a number of German bodies were washed up on the south coast of England in August and September, 1940'* ... and offers the explanation:

> *In August 1940, the Germans were embarking their Army in the barges in harbours along the French coast, but there is no evidence that they ever left harbour as a fleet to invade this country. Bombing raids on those harbours were carried out by Bomber Command and some barges which put to sea,*

264

probably to escape the raids, were sunk either by bombing or on encountering bad weather. During the next six weeks bodies of German soldiers were washed up at scattered points along the coast between Cornwall and Yarmouth (amounting to about 36 over a period of a month).[28]

What is not discussed in the *Hansard* account is how the rumour soon evolved to claim that the bodies were all badly burned because the invasion force had been foiled by a secret coastal defence, whereby the sea was flooded with petrol, set on fire and burned the invasion forces as they approached the shore.

A Petroleum Warfare Department had been established shortly after the Dunkirk evacuation, in response to the invasion threat, and there had been experiments with flame barrage. It proved harder than anticipated to get the oil to ignite, but a notable success was achieved on the northern shores of the Solent near Tichfield and this was all the British propaganda organisations needed. Ten tanker wagons pumped tons of oil onto the sea and it was successfully ignited and '*within a few seconds of the pumps being started a wall*

Demonstration of a flame barrage on the sea at Studland Bay, Dorset, March 1941.

of flame of such intensity raged up from the sea surface that it was impossible to remain on the edge of the cliff, and the sea itself began to boil.'[29]

The successful demonstration could not have come at a more opportune moment. Intelligence sources were suggesting the invasion of Britain by German forces was planned for early September and the demonstration of the barrage with film or photographs could be deliberately planted on German intelligence and through channels calculated to leak stories of burning sea defences out to the invasion forces too. Intelligence sources in Germany fed back that the Germans were aware of the 'new weapon' the British had developed and the Operation Sealion planners were suddenly given a new headache as they hastily attempted to develop countermeasures.[30]

The W Board, established in late September 1940, brought together directors and senior members of intelligence and deception organisations to discuss and co-ordinate information that could be fed back to German intelligence by double-cross agents. It prompted a wider consideration of the co-ordination of the dissemination of rumours. Guy Liddell recorded:

> *MI5's view was that we should get quick answers to any questionnaires or enquiries that we received from the other side. We wanted first of all to know the truth and secondly how much of it could be put over. Having obtained this information, we would then send down our agent to see how much of it he could pick up of his own accord. It had to be borne in mind that we were mainly purveyors of the true information, but that by putting over a half-truth we might be able to assist a line put out by some other department.*
>
> *At the moment it seems that EH* [MI6's Department Electra House, later formed the core of the new Political Warfare Executive in 1941, their task specifically to formulate and disseminate rumours], *MEW* [Hugh Dalton's Ministry of Economic Warfare], *Secret Intelligence Service and Naval Intelligence Division are all circulating false rumours. Some of them have come back to our agents for confirmation. We are thus in the position of having to contradict information put out by another department.*
>
> *It was suggested at the meeting that Inter-Services Security Board was already disseminating false information to cover various operations … Director Military Intelligence suggested that all rumours and false information should be pooled in Inter-Services Security Board and that we should submit our questionnaires to the secretary who would provide the answers … In the meantime the W. Committee could meet about once a fortnight in order to assist on the main rumour policy.*[31]

Intelligence services do not always co-ordinate with each other; sometimes this is because of the need for secrecy and in other instances because of the vanity and pride of those in charge of the branch, or even the whole organisation, who are seeking the glory of a particular coup and are not prepared to share it. Working together the British intelligence organisations co-ordinated a masterful infiltration of the story of the charred German bodies into rumour at home and abroad and the stories were so vivid and compelling they endured for months and even years afterwards.[32] The tale of the flame barrage as a secret weapon and burned bodies was spread as a hush-hush rumour, given even more weight by a block on the story in the British press.

Once progress had been made in Europe after the D-Day landings and war seemed to be very much on the turn in favour of the allies, there began a long run of 'now it can be told' genre stories of secrets from the early war years published in newspapers and magazines. In October 1944 *The People*, which had one of the largest readerships in the country, was at last allowed to run a story, credited to John Parris, British United Press special correspondent, under the headline *40,000 Died in Flaming Channel*. Parris explained that the Belgians with whom he had talked were surprised to learn that the British people had never been told of the attempt and he had heard one particular story from Renée Meurisse, a Belgian Red Cross nurse, who was in charge of a group of Belgian refugees on 17 September 1940:

At seven o'clock that night a German Red Cross train of 40 coaches pulled into Brussels station. We had been expecting a refugee train, so we were surprised when we saw a train load of Germans. The German commandant, who looked tired, approached me and asked if we could help his wounded. He said that the train had been shunted on the wrong line and that his men were dying for lack of treatment. We agreed to help ... I helped to carry a young German soldier from the train. He was horribly burned about the head and shoulders. A doctor helped me put him in a corner and we determined to find out what had happened to him.

Finally, we managed to piece together the whole story. He said they had been told that they were going to invade Britain, that nothing could stop them, that it was just a matter of getting into boats and going across the Channel. He told me, 'It was horrible. The whole Channel was in flames, and the British bombed and machine gunned us. Hell couldn't be worse.' And then he died, there on the stretcher. The Red Cross worker added, 'as did many others on that station. We looked after more than 500 soldiers as best we could. Many of them died there in Brussels railway station. Others died in our hospitals.'[33]

Back in 1940 there were even leaflets dropped by the RAF on German troops in the invasion forces' concentration ports purporting to be sheets of useful phrases for German invasion forces. The leaflets offered phrases in German,

WIR FAHREN GEGEN ENGELLAND

DER KLEINE INVASIONS-DOLMETSCHER	PETIT MANUEL DE CONVERSATION POUR L'INVASION	TAALCURSUS ZONDER LEERMEESTER VOOR DUITSCHE SOLD..

I. Vor der Invasion

1. Die See ist gross — kalt — stürmisch.
2. Wie oft müssen wir noch Landungsmanöver üben?
3. Ob wir wohl in England ankommen werden?
4. Ob wir heil zurückkommen werden?
5. Wann ist der nächste englische Luftangriff? Heute morgens; mittags; nachmittags; abends; nachts.
6. Warum fährt der Führer nicht mit?
7. Unser Benzinlager brennt noch immer!
8. Euer Benzinlager brennt schon wieder!
9. War hat schon wieder das Telefonkabel durchgeschnitten!
10. Haben Sie meinen Kameraden in den Kanal geworfen?
11. Können Sie mir eine Schwimmweste — einen Rettungsring — leihen?
12. Was kosten bei Ihnen Schwimmstunden?
13. Wie viele Invasionsfahrten brauch' ich für das E.K.I?
14. Sieben — acht — neun.
15. Wir werden gegen Engelland fahren!

I. Avant l'invasion

1. La mer est vaste — froide — houleuse.
2. Combien de fois encore devrons-nous faire des exercises de débarquement?
3. Pensez-vous que nous arriverons jamais en Angleterre?
4. Pensez-vous que nous reviendrons jamais d'Angleterre?
5. Quand le prochain raid anglais aura-t-il lieu? — Aujourd'hui, dans la matinée, à midi, dans l'après-midi, dans la soirée, dans la nuit.
6. Pourquoi est-ce que le Fuehrer ne vient pas avec nous?
7. Notre dépôt d'essence continue de brûler!
8. Votre dépôt d'essence a recommencé à brûler!
9. Qui a encore coupé encore d'une telle phonique?
10. Avez-vous jeté mon camarade dans le canal?
11. Pouvez-vous me prêter une ceinture, — une bouée de sauvetage?
12. Quel prix prenez-vous pour les leçons de natation?
13. Combien d'invasions dois-je faire pour recevoir la Croix de Fer de 1ère classe?
14. Sept — huit — neuf.
15. Nous partirons pour l'Angleterre! (Qu'ils disent.)

I. Vóór de invasie

1. De zee is groot — koud — stormachtig.
2. Hoe vaak nog moeten w'exerceeren om 't landen op een kust te leeren?
3. Zullen we ooit in Engeland komen?
4. Zullen we heelhuids wêerom komen?
5. Wanneer komt de volgende Britsche luchtaanval? Heden — morgen, middag, namiddag, avond, nacht.
6. Waarom reist de Führer niet met ons mee?
7. Ons benzinedepot staat nog steeds in lichter laaie!
8. Uw benzinedepot staat alweer in lichter laaie!
9. Wie heeft nu telefoonleiding nou weer doo. geknipt?
10. Heeft U mijn kameraad in de gracht gesmeten?
11. Kunt U mij een zwemvest — een reddinggordel leenen?
12. Hoeveel kost het om bij U zwemmen te leeren?
13. Hoe dikwijls moet ik aan een invasietocht meedoen om het IJzeren Kruis te winnen?
14. Zeven — acht — negen keer.
15. Wij zullen gauw naar Engeland varen! (Plons! Plons! Plons!)

II. Während der Invasion

1. Der Seegang. — Der Sturm. — Der Nebel. Die Windstärke.
2. Wir sind seekrank. Wo ist der Kübel?
3. Ist das eine Bombe — ein Torpedo — eine Granate — eine Mine?

II. Pendant l'invasion

1. Le gros temps — la tempête — le brouillard — la violence de l'ouragan.
2. Nous avons le mal de mer. Où est la cuvette?
3. Est-ce une bombe — une torpille — un obus — une mine?

II. Tijdens de invasie

1. De deining — de storm — de mist — de orkaan.
2. Wij zijn zeeziek. Waar is de kwispedoor?
3. Is dat een bom — een torpedo - granaat — een mijn?

British created leaflet containing some useful phrases in English, French and Dutch dropped by the RAF on German troops embarking on the invasion of Britain.

French and Dutch such as: 'What is that strong smell of petroleum?' 'What is setting the sea on fire?' and 'Does not the Captain burn beautifully?'

Leaflets aside, and despite the stories of invasion troops being thwarted by flame barrage being repudiated by German military authorities, the story reached the ears of German soldiers in France. It spread and remained one of the greatest fears of many German soldiers training to participate in

'Joyous Guard. Surrender, or Die,' Punch 24 July 1940. *Hitler could shout all he liked, the moat remained uncrossed and the defences of fortress Britain remained un-breached.*

the invasion landings against Britain. Flame barrage was, like the plans for Operation Sealion, reliant on ideal conditions, it may not have worked when it was needed most, but it remained at the heart of one of the most successful scare stories of the Second World War.

*   *   *

Many Germans could not understand how the British people managed to keep their sense of humour, even through the darkest hours of Blitz and invasion threat during 1940.

Issued by the Ministry of Information in co-operation with the War Office
and the Ministry of Home Security

Beating the INVADER

A MESSAGE FROM THE PRIME MINISTER

IF invasion comes, everyone—young or old, men and women—will be eager to play their part worthily. By far the greater part of the country will not be immediately involved. Even along our coasts, the greater part will remain unaffected. But where the enemy lands, or tries to land, there will be most violent fighting. Not only will there be the battles when the enemy tries to come ashore, but afterwards there will fall upon his lodgments very heavy British counter-attacks, and all the time the lodgments will be under the heaviest attack by British bombers. The fewer civilians or non-combatants in these areas, the better—apart from essential workers who must remain. So if you are advised by the authorities to leave the place where you live, it is your duty to go elsewhere when you are told to leave. When the attack begins, it will be too late to go ; and, unless you receive definite instructions to move, your duty then will be to stay where you are. You will have to get into the safest place you can find, and stay there until the battle is over. For all of you then the order and the duty will be : " STAND FIRM ".

This also applies to people inland if any considerable number of parachutists or air-borne troops are landed in their neighbourhood. Above all, they must not cumber the roads. Like their fellow-countrymen on the coasts, they must " STAND FIRM ". The Home Guard, supported by strong mobile columns wherever enemy's numbers require it, will immediately come to grips with the invaders, and there is little doubt will soon destroy them.

Throughout the rest of the country where there is no fighting going on and no close cannon fire or rifle fire can be heard, everyone will govern his conduct by the second great order and duty, namely, " CARRY ON ". It may easily be some weeks before the invader has been totally destroyed, that is to say, killed or captured to the last man who has landed on our shores. Meanwhile, all work must be continued to the utmost, and no time lost.

The following notes have been prepared to tell everyone in rather more detail what to do, and they should be carefully studied. Each man and woman should think out a clear plan of personal action in accordance with the general scheme

[signature: Winston S. Churchill]

STAND FIRM

I. What do I do if fighting breaks out in my neighbourhood ?

Keep indoors or in your shelter until the battle is over. If you can have a trench ready in your garden or field, so much the better. You may want to use it for protection if your house is damaged. But if you are at work, or if you have special orders, carry on as long as possible and only take cover when danger approaches. If you are on your way to work, finish your journey if you can.

If you see an enemy tank, or a few enemy soldiers, do not assume that the enemy are in control of the area. What you have seen may be a party sent on in advance, or stragglers from the main body who can easily be rounded up

The Beating the Invader *leaflet of 1941 sent to every British household turned the 'Stay Put' message to the more aggressive and positive 'Stand Firm'. and 'Carry On'.*

The fighter pilots of the RAF ensured Göring did not 'wipe the British air force from the sky' as he bragged would be done.[34] Britain's defences remained un-breached and the Channel, its greatest moat, uncrossed. It took Britain and her Allies years to build the necessary landing craft for the liberation of North Western Europe on the D-Day Beaches in June 1944. The converted

BOROUGH OF LEYTON

INVASION DEFENCE

"STAND FIRM"

The Government have issued a message urging all civilians if invasion takes place, to "Stand Firm"; to keep off the roads; to do everything they can to help each other; to do nothing which will help the enemy, and to help the military and the civil authorities to the fullest extent.

Help can be given by civilians, both men and women, in many ways, and indeed help must be given so as to avoid wasting the services of soldiers in non-combatant work. Cooking and distribution of food, filling craters in streets, clearing debris from streets, digging trenches, first aid, etc., are a few examples of what can be done by civilians.

Although enemy invasion is not imminent, the country must be prepared to repel it, should it appear.

As Controller of the Civil Defence Services, I have, with the consent of the Corporation, been appointed Invasion Defence Officer, to organise a Scheme of Defence, and I appeal to everyone, man and woman, to give a helping hand in carrying out the scheme.

An Invasion Defence Warden has been appointed who will be responsible to me for the organisation in each District Warden's area. He in turn will be assisted by Post Invasion Defence Wardens and Street Leaders. These officers will have great responsibilities and many duties to perform, but these will be lessened considerably by the active assistance which will, I am sure, be willingly given by all residents within the Borough. These Officers will be calling upon you at an early date for information, so that we can know and organise our strength, and I trust you will assist by giving the information required. During invasion conditions they will be of considerable help to you in connection with food and water supplies and other matters; therefore, the greater the assistance given to them now in making preparations, the greater may be the benefits to be derived from the preparations when made.

A large number of volunteers, both men and women, will be needed to perform the work, particulars of which will be given to you when the officer calls. Any person who desires to volunteer his or her services under invasion conditions should inform the officer on his visit what work he or she is prepared to undertake. A person who has been registered for service with a Factory Labour Squad should not enrol, but should tell the officer that he has done so.

Tools such as picks, shovels, wheel barrows, ladders and buckets will be needed, and if any person possesses all or any of these he should offer to lend them, in case of need, during an invasion.

Do not forget the message "Stand Firm" and do everything in your power to help.

Dated this 14th day of September, 1942.

Town Clerk and Invasion Defence Officer.

Town Hall,
Leyton, E.10.

C. 12.1   Crusha & Son, Ltd., Tottenham., Wood Green, Palmers Green and Enfield.

'Stand Firm' invasion defence leaflet for the London Borough of Leyton, September 1942. Britain continued to develop its anti-invasion plans over the years after 1940.

barges required for the Operation Sealion plans never reached the quantities required, nor were they well suited for a Channel crossing. The weather and tides of the English Channel were never in Hitler's favour during 1940. He postponed Operation Sealion on 17 September 1940, and on 19 September gave orders that the strategic concentration of shipping was to cease and existing concentrations of invasion barges were to be dispersed.

On 12 October Hitler postponed Operation Sealion for 1940 but stated it would be reviewed in the spring of the new year. However, he began to release troops from training for the invasion of Great Britain from December 1940. Despite the invasion guides being updated and issued up to 1941, Hitler was concentrating on a new campaign against Russia in 1941. But do not be misled, the war on Britain did not end there. Hitler's bombers continued their bombing campaigns on British mainland targets and agents continued to land by parachute and boat over subsequent years.

If the factors had been different in 1940, if Hitler had had more aircraft to fight the RAF, if he could establish a secure path for his invasion fleet across the Channel and had effective landing craft and the numbers of trained troops outlined in the plans, there is no doubt Operation Sealion would have been attempted. Britain would have put up one hell of a fight, but we should never forget German troops eating their lunch out of their mess tins on the beaches of Northern France during a break from invasion training gazing out across the Channel in 1940 they could just as well have been eating fish and chips out of the last free British newspapers on the seafront at Brighton, Bognor or Broadstairs after a successful invasion.

May we, as a nation, never forget to give thanks for our freedom and the thousands who stood ready to defend our green and pleasant land.

German troops eating their lunch on the beach at Mers-le-Bains, France, 1940, looking out across the Channel to Britain, the country they were in training to invade.

Civil Defence Regions, Commissioners, Headquarters and Regional Security Liaison Officers, December 1940

Region 1 (Northern) HQ Newcastle Upon Tyne
Sir Arthur Lambert MC
Watson House, Pilgrim Street
Newcastle Upon Tyne
RSLO Major Forrest

Region 2 (North Eastern) HQ Leeds
The Rt Hon Lord Harlech GCMG
Bishopgate House, Bishopgate Street
Leeds
RSLO Major Hordern

Region 3 (North Midland) HQ Nottingham
Lord Trent
GPO Buildings, Queen Street
Nottingham
RSLO Major Haylor

Region 4 (Eastern) HQ Cambridge
Sir Will Spens CBE
St Regis, Montague Road,
Cambridge
RSLO Major Dixon

Region 5 (London) HQ London (3 Commissioners)
The Rt Hon Captain David Euan Wallace MP (Senior Commissioner)
Sir Ernest Gowers
Admiral Sir Edward Evans
Geological Museum,
Exhibition Road,
Kensington
RSLO Major Langdon

Region 6 (Southern) HQ Reading
Sir Harold Butler CB
Marlborough House
Parkside Road
Reading
RSLO Major Ryde

Region 7 (South Western) HQ Bristol
Sir Geoffrey Peto KBE
19 Woodland Road
Bristol
RSLO Major Ferguson

Region 8 (Wales) HQ Cardiff
Col G.T. Bruce CB CMG DSO
8 Cathedral Road
Cardiff
RSLO Major Ford

Region 9 (Midland) HQ Birmingham
The Earl of Dudley MC
Civic House, Great Charles Street
Birmingham
RSLO Major Wethered

Region 10 (North Western) HQ Manchester
Sir Harry G. Haig KGSI
Arkwright House, Parsonage Gardens
Manchester
RSLO Major Baxter

Region 11 (Scotland), HQ Edinburgh
The Rt Hon Thomas Johnston MP
25, Palmerston Place
Edinburgh
RSLO Major Perfect

Region 12 (South Eastern), HQ Tunbridge Wells
Sir Auckland Geddes
Bredbury House, Mount Ephraim
Tunbridge Wells
RSLO Major Grassby

Maxwell Knight's Account of
'The Wolkoff – Kent Case'

The history of the investigation which led up to the case against Tyler Kent and Anna Wolkoff provides an interesting example of the various phases of intelligence work; in particular the happy results which may be achieved by close co-operation and friendly relationships with the Police.

The investigation really started in the late summer of 1939 before the outbreak of war when reports from various agents drew attention to the activities of Captain A.H. Maule Ramsey MP, and his Right Club. At first information was received from casual sources which showed that although outwardly professing to be unconnected with other Fascist movements, the Right Club had among its members, people who were working for such extreme organisations as the British Union, the Imperial Fascist League and the Nordic League. In fact, Captain Ramsay actually addressed meetings of the Nordic League at which he made statements regarding his policy of anti-Semitism which were frankly pro-German in tone and almost amounted to incitement to riot.

These early reports showed that it was clearly necessary to have an agent inside the Right Club, and a certain lady who will be referred to as Miss A. and who, by a fortunate chance, was already acquainted with Captain and Mrs Ramsay, was introduced. (It may be of interest to note that Miss A. had previously worked for MI5 in connection with other matters, and had, therefore, received some training.)

After the outbreak of war reports from Miss A. showed quite clearly that part of the Right Club's policy was an effort to penetrate not only other anti-Semitic and anti-Communist organisations, but actually into the service of government departments. In fact Captain Ramsay boasted that he had contacts in the Admiralty, the War Office, the Foreign Office, the Army, and even, in his most enthusiastic moments, in Scotland Yard. At one period he lamented the fact that he had no one in the Postal Censorship, and when this fortunate occurrence was reported to Captain Ramsay, both he and his wife welcomed the news with glee, and throughout the ensuing months continually tried to get from Miss A. confidential information about the personnel and working of the censorship.

It is unnecessary here to go into the activities of the Right Club to any great extent, but it is important to note that it was through the Right Club that Miss A. was introduced to Anna Wolkoff – incidentally by Mrs Maule Ramsay. This introduction took place on 6 December 1939. Anna Wolkoff had, of course, been considered a suspect by MI5 for some considerable time, together with her father, Admiral Wolkoff, and her sisters. The Wolkoff family were White Russians and the admiral had been Russian military attaché in London during the Tsarist regime. The admiral is not a British subject, but Anna Wolkoff was naturalised in 1935.

Between December 1939 and the early spring of 1940 the reports received from Miss A. and other sources showed that there was an 'inner ring' of Right Club members which, in addition to carrying out anti-war propaganda camouflaged as anti-Communist propaganda, was interesting itself in political and diplomatic matters which suggest that espionage might not be so far removed from its activities as might, at first, have been supposed. The most active person in this inner circle was Anna Wolkoff, and it was upon Wolkoff that Miss A. was instructed to concentrate her attention.

In late February 1940 it was discovered that Anna Wolkoff had become acquainted with a young man employed in the United States Embassy. This young man subsequently turned out to be Tyler Kent. In the same month it was thought wise to introduce another agent into the group of persons around Captain Ramsay and Anna Wolkoff, and for this purpose a young Belgian girl, Miss Z. was used. That she had a very useful background and many contacts which could be exploited on our behalf, will transpire later, and she had the additional advantage of having met the Wolkoff family some few years previously.

At about the same time that Anna Wolkoff's contact with Kent was first reported it was discovered that Wolkoff had a contact in the Belgium Embassy, the second secretary Jean Nieumanhuys. This man used to enable Wolkoff to make use of the diplomatic bag for communication with the Continent. Wolkoff confided in Miss A. that by this means it was possible for her to communicate with William Joyce (Lord Haw Haw) in Germany, and the method was that letters would be given to Nieumanhuys addressed to the Comte or Comtesse de Laubespin, an official at the Belgian Foreign Office in Brussels who was also a friend of Anna Wolkoff.

The main events out of which the case against Wolkoff and Kent arose, took place in April 1940 and may be summarised as follows. (Some of these events chiefly concern Miss A. while others concern Miss Z. Every effort, however, will be made to make the account as clear as is consistent with the necessary brevity. For the sake of clarity the events which concern the subject charge against Anna Wolkoff of committing an offence contrary to section 2a of the Defence Regulations, i.e. acts done with intent to assist the enemy, will be dealt with first, as most of the facts are centred round Miss Z.)

On instructions from the officer in charge of the case Miss Z. had been told to create in Anna Wolkoff's mind the impression that she (Miss Z) also had many contacts in the diplomatic world. On 9 April, at the Russian Tea Rooms in Harrington Road, S.W. (the family business of the Wolkoffs) Miss Z. mentioned to Admiral Wolkoff a fictitious friend of hers in the Rumanian Legation. Admiral Wolkoff communicated the news to Anna who was also in the tea room. Anna immediately spoke to Miss Z., and asked her whether, through her friend, it would be possible to get a letter to Germany by other channels than the ordinary post. Her reply was that it might be possible.

Anna then produced an envelope addressed to Joyce in Berlin and asked Miss Z if she could arrange for its dispatch via the diplomatic bag. This letter was, of course, passed to MI5. The officer in charge, photographed and returned it to Miss Z. On 10 April Anna Wolkoff was told that all the arrangements had been made for the letter to be conveyed. She then intimated that she wished to add something to the letter, and Miss Z. was asked if she could possibly get it back for a short time. This unexpected development was coped with, and on the morning of 11 April, Anna Wolkoff visited Miss Z's flat, received the letter back, re-opened it, and added to the material already in the letter, a note in German which she signed with the badge of the Right Club. The letter was then handed back to Miss Z.

Note on the actual letter

The original content of the letter was a message, in code, which when deciphered, was shown to be a commentary on Haw Haw's broadcast, together with suggested improvements, together with items of political news.

Certain arrangements were then made for the forwarding of the letter as it was obviously desirable to ascertain (a) if the letter reached Joyce what acknowledgement would be made; and (b) to explore further activities of these treacherous individuals.

After the incident of the Haw Haw letter, Miss Z. rose in Anna Wolkoff's esteem, and she was instructed to talk about her family in Belgium and the possibility of her paying a visit to her relatives there, this of course, for the purpose of investigating further Wolkoff's use of the Belgium diplomatic bag and the extent of the Right Club's contacts in Belgium.

Round about the middle of April Anna Wolkoff confided to Miss Z the same information about Nieumanhuys that she had confided to Miss A. She further stated that if Miss Z went to Belgium she would like her to contact an individual, Guy Miermans, whom she described as 'our principal agent in Belgium', in order to obtain from him translations of some Russian document; to visit de Laudespin for the purpose of finding out whether Nieumanhuys was entirely to be trusted; and also to obtain news on how anti-Semitic and similar propaganda was faring in Belgium.

Arrangements were made for Miss Z to go to Belgium, and she left on 16 April, having first received from Anna Wolkoff typewritten instructions in French. Miss Z carried out all the instructions given her by Wolkoff, and incidentally obtained for us a considerable amount of information of interest. The principal interest centred round the undoubted fact that Nieumanhuys was an agent working for the Germans, and that both he and the de Laudespins were alarmed at the extent to which Anna Wolkoff's activities were being pushed in England. This alarm was probably due to their mistrust of Wolkoff's Russian temperament, and fear for their own safety. Miss Z returned to England on 20 April and subsequently reported on her mission to Anna Wolkoff.

We will now leave this aspect of the case and return to Miss A and the case of Tyler Kent. It will be appreciated that both in regard to the investigation into Kent and with regard to the court proceedings, there are many details which cannot be referred to in this account. As is well known, the case was held entirely in camera and it is impossible to disseminate as much information as one would like. For the purposes of this account, however, it is not considered that the details which have to be left out make any material difference.

Between the end of February 1940 and the middle of May 1940 Miss A reported on several occasions incidents which made it increasingly clear that Anna Wolkoff was obtaining through Tyler Kent, a copy-clerk in the American Embassy, information which Kent had no right to be conveying to any person outside the United States government service. This information was, in the main, not concerned with United States domestic affairs, but was information which would be of the greatest value to the enemy and which might do incalculable harm to the Allies were they to be conveyed to Germany.

We discovered, also through the agency of Miss A, that Anna Wolkoff was in close contact with an important official at the Italian Embassy – in fact Wolkoff went so far as to boast that information which she obtained from Kent, had been successfully communicated by her to the Italian Government via her contact in the Embassy. As investigations proceeded it became increasingly obvious that in Tyler Kent, Anna had a source of information which she was using to the detriment of this country.

It will be remembered that by the middle of April 1940 it had been established that Anna Wolkoff was communicating with William Joyce; that she was in the habit of using the Belgian diplomatic bag for communication to persons abroad – probably including Joyce – and there was, therefore, abundant evidence that Anna Wolkoff was indeed to be classed as an enemy agent.

On 20 May 1940 Kent was dismissed from United States government service, his private residence was searched and on the premises documents and material were found which showed that Kent had for some time, been abstracting originals of secret documents from the embassy which he had been copying and, in some cases, lending to Anna Wolkoff. In one particular incident it was clear that these documents had been photographed. Kent was detained, and on the same day Anna Wolkoff was arrested and interned under Section 18B of the Defence Regulations.

Further enquiries subsequent to the arrests disclosed the identity of the person who had photographed for Anna Wolkoff some of the documents stolen by Kent. In due course both Kent and Wolkoff were charged with offences under the Official Secrets Act and Defence Regulations and, as is now well known, were convicted at the Old Bailey, receiving sentences of seven years penal servitude in the case of Kent, and ten years penal servitude in the case of Anna Wolkoff.

From the point of view of intelligence officers there are certain lessons to be learnt from this case. The first is that during war-time there will always come a point in an investigation where an agent must be sacrificed in order to achieve satisfactory results and the intelligence officer in charge of the case must face the responsibility of deciding the exact point at which such sacrifices must be made.

The second lesson is that in the collection of information about suspects in the form of agents' reports, it is impossible to overestimate the importance of distinguishing in each report which material is useless for this purpose.

The third lesson is that when any search of premises is conducted and documents are taken away by an MI5 officer, the greatest care must be taken to see that these are properly listed and recorded, for one can never tell when a document which appears to be unimportant at the time, may become vital at a later stage in the case.

And the fourth, and by no means least important lesson, is that when investigations have reached the point when proceedings are contemplated, it is absolutely essential that the senior officers of the Police in the force concerned, should be taken fully into the confidence of the Intelligence Service, for it is the Police who have to make the arrests, who have to take statements and perform a number of functions outside the scope of an Intelligence officer. Therefore, to have any reservations with the Police is not only short-sighted but may be disastrous from the point of view of the case.

With regard to the 'affair' of Kent and Wolkoff, the most complete co-operation existed between ourselves and Special Branch, and a very great measure of the success of the case is due to the work of the Police officers concerned.

Major Maxwell Knight B.5.b.[35]

Victor Rothschild on Sabotage

Baron Victor Rothschild (1910–1990), was born into the wealthy Jewish family of bankers and was educated at Trinity College, Cambridge where he became known for his love of fast cars and playboy lifestyle. He inherited the baronetcy aged 26. Shortly after the outbreak of the Second World War Rothschild was recruited to work for MI5 and became head of their explosives and sabotage section known as B.18 that took a particular interest in the activities of the Fifth Column in Britain. Being one of the newest sections of MI5 its scope and specialisms were outlined for the benefit of Regional Security Liaison Officers and MI5 in general in a *B Division Weekly Intelligence Summary* published in October 1940:

> *The functions* [of B.18] *are to assist the Police in the investigation of cases of sabotage where enemy or subversive activity is suspected, to collate information regarding sabotage all over the country and to provide technical experts where necessary.*

> *The personnel of the section is:-*
> *Lord Rothschild – General*
> *Miss Sherer – General*
> *R. Egerton Johnson – General*
> *W.S. Burn (specialist) – Naval and marine sabotage*

The following specialists are attached to the section for technical advice re technical investigation.

Television and Radio	Dr. A.F. Rawdon Smith, Cambridge
Poisoning of wells or supplies	Lt. Col. Professor A.J. Clark, F.R.S. Edinburgh
Optics & non-atomic physics	Professor E.N. DaC. Andrade, F.R.S. London
Chemical analysis	Mr W.C. Adams (Government Chemist), London
Machine tools	"D" (not to be confused with another "D")

Industry in general and non-biological science	Brig-Gen Sir Harold Hartley, F.R.S. Watford
Corrosion in industry	Dr. G Bengough, F.R.S. London
Bacteria and viruses	Professor Topley, F.R.S. London
	Dr. Bruce White, London
	Lord Hankey's organisation
Fuel contamination	Professor Heilbron, F.R.S. London
	Professor Ememeus, London
	Professor Egerton, F.R.S. London
	Professor Briscoe, London
General chemical sabotage	Dr. Jones
	Professor Briscoe, London
	Dr. King
Sabotage through chemical warfare agents & special chemical enquiries	Professor Sir Robert Robinson, F.R.S. Oxford and Chemical Defence Research Dept. Porton
Catalytic & surface reactions or special psycho-chemical enquiries	Professor C.N. Hinshelwood, F.R.S. Oxford
Rolling Mills	Mr. J. Perry, 19 Royal Mint Street
R.D.F.	Mr. A.L. Hodgkin, Swanage

Arrangements have been made whereby the details of all fires in which incendiarism is suspected shall be sifted by a committee and reported to B.18.

An attempt is being made to set up a similar organisation with regard to sabotage connected with ships and ship cargoes and shipbuilders, though this is not running yet.

We have also an arrangement with Colonel Symonds of the Home Office to assist us in cases where his technical knowledge of fires may be of use.

For the purposes of enquiry, B.18 also has the services of B.27, the head of whom is Superintendent Burt. It is well known that Superintendent Burt is a specialist on fires, while the other officers under him have technical qualifications apart from their police experience.[36]

Rothschild worked all over Britain during 1940 investigating reported cases of sabotage and spoke at regional security meetings in the provinces. The declassified notes of the meeting of police security officers for the Northern Civil Defence Region on 5 November 1941 provide a rare insight into what

Rothschild himself had to say on the subject and his conclusions drawn from the work of B.18 over its first 12 months of existence:

> *MI5 is of course most interested if sabotage should turn out to be the work of the German Secret Service, but there are other subversive organisations which might commit sabotage in this country. The first of these is the BUF, but apart from one trivial and unsuccessful attempt at Leeds, the Fascists are not known to have made any serious sabotage attempts.*
>
> *The second subversive organisation is the Communist Party which has for a long time appreciated the value of sabotage as a weapon in the final struggle for political ends. Several members of the British Party have received instruction at sabotage schools in the Soviet Union. However, since the entry of the Soviet Union into the war it is extremely unlikely that any orthodox Communists will attempt sabotage, nor were attempts we made during the war before the Soviet Union came in.*
>
> *MI5 receives many reports of sabotage which has sometimes been of a fairly serious nature and which has been committed by disgruntled workmen. Such cases are not, strictly speaking sabotage but can be classified as wilful damage. From the MI5 angle they are not of great importance. So far there has been no sabotage here attributable either to the German Secret Service or to subversive organisations, although several successful acts of sabotage have been perpetrated abroad. So far as the German Secret Service is concerned, we know that sabotage is an integral part of Germany's war tactics and it is possible that plans are laid on for implementation in the event of an invasion.*
>
> *At the same time, several German agents have arrived in this country trained and equipped for committing sabotage. It is naturally difficult for an enemy agent to bring high explosive into this country owing to its bulk, so in general the Germans have instructed their agents to purchase the raw materials for manufacturing their incendiary or explosive bombs from chemist shops in Great Britain ...*
>
> *There are, however, two essential parts of a bomb which it is difficult for the saboteur to make himself. These are the initiating mechanism and the delay mechanism. The Germans are mistakenly under the impression that it is difficult to obtain detonators on this country and therefore detonators have usually been included in the saboteur's equipment, concealed in such innocuous looking objects as shaving brushes or clothes brushes. Delay mechanisms, which vary from common Bickford fuse to intricate clock mechanisms and acid delays can be brought into the country in a variety of different covers which are easily included in the normal traveller's personal luggage. Such things as shaving soap, torch batteries, leather belts (for fuse wire), fountain pens and pencils have been used as covers ... MI5 has set up an organisation*

which has specialised knowledge of such matters and if suspicious articles are found the RSLO should immediately be informed so that he can arrange for the objects to be examined.

Enemy agents coming to this country have been instructed in the type of objective they should attempt to sabotage, although the inadequacy of some of these instructions makes it appear unlikely that these attempts would have been successful. For example, one saboteur was told to blow up a bridge, which would have been impossible with the small amount of explosive with which he was provided. For successful sabotage, targets which are to a certain extent self-destroying should be selected. Such objectives are petrol and ammunition stores, factories which are flammable and railway lines, when a small charge can blow a line and derail a train, which will then do a great deal of damage through its own impetus.

Among the objectives given to German saboteurs are telephone wires and H.T. Cables and agents have been supplied with rubber insulated pliers for attacking these. MI5 is therefore interested in the incidence of cases of cut telephone wires, even though it frequently turned out the wires were cut accidentally or by irresponsible people.[37]

Notes

Introduction

1. Kell, Constance *A Secret Well Kept: The Untold Story of Sir Vernon Kell, Founder of MI5* (London 2017)
2. Christopher Andrew, *The Defence of the Realm: The Authorized History of MI5* (London 2009)
3. Recalled by Toby Pilcher in an after-dinner speech about the early days at Wormwood Scrubs, *Guy Liddell Diary* 21 October 1942 KV4/190
4. *The Times*, 6 December 1958
5. *The Times* 21 January 1980
6. KV4/111
7. *The Times* 21 January 1980
8. *Liddell Diary* KV4/189
9. *The Times*, 22 January 1980
10. *Liddell Diary* 25 September 1940 KV4/186
11. *The War Weekly* 5 January 1940
12. *Liddell Diary* 4 February 1940 KV4/185
13. *Liddell Diary* 18 March 1940
14. *Liddell Diary* 27 June 1940
15. *Liddell Diary* 28 July 1940

Chapter 1

1. *Manchester Guardian* 7 December 1931
2. *Daily Herald* 7 December 1931
3. FO 371/15216
4. Ansel, *Hitler Confronts England*
5. Article by Basil Liddell Hart, *John Bull Magazine* 13 May 1950
6. FO 395/468
7. *The Times* 29 April 1933
8. *The Times* 11 May 1933
9. *The Times*, 12 May 1933
10. *Sydney Morning Herald*, 13 May 1933
11. O'Keeffe, Paul *Some Sort of Genius: A Life of Wyndham Lewis* (Counterpoint 2015)
12. *The Times*, 20 February 1934

Chapter 2

1. Home Defence Sub-committee, Report 118a *Continental Air Menace* (1923) p.4
2. Wells, H.G. *The War In The Air* (reprint London 1967) p.8
3. *Hull Daily Mail* 4 April 1935
4. *Evening News* 5 April 1935
5. *Times* 6 April 1935
6. *Daily Mail* 5 April 1935

7. KV-2-2834
8. KV2/834
9. Report by Inspector Jempson, MI5 file on Hans Wesemann KV2/2834
10. Statement of Divisional Detective Inspector Clarence Campion MEPO3/871
11. Ibid
12. Statement of Mrs Elizbeth Allworth MEPO 3/871
13. Statement of Karl Korsch MEPO 3/871
14. Statement of Ika Olden MEPO 3/871
15. Statement of Arthur William Campbell MEPO 3/871
16. Statement of Mrs Elizbeth Allworth MEPO 3/871
17. Statement by Mary Omerod 6 April 1935 MEPO 3/871
18. Statement of PC George Hall 4 April 1935 MEPO3/871
19. Case Report by Divisional Detective Inspector Clarence Campion p.4 MEPO3/871
20. Case Report by Divisional Detective Inspector Clarence Campion pp7–8 MEPO3/871
21. *Manchester Guardian* 5 April 1935
22. KV2/1743
23. *Daily Herald* 5 April 1935
24. HC Deb 8 April 1935 vol 300 col 678–80
25. MEPO 3-871
26. *Nottingham Evening Post* 10 April 1935
27. MEPO 3-871
28. MEPO 3-871
29. German Embassy London to Foreign Office Berlin 15 May 1936, Politisches Archiv des Auswärtigen Amts, Berlin, Rechtabteilung, Schweiz, Streitfall Jakob, R42532 translated in Brinson, Charmian and Dove, Richard *A Matter of Intelligence* (Manchester 2014) p.39
30. MEPO3/871
31. KV2/2834
32. KV2/2834
33. Ibid
34. HO 382/214
35. MEPO 3/871
36. See Cohen, John *A Study of Suicide Pacts, Medico-Legal Journal* vol. 23 issue 3 (1961) pp144–151
37. See Ramsland, Katherine *Suicide:Pacts versus Clusters*, *Psychology Today* website, posted 14 July 2017
38. See Joiner, T.E. *Myths about Suicide* (Harvard 2010)
39. KV2/2834
40. Kendal to Brook, HO Aliens Department W2024
41. Deposition given to Swiss Authorities by Hans Wesemann after his capture KV2/2834
42. *The Times* 11 April 1936 p.14
43. *The Times*, 16 April 1936

Chapter 3
1. *The Times* 10 March 1936
2. KV5/75
3. *Central Somerset Gazette* 22 May 1936
4. *Yorkshire Post* 3 August 1936
5. See MEPO 2/3043
6. *Birmingham Daily Gazette* 10 April 1937
7. KV5/75
8. KV5/85

9. KV5/85
10. *Colwyn Bay and North Wales Weekly News* 22 July 1937
11. *Daily Herald*, 24 May 1937
12. See *The Sun* 16 October 2018
13. KV5/85
14. Matthews, Stanley and Scott, Les *The Way It Was* (London 2001) p.117

Chapter 4
1. Kell to Scott 24 April 1936 HO45/25385
2. Ibid
3. KV2/1743
4. *Evening Telegraph* 12 March 1937
5. Ibid
6. *Evening Standard* 10 August 1937
7. *Jewish Telegraphic Agency* (New York) 12 August 1937
8. Baker-White, John *The Big Lie* (London 1955)
9. Rosel, Rudolph Gottfried KV2/3187
10. *Liddell Diary* 30 September 1939 KV4/185
11. FO371/21649
12. *Western Mail* 8 April 1938
13. See HC Deb 29 March 1938 vol 333 cc1824–5
14. See *HC Deb 06 April 1939 vol 345 cc2971-32971*
15. *Midland Daily Telegraph* 6 April 1939
16. Quoted by Urbach, Karina in *Go-Betweens of Hitler* (Oxford 2015) p.192
17. See HO 283/70 Raven-Thomson's MEPO file has still not been released.
18. Margaret Elizabeth Newitt KV2/3326
19. Ibid
20. B Division Security Summary 31 October 1940 KV4/122
21. Ibid
22. *Liddell Diary* 8 September 1940 KV4/185
23. KV2/1293
24. KV2/1293
25. KV2/1293
26. KV2/537
27. Quoted in *Report on the Case of Anna Sonia Chateâu-Thierry* p.5 KV2/357
28. *Case of Anna Sonia Chateau-Thierry* pp. 1–5 KV2/357
29. KV2/15
30. Morrish Interview 3 December 1940 KV2/357 e
31. KV2/357
32. KV2/15
33. Sweet, Matthew *The West End Front* (London 2011) p25
34. *Liddell Diary* 8 March 1940 KV4/186
35. *Liddell Diary* 8 March 1940 KV4/186
36. B Division Weekly Intelligence Summary No 5 1940 KV4/122
37. B Division Weekly Intelligence Summary No 5 1940 KV4/122
38. Weil, Otto KV2/3303
39. Ibid
40. After the First World War, the Saar region of Germany, a major source of coal, was given to the League of Nations to control. The Treaty of Versailles stated that there should be a vote or plebiscite to decide who should rule the Saar in the future. In 1935, the Saar

region voted 90 per cent in favour of returning to Germany which Hitler regarded as a great success.

41. KV2/3303
42. Ibid
43. KV2/192
44. KV2/3421
45. *Dundee Courier* 17 May 1938
46. Schut, Gerrit, KV2/3546
47. Statement by Annovazzi, Elizabeth 18 June 1940, KV2/3546
48. KV2/3546
49. KV2/3546
50. KV2/3546
51. See *De Schut-groep* (*Nest Keulen/Ast Wilhelmshaven*) nisa-intelligence.nl
52. KV2/3546
53. Ibid
54. Ibid

Chapter 5

1. *Birmingham Daily Post 9 December* 1939
2. See *The Times*, 3 November 1939 p.10
3. *Evening Despatch* 2 November 1939
4. *The Times* 3 November 1939
5. *The Times* 4 November 1939
6. *Derby Evening Telegraph* 8 November 1939
7. *Liddell Diary* 8 December 1939 KV4/185
8. *Birmingham Daily Post* 9 December 1939
9. See Kaplan, R M (2017) *The Fallible Inflexibility of Bernard Spilsbury* Forensic Res Criminol Int. 4 (2) 00105

Chapter 6

1. *Liddell Diary* 18 September 1940 KV4/186
2. See Dilks, David *The Diaries of Sir Alexander Cadogan, 1938 – 1945* (London 1971) pp. 218–219
3. War Cabinet No67 of 1939 1 November 1939, Minute 15, Confidential Annexe: Cabinet Papers, 65/4
4. See Putlitz, Wolfgang zu, *The Putlitz Dossier* (London 1957) pp.180–181
5. See Putlitz, Wolfgang zu, *The Putlitz Dossier* (London 1957) p.185
6. Schellenberg, Walter, *Hitler's Secret Service* (New York 1958) p.77
7. Ibid p.78
8. See Protze, Traugott Anreas Richard KV2/1740
9. See de Graaff, Bob *The Venlo Incident* in *World War Investigator*, No 13 (London 1990)
10. Best, Captain S. Payne *The Venlo Incident* (London 1950)
11. Hankey to Sinclair, 31 October 1939, NMM Sinclair MSS 81/091
12. See Putlitz, Wolfgang zu, *The Putlitz Dossier* (London 1957) pp.185–6
13. See Dilks, David (ed.) *The Diaries of Sir Alexander Cadogan 1938–1945* (London 1971) pp230–33
14. Schulze-Bennett, Oberstleutnant Walter, *Der Grenzzwischenfall bei Venlo*, *Die Nachut* 23/24 (1973)
15. *Liddell Diary* 12 November 1940 KV4/186
16. Deacon, Richard *A History of British Secret Service* (London 1984) p.339
17. See West, Nigel *Historical Dictionary of International Intelligence* (Oxford 2006) p. 27

18. KV2/1740
19. Schulze-Bernett interrogation report, in Protzes KV2/1740
20. Koutrik, Folkert Arie Van alias 'WALBACH' KV2/3643
21. KV2/1740
22. KV2/1740
23. KV2/3643
24. Andrew, Christopher *The Defence of the Realm* p.245
25. Kluiters, FAC *Bill Hooper and Secret Service* article published on nisa-intelligence.nl
26. KV2/3643
27. Ibid
28. KV2/13
29. *Liddell Diary* 24 November 1939 KV4/185

Chapter 7
1. See KV2/1700
2. Kluiters, FAD and Verhoeyen, E. *An International Spymaster and Mystery Man Abwehr Officer Hilmar G. J. Dierks* (Nisa-intelligence.nl) pp 4–5
3. KV2/1699 and KV2/1700
4. KV2/1699
5. KV2/13
6. KV2/1452
7. *Liquidation Report on Waldberg, Meier, Pons and Kieboom* in Pons, Sjoerd KV2/13
8. KV2/1700.
9. Letter from Silvester, R M KV2/12
10. Ibid
11. Ibid
12. See KV2/1452
13. Jowitt, The Earl *Some Were Spies* (Hodder 1954) pp.30–31
14. KV2/1700
15. KV2/13
16. Ibid
17. *Liddell Diary* 6 September 1940 KV4/186
18. HO144/ 21472
19. Ibid
20. *Liddell Diary* 6 September 1940 KV4/186
21. Ibid
22. KV2/13
23. *The Times* 15 August 1940 p3
24. *Newcastle Evening Chronicle* 14 August 1940
25. *Daily Herald* 15 August 1940
26. *Aberdeen Evening Express* 15 August 1940
27. Ibid
28. *Midland Daily Telegraph* 16 August 1940 for the full report to the Home Security Committee on 21 August 1940 see Security Intelligence Centre: Papers CAB 93/5
29. Telegram to Combined Intelligence Committee 20 July 1940 HW 48/1
30. *Western Mail* 16 August 1940
31. Masterman, *The Double-Cross System* (London 2007) p50
32. *Northampton Mercury,* 18 May 1945
33. *Liddell Diary*, 7 September 1940 KV4/186
34. *Liddell Diary*, 8 September 1940 KV4/186
35. *Liddell Diary* 8 September 1940 KV4/186

36. *Liddell Diary* 22 September 1940 KV4/186
37. Memories and stories from residents in Willingham collected by the author when he researched the story in the 1990s, also see West, Nigel *Seven Spies Who Changed the World* (London 1991) pp.34–7
38. *Northern Whig* 4 September 1940
39. *Liddell Diary* 22 September 1940 KV4/186
40. Ibid
41. *Liddell Diary* 23 September 1940 KV4/186
42. *Liddell Diary* 23 September 1940 KV4/186
43. *Liddell Diary* 11 October 1940
44. KV 2/60
45. *Liddell Diary* 13 January 1941
46. *Liddell Diary* 16 January 1941
47. KV 2/2593
48. Masterman, J C *The Double-Cross System* (London 2007) p54
49. *Liddell Diary* 16 October 1940
50. *New York Times*, 23 October 1992
51. KV2/15
52. KV2/18
53. KV2/1701
54. KV2/1701
55. Ibid
56. KV2/1701
57. KV2/ 1701
58. Ibid
59. KV2/17
60. KV2/17
61. *Daily Herald* 2 October 1940
62. KV2/17
63. See *Dr Dearden's Report of an Interview with Vera on 9. 1.41* p.3 in KV2/15
64. Quoted by Petrie in his minute of 28.2.42 KV2/15
65. Report by U.35 (Ustinov) KV2/15
66. Minute by D G White ADB1 26.2.42 KV2/15
67. *Liddell Diary* 4 October 1940
68. KV2/17
69. Butler, Memo 20.6.41 KV2/15
70. *Liddell Diary* 1 October 1940 KV4/186
71. KV2/357
72. KV3/76
73. KV2/15
74. KV2/15
75. KV2/15
76. KV2/15
77. Butler, Note on Room 055 interview with Morrish KV2/357
78. Interview with Morrish KV2/357
79. Butler, Richard, note of interview with Wilkinson 17.12.40 KV2/357
80. Ibid
81. KV2/15
82. KV2/15
83. KV2/15
84. Petrie to Maxwell KV2/15

85. Milmo to Davies, Home Office 12.2.42 KV2/15
86. *Liddell Diary* 8 October 1940
87. KV2/546
88. See article and statements by Smith, Keggin, Penn and Forth contributed by John Forth, WW2 People's War website.
89. *Liddell Diary* 5 October 1940
90. Ibid
91. Recollections of PC Forth contributed by his son John E. Forth, WW2 People's War website.
92. *Liddell Diary* 25 October 1940 KV4/187
93. Cases of Edvardsen and Lund complied by Milmo, 31 October 1941 KV2/21
94. B.8 (L) Report 29 October 1940 KV2/21
95. Translation of statement by Edvardsen, 28 October 1940 KV2/21
96. Hinsley, F H and Simkins, C A G *British Intelligence in the Second World War* vol. 4 p.325 (London 1990)
97. *B.8 (L)* Report 28 October 1940 KV2/21
98. Statement by Supt A W Stuart 27 October 1940 KV2/21
99. Letter from Scottish RSO to Dick White MI5 27 October 1940 KV2/21
100. A term used by Drüke to describe himself and his fellow agents see KV2/15
101. *B.8 (L)* Report by Robin Stephens dated 18 October 1940 KV2/21
102. *Liddell Diary* 7 October 1940 KV4/187
103. Statement by Charles Baldock KV2/27
104. Statement by Captain William Henry Newton KV2/27
105. Translation of Statement by Josef Jakobs presented at his Court Martial KV2/27
106. Statement by Hinchley-Cooke KV2/27
107. See Ramsay, Winston G., *After the Battle, Number 11, German Spies in Britain* (London 1976) pp24–25
108. *Liddell Diary* 16 September 1940 KV4/186
109. Masterman, *The Double-Cross System* (London 2007) p.61
110. Ibid
111. *Liddell Diary* 1 October 1940 KV4/186
112. Ibid p.62
113. *Scottish Daily Mail* 1 April 2017
114. Masterman, *The Double-Cross System* (London 2007) p3

Chapter 8

1. Selected Historical Papers from the SNOW case KV2/445-453
2. Farago, Ladislas *The Game of Foxes* (London 1971) pp xi-xiv
3. KV2/449, KV2/674,
4. Farago, Ladislas, *The Game of Foxes* (London 1972) p.266
5. *The Times* 3 November 1939
6. Brooks, Peter *Coastal Towns at War* (Cromer 1988)
7. HO 45/25568
8. *Liddell Diary* 4 October 1940 KV4/187 and Statement by Jose Waldberg KV2/1700
9. KV3/76
10. Dewar, Tom *Norfolk Front Line* (Brancaster Staithe 1998) pp71–5
11. Letter Johnson to Collis 13 March 1990, private correspondence
12. *Yorkshire Evening Post* 26 August 1947
13. *Yorkshire Evening Post* 28 August 1947
14. *Hull Daily Mail* and *Yorkshire Evening Post* 25 November 1947
15. *Liddle Diary* 5 November 1940 KV4/187

16. Bucks Constabulary Report KV2/114
17. Cambridge Borough Police Report KV2/114
18. *Liddle Diary* 1 April 1941 KV4/187
19. Cambridge Borough Police report re: Ter Braak KV2/114
20. Cambridge Borough Police report re: Ter Braak KV2/114
21. *Liddell Diary* 3 April 1941 KV4/187
22. Cambridge Borough Police report re: Ter Braak KV2/114
23. Report on W/T sets of Agents KV2/114
24. See Braak, Jan Willem Van den *Spion Tegen Churchill* (Zutphen, Netherlands 2017)
25. Masterman, J C *The Double-Cross System* (London 2007) p54
26. SIS report on Mörz dated 23 July 1939 KV2/1206
27. Statement by Heinrich Grunov translated and sent to Curry MI5 12.12.39 KV2/1206
28. SIS report on Mörz dated 23 July 1939 KV2/1206
29. Statement quoted in correspondence White to Vivian 30 December 1939 KV2/2106
30. KV2/2106
31. *Liddell Diary* 10 May KV4/186
32. KV2/2106
33. KV2/2106
34. KV2/2106
35. *Liddell Diary* 12 March 1940 KV4/186
36. See Metropolitan Police Special Branch report 4 September 1940 KV2/106
37. KV2/2106
38. KV2/2106
39. KV2/2106
40. KV2/2106
41. KV2/2106
42. Minute 53 KV2/2106
43. Security Control Office circular 1 March 1941 KV2/2106
44. White to DAC Special Branch 7 August 1941 KV2/2106

Chapter 9
1. *Daily Express*, 13 May 1940
2. *The Times* 14 May 1940
3. *Dundee Courier* 13 May 1940 and *Birmingham Daily Gazette* 13 May 1940
4. Ibid
5. *Western Daily Press* 13 May 1940
6. *The Times* 14 May 1940
7. Mackenzie, S P *The Home Guard: A Military and Political History* (Oxford 1995) p.18
8. Gillman, Peter and Gillman, Leni, 'Collar the Lot' *How Britain Interned & Expelled its Wartime Refugees* (London 1980) pp45–6
9. *Liddell Diary*, 21 May 1940 KV4/186
10. *Liddell Diary*, 21 May 1940 KV4/186
11. *Liddell Diary*, 21 May 1940 KV4/186
12. *Liddell Diary* 21 May 1940 KV4/186
13. Tyne & Wear Archives *Northern Civil Defence Region meetings of Police Security Officers PA.NC/2/2/46*
14. *Daily Herald* 24 May 1940
15. *Yorkshire Post and Leeds Intelligencer* 23 May 1940
16. *Daily Herald* 24 May 1940
17. Tyne & Wear Archives *Northern Civil Defence Region meetings of Police Security Officers PA.NC/2/2/46*

18. *Liddell Diary* 7 June 1940 KV4/186
19. *Liddell Diary* 12 March 1940 KV4/186
20. *Liddell Diary* 26 May 1940 KV4/186
21. *Liddell Diary* 2 July 1940 KV4/186
22. *Liddell Diary* 15 July 1940 KV4/186
23. *Liddell Diary* 22 June 1940 KV4/186
24. MI5 *B Division Weekly Intelligence Summary* No 2 16 October 1940 KV4/122
25. MI5 *B Division Weekly Intelligence Summary* No 2 16 October 1940 KV4/122
26. Ibid
27. *HC Series 5 Vol. 362 Written Answers* 3 July 1940
28. *Aerodromes in UK Obstruction Blockage Policy Against Enemy Use* AIR 2/4557
29. *Liddell Diary* 22 May 1940 KV4/186
30. AIR 2/4557
31. *Liddell Diary* 26 May 1940 KV4/186
32. *Liddell Diary* 17 June 1940 KV4/186
33. *No 10 Region Summary* 13 September 1940 KV4/122
34. Macleod, Colonel R & Kelly Denis, *The Unguarded: The Ironside Diaries 1937–1940* (New York 1963)
35. *Liddell Diary* 26 June 1940 KV4/186
36. *Liddell Diary* 21 August 1940 KV4/186
37. Ibid
38. MI5 B Division Intelligence Summary 24 October 1940 KV4/122
39. *Yorkshire Evening Post* 8 August 1940
40. *Belfast Telegraph* 9 August 1940
41. *Coventry Evening Telegraph* 27 August 1940, *Newcastle Journal* 27 August 1940
42. *Evening Despatch* 29 August 1940
43. *Sunderland Daily Echo* 5 September 1940
44. *North Eastern Gazette* 5 September 1940
45. *No 2 Region Summary* 5 September 1940
46. *Liddell Diary* 7 October 1940 KV4/187
47. MI5 *Weekly Intelligence Summary* No 1 9 October 1940 KV4/122
48. Tyne & Wear Archives *Northern Civil Defence Region meetings of Police Security Officers PA.NC/2/2/46*
49. HO 45/25568
50. HO 45/25568
51. *Sunderland Daily Echo* 2 March 1938
52. Ibid
53. HO 45-25568
54. *Liddell Diary* 3 December 1939 KV4/185
55. HO 45-25568
56. HO45/ 25569
57. HO45/ 25569
58. HO45/ 25569
59. HO45/ 25569
60. HO45/ 25569
61. HO45/ 25569
62. *West Sussex Gazette* 6 June 1940
63. *Daily Express* 5 March 1950
64. *Liddell Diary* 12 September 1940 KV4/186
65. *Liddell Diary* 17 September 1940 KV4/186
66. *Liddell Diary* 17 December 1940 KV4/187

67. *West Sussex Gazette* 13 February 1941
68. TS/27/533
69. Ibid
70. Tate, Tim *Hitler's British Traitors* (London 2018) pp209–14, 216–25
71. Baker White, John *The Big Lie* (London 1955) pp26–27
72. *Daily Telegraph* 27 February 2014
73. Jago, Michael *The Man who was George Smiley: The Life of John Bingham* (London 2013)
74. Jones, Westminster Bank to Harker, MI5 11 June 1940 KV2/3874
75. Hutton, Robert *Agent Jack* (London 2018) pp36–37
76. KV2/3874
77. KV2/680
78. MI5 *B Division Weekly Intelligence Summary No 2 10 October 1940* KV4/122
79. KV2/3874
80. MI5 *B Division Intelligence Summary 10 October 1940* KV4/122
81. *Liddell Diary* 30 August 1940 KV4/186
82. MI5 *B Division Intelligence Summary 10 October 1940* KV4/122
83. KV2/680
84. KV2/680
85. Trythall, Anthony John *'Boney' Fuller: The Intellectual General* (London 1977)
86. McKinstry, Leo *Operation Sealion* (London 2014)
87. KV2/680
88. MI5 *B Division Intelligence Summary 10 October 1940* KV4/122
89. KV2/680
90. KV2/680

Chapter 10
1. Letter from White MI5 to Stephenson SIS 28 July 1941 KV3/76
2. *Liddell Diary* 27 May 1940 KV4/186
3. *Liddell Diary* 20 June 1940 KV4/186
4. *Liddell Diary* 24 June 1940 KV4/186
5. *Liddell Diary* 21 July 1940 KV4/186
6. KV2/122
7. Tyne & Wear Archives *Northern Civil Defence Region meetings of Police Security Officers PA.NC/2/2/46*
8. MI5 *B Division Weekly Intelligence Summary No2, Part II Regional Summary* 16 October 1940 KV4/122
9. HO 45/25568
10. HO 45/25568
11. HO 45/25568
12. HO 45/25568
13. HO 45/25568
14. KV4/122

Chapter 11
1. WO 199/1446
2. ADM 116/4469
3. Montgomery, Field Marshal Bernard Law The *Memoirs of Field Marshal Montgomery* (London 1958)
4. Churchill, *The Second World War*, Vol 2 (London 1949)
5. WO 199/44 Keeps and Fortified Villages, nodal points and anti-tank islands
6. WO 199/44

7. WO 199/2528
8. WO199/287
9. WO199/287
10. Stewart, Andrew *The King's Private Army* (Solihull 2003)
11. Stewart MC, P. F., *History of the XII Royal Lancers* (London 1950) p376
12. WO199/297
13. Stewart, Andrew *The King's Private Army* (Solihull 2003)
14. WO 199/293
15. *The Times*, 12 January 2018
16. Draper, A. *Operation Fish: The Race to Save Europe's Wealth 1939–1945* (London 1979)
17. Bosman, Suzanne *The National Gallery in Wartime* (London 2008)
18. Stewart MC, P. F., *History of the XII Royal Lancers* (London 1950) p376
19. HC Deb 16 October 1940 vol 365 cc695-6
20. ADM 116/4493
21. Tyne & Wear Archives *Northern Civil Defence Region meetings of Police Security Officers PA.NC/2/2/46*
22. TV Interview with Geoff Devereux, *Hitler's Britain* Echo Bridge (2008)
23. *Newcastle Evening Chronicle* 18 February 1981
24. *Newcastle Evening Chronicle* 18 February 1981

Chapter 12

1. Bushby, John R. *Air Defence of Great Britain* (Shepperton 1973)
2. Clarke, *Comer England Under Hitler* (New York 1961)
3. Forczyk, Robert *We March Against England* (London 2016) p.43
4. Wheatley, Ronald *Operation Sealion* (London 1958)
5. Ansel, Walter *Hitler Confronts England* (London 1960)
6. Wheatley, Ronald *Operation Sealion* (London 1958)
7. Ansel, Walter *Hitler Confronts England* (London 1960)
8. Engel, Major Gerhard *At the Heart of the Reich* (Barnsley 2005)
9. Quoted in Glover, Michael *Invasion Scare 1940* (London 1990)
10. Ansel, Walter *Hitler Confronts England* (London 1960) pp140–41
11. Lee, John *A Soldier's Life: General Sir Ian Hamilton 1853–1947* (London 2000) p.146
12. CIA Report (Declassified 1999) *Mil-Geo: The Geographic Service of the German Army* (USA 1951)
13. CIA Report (Declassified 1999) *Mil-Geo: The Geographic Service of the German Army* (USA 1951)
14. *Generalstab des Heeres Abteiling für Kriegskarten un Vermessungswessen* (IV.Mil.-Geo.) *Militärgeographische Angaben über England* (Berlin 1940)
15. *Generalstab des Heeres Abteiling für Kriegskarten un Vermessungswessen* (IV.Mil.-Geo.) *Grosbritannien: Liste geographischer Eigennamen mit Angabe ihrer Aussproche* (Berlin 1940)
16. CIA Report (Declassified 1999) *Mil-Geo: The Geographic Service of the German Army* (USA 1951)
17. Clarke, Comer *England Under Hitler* (New York 1961)
18. McKale, Donald M. *The Swastika Outside Germany* (Kent State University, USA 1977)
19. Clarke, Comer *England Under Hitler* (New York 1961)
20. Six was appointed chief of the *Vorkommando Moscow*, an *Einsatzgruppe* responsible for for the execution of hundreds of known victims. Found guilty of war crimes at Nuremberg he was and sentenced to 20 years, later commuted to ten years and he ended up serving a sentence of just over seven years. On release he obtained a job in public relations. He died in 1975.
21. HC Deb 18 November 1946 vol 430 cc56 W

22. HC Deb 18 November 1946 vol 430 cc56–7W
23. HC Deb 18 November 1946 vol 430 cc57W
24. Addison, Paul and Crang, Jeremy A. eds. *Listening to Britain* (London 2011)
25. Glover, Michael Invasion Scare 1940 p189
26. Hayward, James *Myths and Legends of the Second World War* (Stroud 2003)
27. *Nottingham Journal* 12 September 1940
28. HC Deb 18 November 1946 vol 430 cc55–56 W
29. Banks, Sir Donald *Flame Over Britain* (London 1946)
30. Hayward, James *Burn the Sea* (History Press 2016) pp38–40
31. *Liddell Diary* 1 October 1940
32. See Hayward, James *Burn the Sea* (Stroud 2016)
33. *The People* 1 October 1944
34. Enigma signal from Göring to all units in *Luftlotten* I, II and V deciphered at Bletchley Park 8 August 1940
35. MI5 *B Division Weekly Intelligence Summary*, No.7 21 November 1940 KV4/122
36. MI5 *B Division Weekly Intelligence Summary* No. 2 16 October 1940 KV4/122
37. Tyne & Wear Archives *Northern Civil Defence Region meetings of Police Security Officers PA.NC/2/2/46*

Bibliography

Addison, Paul & Crang, Jeremy A, *Listening to Britain: Home Intelligence Reports on Britain's Finest Hour – May to September 1940* (London 2011)

Andrew, Christopher, *The Defence of the Realm: The Authorized History of MI5* (London 2009)

Andrew, Christopher, *Secret Service: The Making of the British Intelligence Community* (London) 1985

Ansel, Walter, *Hitler Confronts England* (London 1960)

Atkin, Malcolm, *Fighting Nazi Occupation: British Resistance 1939–1945* (Barnsley 2015)

Banks, Sir Donald, *Flame Over Britain* (London 1946)

Barnes, James J & Barnes, Patience P, *Nazis in Pre-War London 1930–1939: the fate and Role of German Party members and British Sympathizers* (Brighton 2005)

Best, Captain S. Payne, *The Venlo Incident* (London 1950)

Bosman, Suzanne, *The National Gallery in Wartime* (London 2008)

Braak, Jan Willem Van den, *Spion Tegen Churchill* (Zutphen, Netherlands 2017)

Brammer, Uwe, *Spionageabwehr und Geheimer Mleldedienst. Die Abwehrstelle X im Wehrkreis Hamburg 1935–1945*, (Freiburg, Rombach, 1989)

Briggs, Susan, *Keep Smiling Through: The Home Front 1939–45* (London 1975)

Brinson, Charmian & Dove, Richard, *A Matter of Intelligence: MI5 and the Surveillance of Anti-Nazi Refugees 1933–50*, (Manchester 2014)

Brooks, Peter, *Coastal Towns at War* (Cromer 1988)

Bushby, John R, *Air Defence of Great Britain* (London 1973)

Churchill, Winston S. *The Second World War*, Vol 2 (London 1949)

Clarke, Comer, *England Under Hitler* (New York 1961)

Collier, Basil, *The Defence of the United Kingdom* (London 1957)

Deacon, Richard, *A History of British Secret Service* (London 1980)

Demarne, Cyril, *The London Blitz: A Fireman's Tale*, London 1980

Dewar, Tom, *Norfolk Front Line* (Brancaster Staithe 1998)

Dilks, David, *The Diaries of Sir Alexander Cadogan, 1938 – 1945* (London 1971)

Draper, Alfred, *Operation Fish: The Race to Save Europe's Wealth 1939–1945* (London 1979)

Dunford-Slater, Brigadier John Frederick, *Commando* (London 1955)

Engel, Major Gerhard, *At the Heart of the Reich* (Barnsley 2005)

Erickson, John, I*nvasion 1940: The Nazi Invasion Plan for Britain by SS General Walter Schellenberg* (London 2000)

Farago, Ladislas, *The Game of Foxes: British and German intelligence operations and personalities which changed the course of the Second World War* (London 1971)

Fleming, Peter, *Invasion 1940* (London 1959)

Forczyk, Robert, *We March Against England* (London 2016)

Garnett, David, *The Secret History of PWE: The Political Warfare Executive 1939–1945* (London 2002)

Generalstab des Heeres Abteilung für Kriegskarten und Vermessungswesen (IV. Mil.-Geo.) *Militärgeographische Angaben über England* (Berlin 1940–41)

Gilbert, Martin, *Finest Hour: Winston Churchill 1939–1941* (London 1983)

Gillies, Midge, *Waiting For Hitler: Voices from Britain on the Brink of Invasion*, London 2006

Gillman, Peter and Gillman, Leni, *'Collar the Lot' How Britain Interned and Expelled its Wartime Refugees* (London 1980)

Glover, Michael, *Invasion Scare 1940* (London 1990)

Hayward, James, *Burn the Sea: Flame Warfare, Black Propaganda and the Nazi Plan to Invade England* (Stroud 2016)

Hayward, James *Hitler's Spy* (London 2012)

Hayward, James, *Myths & Legends of the Second World War* (Stroud 2006)

Higgins, Jack, *The Eagle Has Landed* (London 1975)

Hinsley, F.H. & Simkins, C.A.G., *British Intelligence in the Second World War Volume IV Security and Counter Intelligence* (London 1990)

Hutton, Robert, *Agent Jack: The Story of MI5's Secret Nazi Hunter* (London 2018)

Irving, David, *Hess, The Missing Years 1941–1945* (London 1989)

Jago, Michael, *The Man who was George Smiley: The Life of John Bingham* (London 2013)

Jakobs, Giselle, *The Spy in the Tower* (Stroud 2019)

Jeffery, Keith, *MI6 The History of the Secret Intelligence Service 1909–1949* (London 2010)

Joiner, T.E,. *Myths about Suicide* (Harvard 2010)

Jonason, Tommy & Olsson, Simon, *Agent Tate: The Wartie Story of Harry Williamson*, Stroud 2011

Jowett, The Earl, *Some Were Spies* (London 1954)

Kieser, Egbert, *Hitler on the Doorstep Operation 'Sea Lion': The German Plan to Invade Britain 1940* (Annapolis 1997)

Lampe, David, *The Last Ditch: Britain's Secret Resistance and the Nazi Invasion Plan* (London 2007)

Lee, John, *A Soldier's Life: General Sir Ian Hamilton 1853–1947* (London 2000)

Lehmann-Russbueldt, Otto, *Germany's Air Force* (London 1935)

Lett, Brian, *SOE's Mastermind: An Authorised Biography of Major General Sir Colin Gubbins KCMG, DSO, MC* (Barnsley 2016)

Levine, Joshua, *The Secret History of the Blitz* (London 2016)

Lucas, James, *Reich: World War II Through German Eyes* (London 1990)

Mack, Joanna & Humphries, Steve, *The Making of Modern London: London at War 1939–1945* (London 1985)

Mackay, Robert *The Test of War: Inside Britain 1939–45* (London 1999)

Mackenzie, S.P., *The Home Guard: A Military and Political History* (Oxford 1995)

Macleod, Colonel R & Kelly Denis, *The Unguarded: The Ironside Diaries 1937–1940* (New York 1963)

Masterman, J.C., *The Double-Cross System* (London 2007)

Matthews, Stanley and Scott, Les, *The Way It Was* (London 2001)

McKinstry, Leo, *Operation Sealion* (London 2015)

Montgomery, Field Marshal Bernard Law, The *Memoirs of Field Marshal Montgomery* (London 1958)

Morshead, Sir Owen, *Windsor Castle an Illustrated History* (London 1957)

Morshead, Sir Owen, *Windsor Castle* (London 1951)

Morton, Andrew, *17 Carnations: the Windsors, The Nazis and the Cover-up* (London 2015)

Mosley, Leonard, *Backs to the Wall: London Under Fire 1939–1945* (London 1974)

Nixon, Barbara, *Raiders Overhead: A Diary of the London Blitz* (London 1980)

O'Keeffe, Paul, *Some Sort of Genius: A Life of Wyndham Lewis* (Counterpoint 2015)

Pawle, Gerald, *The Secret War 1939–1945* (London 1956)

Putlitz, Wolfgang zu, *The Putlitz Dossier* (London 1957)

Ramsay, Winston G., *After the Battle, Number 11, German Spies in Britain* (London 1976)

Rett, Seymour, *The Hidden War: The Amazing Camouflage Deceptions of World War II* (London 1980)

Ritter, Nikolas, *Deckname Dr. Rantzau*, (Hamburg, 1972)

Rowe, Mark, *Don't Panic: Britain Prepares for Invasion 1940* (Stroud 2010)

Schellenberg, Walter, *Hitler's Secret Service* (New York 1971)

Schenk, Peter, *Invasion of England 1940: The Planning of Operation Sealion* (London 1990)

Scotland, Lt. Col. A.P., *The London Cage* (London 1957)

Simpson, A.W. Brian, *In the Highest Degree Odious: Detention Without Trial in Wartime Britain* (Oxford 1994)

Smart, Nick (ed.) *The Bickersteth Family World War II Diary: 1939–1942* (Michigan 1999)

Stewart, Andrew, *The King's Private Army: Protecting the British Royal Family During the Second World War* (Solihull 2015)

Stewart MC, P.F., *History of the XII Royal Lancers* (London 1950)

Storey, Neil R. *Norfolk in the Second World War* (Wellington 2015)

Storey, Neil R. *The Home Front in World War Two* (Stroud 2017)

Stourton, Edward, *Auntie's War: the BBC During the Second World War*, (London 2017)

Strong, Major General Sir Kenneth, *Intelligence at the Top: The Recollections of an Intelligence Officer* (New York 1969)

Tate, Tim, *Hitler's British Traitors: The Secret History of Spies, Saboteurs and Fifth Columnists*,

Sweet, Matthew, *The West End Front: The Wartime Secrets of London's Grand Hotels* (London 2011)

Taylor, James, *Careless Talk Costs Lives* (London 2010)

Todd, Nigel, *In Excited Times: The People Against the Blackshirts* (Whitley Bay 1995)

Toller, Ernst, *Letters from Prison* (London 1936)

Tremain, David, *The Beautiful Spy: The life and Crimes of Vera Eriksen* (Stroud 2019)

Trythall, Anthony John, *'Boney' Fuller: The Intellectual General* (London 1977)

Urbach, Karina, *Go-Betweens of Hitler* (Oxford 2015)

Verhoeyen, *Etienne Spionnen aan de achterdeur: de Duitse Abwehr in België, 1936–1945* (Antwerp 2011)

Warner, Philip, *Phantom* (Barnsley 2005)

Wells, H.G., *War of the Worlds* (London 1897)

Wells, H.G., *The Shape of Things to Come* (London 1933)

Wells, H.G., *The War In The Air* (reprint London 1967)

West, Nigel, *The Guy Liddell Diaries Vol I: 1939–1942* (London & New York 2005)

West, Nigel, *Historical Dictionary of International Intelligence* (Oxford 2006)

West, Nigel, *Secret War: The Story of SOE, Britain's Wartime Sabotage Organisation* (Sevenoaks 1993)

West, Nigel, *Seven Spies Who Changed the World* (London 1991)

Wheatley, Ronald, *Operation Sealion* (London 1958)

White, John Baker, *The Big Lie* (London 1955)

Wighton, Charles & Peis, Günter, *They Spied on England* (London 1958)

Wilks, Mick, *Chronicles of the Worcestershire Home Guard* (Herefordshire 2014)

Newspapers, Magazines and Journals

Aberdeen Evening Express

After the Battle

Anglo-German Review

Belfast Telegraph

Birmingham Daily Gazette

Central Somerset Gazette

Colwyn Bay and North Wales Weekly News

Coventry Evening Telegraph

Cyclist, The

Daily Express

Daily Herald

Daily Mail

Derby Evening Telegraph

Die Nachut

Dundee Courier

Evening News

Evening Despatch

Hansard

Hull Daily Mail

Jewish Telegraph, The

John Bull

Leichtathlet, Der

Manchester Guardian

Medico-Legal Journal

Midland Daily Telegraph

Nachut, Die

New York Times, The

Newcastle Chronicle

Newcastle Evening Chronicle

Newcastle Journal and North Mail

Northampton Mercury

Northern Whig

Nottingham Evening Post

Nottingham Journal
People, The
Picture Post
Psychology Today
Punch
Scottish Daily Mail
Spectator, The
Sun, The
Sunderland Daily Echo
Sydney Herald

Times, The
Yorkshire Post
Völkisher Beobachter
Volkswille
War Illustrated
West Sussex Gazette
Western Mail
World War Investigator
Yorkshire Evening Post
Yorkshire Post

Archives & Libraries

Aberdeen City and Aberdeenshire Archives
British Library
British Newspaper Archive
Bundesarchiv-Militärarchiv
Cambridgeshire Archives
Centre for Historical Research and Documentation on War and Contemporary
  Society (SOMA-CEGES), Brussels
Central Intelligence Agency Historical Collections
Manx National Heritage and Archives
Ministerie van Justitie: Contraal Archief van de Bijzondere Rechtspleging
Museum of the British Resistance Organisation (B.R.O.) Parham, Suffolk
National Archives and Records Administration, Washington
Netherlands Ministry of Justice Central Archives of the Special Judicial
  Administration (CABR) deposited at the Netherlands Nationals Archives
Newcastle Local Studies Library
Norfolk Record Office
Office des Etrangers/Dienst Vreemdelingenzaken, Brussels
Suffolk Record Office
The National Archives (TNA) (UK) (All KV, HO, ADM, FO, AIR and MEPO
  files cited in the text are held at The National Archives at Kew)
Tyne & Wear Archives

Online:

BBC WW2 People's War website: www.bbc.co.uk/history/ww2peopleswar/
Chain Home (CH) RDF System: ventnorradar.co.uk/CH.htm
Coldspur, incisive analysis and research into spies and espionage: www.coldspur.
  com
Great Shelford Village: www.greatshelford.info/home
Josef Jakobs website: www.josefjakobs.info
Netherlands Intelligence Studies Association: Nisa-intelligence.nl
The Einsatzgruppen Trial: www.jewishvirtuallibrary.org/the-einsatzgruppen-2

Index

East Anglian Real Estate Company, 171
Eastern Command, 171, 196–7, 216
Easton Maudit, Northamptonshire, 129, 130–1
Ebbutt, Norman, 46
Ebertsen, Cornelius, 129
Eden, Anthony, 11, 162
Edinburgh, 64, 120–3, 155, 179, 198, 257, 275, 282
Edvardsen, Gunnar, 132, 133–4
Einsatzgruppen, 257
Electra House, 266
Elser, Georg, 81
Enemy aliens, 52, 55, 103 162–4, 167, 169, 199, 202
Engel, Gerhard, 243
England Football Team, 43
Epstein, Julius, 21
Eriksson, Josephine Fillipine Emilie 'My', 52–3, 55, 124
Evacuation, UK, 207, 211–12, 228-29
Executions, 101, 114, 124, 136, 137

Fabian, Dr Dora, 11–24, 26–7, 45, 70, 125
Farago, Ladislas, 140
Fascists, British Union of, *viii, xv,* 17, 33, 36, 50, 65, 166, 178, 181, 202, 276
Fenner Brockway, Archibald, 12
Fifth Column, *x, xi, xiv, xv,* 87, 106, 154, 157, 174–8, 187–8, 195–7, 282
Fischer, Dr Franz, 77–9, 153
FISH, Operation, 224
Flame barrage, 265, 267–9
Fleming, Peter, 231
Flossack flotille, 257, 259
Foot, Isaac, 22
Foreign Office (FO), 3–4, 14, 23, 30, 46–7, 74, 138, 276–7
Forth, John William, 130–1
France, 31, 33, 44, 50–1, 62, 72, 74–5, 82, 87–8, 98, 103, 153, 160, 168–9, 196, 200, 204, 221, 237, 239, 241, 243–5, 68
Fricke, *Konteradmiral* Kurt, 241
Frost, Malcolm, 109
Führer Directive No.16, 244
Fuller, Major General JFC 'Boney', 192, 194, 214, 253

Gallacher, William, 49
Gallus, Fritz, 54, 56
Ganz, Dr (Anton) Roy, 16, 18, 19–20, 23, 25–6
Gebirgs (Mountain) Division, 133
Gebirgsjäger, 257
Geddes, Sir Eric, *viii*
Geddes, John, 118
General Post Office (GPO), *xv,* 193
German Embassy, London, *viii,* 20, 23, 25, 27, 28–32, 49, 50–1, 76
Gestapo, 14, 28–30, 44–5, 48–9, 73, 81, 111, 152, 156, 189–90, 254
GHQ Line, 210, 212
Gibraltar, 69
Glasgow, 63, 65
Gloucester Place, Marylebone, 54, 122, 165
Gloucestershire, 127, 224
Goebbels, Dr Joseph, 5
Gold reserves, 223
Goose, Karl (GANDER), 131, 141
Göring, *Reichsmarschall* Hermann Wilhelm, 53, 243, 254, 271,
Görtz, Hermann, 34
Gubbins, Colonel Colin McVean, 229–30
Gunther, Elizabeth Anna Maria, 25–7

Hague, The, 76–9, 80, 83–4, 151, 153, 155
Halder, General Franz, 3, 244
Halifax, Lord Edward, 50, 74, 75, 160
Hamburg, 16, 54, 61, 63, 83, 84, 87–9, 108, 115, 122, 134, 142, 151–2
Hampshire Regiment, 262
Hankey, Lord Maurice, 79, 283
Harker, Oswald Allen 'Jasper', *x, xi,* 113, 154
Henderson, Neville, 7, 43
Heydrich, SS-*Gruppenführer* Reinhard Tristan Eugen, 77, 254
Higgins, Jack, 142, 144
Hinxton, Cambridgeshire, 113
Himmler, *Reichsführer-SS* Heinrich Luitpold, 80–1
Hinchley-Cooke, Edward, 108, 136, 137, 187
Hindlip Hall, Worcestershire, 225